LESSON

READY TO GO

and

BOOK 4

longman.com

Joan Saslow

Lesson Plans: Ready to Go and Workplace Plus
Book 4

Copyright © 2004 by Pearson Education, Inc.
All rights reserved.

The black line masters in this publication are designed to be used with appropriate duplicating equipment to reproduce copies for classroom use. Pearson Education grants permission to classroom teachers to reproduce these masters.

Pearson Education, 10 Bank Street, White Plains, NY 10606

Editorial director: Pam Fishman
Vice president, director of design and production: Rhea Banker
Director of editorial production: Linda Moser
Director of electronic production: Aliza Greenblatt
Senior production editor: Robert Ruvo
Marketing manager: Oliva Fernandez
Director of manufacturing: Patrice Fraccio
Senior manufacturing buyer: Nancy Flaggman
Associate digital layout manager: Paula D. Williams
Cover design: Paula D. Williams

ISBN 0-13-148760-4

Printed in the United States of America
6 7 8 9 10 OPM 09 08 07

Contents

Introduction
Unit 1   Your life
Unit 2   The community
Unit 3   Technology
Unit 4   The consumer world
Unit 5   Time
Unit 6   Supplies and services
Unit 7   Relationships
Unit 8   Health and safety
Unit 9   Money
Unit 10   Your career

Introduction

These downloadable Lesson Plans divide each unit into six lessons, with each lesson taking approximately one hour.

Note that the Workbook is assigned as supplemental material for outside of class (homework) and as such is not included in scheduling, except for checking completion and comprehension of assignments.

Also, teaching time has not been calculated for expansion activities such as those outlined in the Teacher's Resources Binder. Use of these resources will largely depend on the class and teacher. Whenever possible, and time and resources permit, additional activities should be included either as review, warm up, or to motivate students.

LESSON PLAN, UNIT 1: PREVIEW/PRACTICAL CONVERSATIONS *(for Student pages 1-3)*

Summary of Lesson Plan

➤ **Preview and Practical conversations** (Student pages 1-3)
Suggested teaching time: 60 minutes
includes Cultural Notes & Discussion
Your actual teaching time: _____

➤ **Preview and Practical conversations** (Student pages 1-3)

Suggested teaching time: 60 minutes
Your actual teaching time: _____

Warm up. Have you ever been interrupted at dinner by a telemarketer? What happened? What did you do?

Procedure:
➤ Before you open the book, provide students with an opportunity to get to know each other. Have them complete a "Find someone who" activity. You can create your own or use the one following. You can hand out photocopies with the sentences on them or write the sentences on the board and ask students to copy them on a piece of paper. Tell students to walk around the classroom and talk with their classmates. Next to each phrase, they should write the name of one student for whom the statement is true. They can use each name only once. If, for example, they write *Sandra* next to *is wearing jeans today*, they cannot write *Sandra* next to anything else. Share the completed sentences as a class.

Note: The structures used in this sample activity can be incorporated into the *Practical grammar* explanations on pages 4 and 5, so have students save their work.

Find someone who

1. is wearing jeans today _____
2. is working today _____
3. is studying at this school for the first time _____
4. drives to class every day _____
5. is planning a trip soon _____
6. never comes late to class _____
7. feels happy to be here _____
8. has a dog or a cat _____
9. thinks your city is exciting _____
10. likes pizza _____

➤ Have students open their books and look at the pictures. Ask questions about the pictures, such as *Who is in the picture on the left?* (a family) *What are they doing?* (eating dinner) *What interrupts them?* (a telephone call) *Who is in the picture on the right?* (The man is talking to a woman on the phone.) *Who is the woman?* (a telemarketer) *What is her job?* (maybe selling something) *Why do you think she is calling?* (She probably wants the man to buy something or give her something.)

➤ Read the *Warm up* questions. Have students look at the picture on the right and imagine the rest of the conversation. Elicit a variety of ideas from the class, such as *I'm sorry. We're having dinner right now; We're not interested; Can you send me something in the mail?*

If your students are ready . . .

Culture / Civics note: In the United States and Canada, people often tell a phone solicitor that they are not interested, and sometimes hang up. Students from other countries may have a different response to such a caller and find it difficult to do something that seems rude.

Unit 1 objectives

Procedure:
Note: Legislation passed in 2003 has changed the telemarketing business. Consumers can now place their names on a national "do not call" list. Telemarketers who call people on the list can be fined.

➤ Have students read the objectives. Ask them to put a check next to the objectives that they can do now and circle those they want to work on most.

➤ Ask students to underline any words they do not understand. Write any unfamiliar terms on the board. Some students may not be familiar with the concepts *good cause, telemarketer's sales solicitation, volunteerism,* and *fraud*. Give a quick explanation of these terms.

(continued on p. 2)

Lesson Plan, Unit 1: Preview and practical conversations (for Student pages 1-3)–*continued*

Model 1

Content: agreeing to contribute to a good cause, using the present continuous for an action in progress, identifying ways to volunteer, identifying good causes

Procedure:

A. Listen and read.

➤ Read the bar for *Model 1*. Ask students what *a good cause* is. If they don't know, give examples of causes and ask if each is a good cause. For example: *Is cancer research a good cause? Is freeing convicted murderers a good cause? What about giving money to a political party or enforcing a leash law for dogs?* Elicit from students that believing something is a good cause is subjective and that some people may think a cause is good, while others might find it silly or even wrong.

➤ To set the scene for the conversation, point to the photo and ask questions such as *Who do you see in the picture?* (a man at a table, a woman walking by) *What do you think the man is doing?* (collecting money) *What's on the table in front of him?* (a container for money donations) *Where are the people?* (in front of a store) *What do you think the woman is doing?* (shopping)

➤ Play the cassette or read the conversation. After students listen and read, ask comprehension questions such as *What is the man doing?* (collecting for the food pantry) *What does he want the woman to do?* (make a donation) *What is the woman's response?* (That's a good cause. She would be happy to make a donation.) *What is the cause that the man is collecting for?* (a food pantry, a place that gives food to people who need it)

B. Pronunciation and intonation practice.

➤ Tell students that they will listen to the conversation again and have the opportunity to repeat each speaker's lines. Play the cassette or read the conversation again. Encourage students to imitate the rhythm, stress, and intonation of the conversation as closely as possible. Correct where necessary.

Option: To help students improve their intonation, have them practice reading the conversation in pairs. Remind them that native speakers often link words when the first word ends in a vowel or when the second word begins with a vowel. For example, native speakers might join *say* and *it*, creating *sayit*. Then have volunteers read the conversation aloud. Ask the other students to listen and note any linkages. Phrases that might naturally be linked because of vowel sounds include *yoube, tomakea, sayit, that'sa*.

Vocabulary

➤ Point to each picture and ask students what they see.

➤ Play the cassette or read the phrases and have students repeat the ways to volunteer.

Option: To elicit students' own experience, ask *Have you ever been asked to do one of these volunteer activities? Have you ever volunteered in one of these ways? Which ones? Which of these do you like doing?*

Option: Write on the board three headings: *Ways to volunteer, Advantages,* and *Disadvantages*. On the left, write each of the ways to volunteer listed in the *Vocabulary*. Ask students to brainstorm the advantages and disadvantages of each way. The chart might look something like the following:

Ways to volunteer	Advantages	Disadvantages
• Make a donation	Helps many causes	Costs you money
• Volunteer some time	Help people directly	Time consuming
• Bake something for the bake sale	Good if you like to cook	Have to be able to cook
• Make a few phone calls	Can do at home on your own time	Have to speak to people you don't know
• Mail some letters	Can fit into a busy schedule	You usually buy the postage
• Distribute some flyers	Meet people	May have to talk to people in English

C. Pair work...

➤ Brainstorm other causes that people might volunteer for, including *health clinics, social services, refugee programs, mentoring programs such as Big Brother / Big Sister, adult ESL programs, elementary schools, sports programs, holiday gift drives.*

➤ Model the conversation with a more advanced student. Play the role of Student A. Demonstrate that Student A mentions a good cause in the first slot and a way to volunteer in the second slot. Make sure students understand that they can use any of the ways to volunteer from the *Vocabulary* in the second slot. Student A then repeats the good cause in the third slot and expresses thanks in the last.

➤ Students practice the conversation with a partner, taking turns playing the roles of Student A and Student B. Circulate and offer help as needed.

Workbook Link: Exercises 1, 2

(continued on p. 3)

Lesson Plan, Unit 1: Preview and practical conversations (for Student pages 1-3)–continued

Model 2

Content: declining a telemarketer's sales solicitation, using the simple present tense with non-action verbs, identifying ways to decline an offer

Procedure:

🎧 A. Listen and read.

➤ Read the bar for *Model 2*. Tell students to notice what the telemarketer's sales offer is.

➤ Direct students' attention to the photo. Ask questions such as *What is going on in the picture?* (A woman is on the phone.) *What is the man in the round photo looking at?* (a telephone book or other directory)

➤ After students listen to the conversation, check comprehension by asking *Who is the man?* (a telemarketer) *What is he selling?* (cell phone service) *What does the woman ask?* (Is this a sales call?) *How does she decline the telemarketer's offer?* (We don't take offers over the phone.)

🎧 B. Pronunciation and intonation practice.

Option: Divide the class in half. Play the cassette or read the conversation and have half the class repeat Student A's lines and the other half repeat Student B's lines. Read the line with students if they have trouble.

🎧 Vocabulary

➤ Have students look at the photo in the *Vocabulary* box. Have them describe the look on the woman's face or speculate about what she just heard.

➤ Play the cassette or read the expressions and have students repeat the ways to decline an offer, imitating the authentic intonation as closely as possible.

➤ Brainstorm other ways to decline an offer. Let students know that they can tell the telemarketer *Please take us off your list*. Then the company cannot call them again.

C. Pair work...

➤ Model the activity with a more advanced student. Play the role of Student A to demonstrate using an expression from the *Vocabulary* to decline an offer.

➤ Have students practice the conversation in pairs, switching the roles of A and B. Circulate, answering questions if necessary.

If your students are ready...

Language note: The telemarketer says *We have a special offer on cell phone service this evening.* Tell students that they may also hear *We're having a special offer*, which means we are running or conducting a special offer, not that we possess a special offer. In some regions, callers may say *We've got a special offer*, which is idiomatic and does not mean ownership.

If your students are ready...

Culture / Civics note: In the United States, there are laws that restrict telemarketing. These restrictions include the following:

   A telemarketer may only call between 8:00 a.m. and 9:00 p.m. A telemarketer may not call you if you have previously asked not to be called. According to legislation passed in 2003, consumers can place their names on a national "do not call" list. Telemarketers who call people on the list can be fined. Before starting a sales pitch, the telemarketer must tell you that the call is a sales call, the name of the seller, and what is being sold. If it is a prize promotion, the telemarketer must tell you that no purchase or payment is necessary to enter the contest or win the prize.

Workbook Link: Exercises 3, 4

➤ Do it yourself!

Procedure:

A–B.

➤ Students should write down the name of one charity solicitation and one sales solicitation that they have actually received.

➤ Ask students for the names of the solicitors who have called them and list some of these names on the board or a transparency.

➤ Model a role play with a more advanced student. Ask the student to play the part of a telemarketer. Before you begin, make sure the student chooses a name for the company he or she represents and the product or cause. If the student is unsure, he or she can pick a name from the list. You will decline the offer. Role-play the conversation again and agree to the offer.

➤ Have students role-play the conversation, changing roles of telemarketer and recipient for more practice. Invite pairs to present their role play.

LESSON PLAN, UNIT 1: PRACTICAL GRAMMAR (for Student pages 4-5)

Summary of Lesson Plan

▶ **PRESENTATION**
Practical grammar (Student pages 4-5)
Suggested teaching time: 60 minutes
includes Language Note (10 minutes)
Your actual teaching time: _____

▶ **Practical grammar**
(Student pages 4-5)

Suggested teaching time: 60 minutes
Your actual teaching time: _____

The simple present tense and the present continuous

Procedure:

▶ Ask students to take out the "Find someone who" activity that they completed on page T1. Put students in small groups to identify the verb form used in each clause in items 1 through 6. Ask them to answer these questions: *Which verb form—simple present tense or present continuous—is used? What cue words suggest the verb form to use?*

▶ Write student responses on the board. Ask for additional cue words used with the simple present tense and the present continuous. You may end up with a chart like this:

The simple present tense	The present continuous
Cue words: (item 4) *every day,* (item 6) *never.* Others: *often, sometimes, always, rarely, usually*	Cue words: (items 1, 2) *today,* (item 3) *for the first time,* (item 5) *soon.* Others: *now, right now, at this moment*

▶ Ask students to read the rules in the grammar box. Go over the example sentences and have students point out the cue words that suggest the verb form to use. Ask for additional example sentences that use the simple present tense to talk about habitual actions and unchanging facts and the present continuous to talk about actions in progress. Write students' examples on the board and underline the cue words.

A. Complete each sentence...

▶ To model item 1, write out the sentence with each possible answer inserted. Have students choose the correct sentence.

▶ Advise students to look for cue words as they are deciding whether to use the simple present tense or the present continuous.

▶ Have students complete the exercise individually and then check their answers with a partner. Review with the entire class.

Option: Have students add an adverb of frequency to each of the following statements to best describe their own behavior. For example, students may write *I usually contribute to charitable organizations* or *I never accept sales offers over the phone.* Have students read their sentences aloud. Elicit that the simple present tense is used in each of these sentences. Remind students that the simple present tense is used with *sometimes, always, never,* and *often.*

1. I contribute to charitable organizations.
2. I receive telephone solicitations during dinner.
3. I accept sales offers over the phone.
4. I tell telemarketers to take me off their lists.
5. I volunteer my time to help others.

Ask students to read their sentences aloud.

B. Complete each sentence...

▶ Write item 1 on the board and ask for volunteers to choose the appropriate verbs from the box to fill in the two slots *(donate, ask).* Once students have decided on the verbs, ask for the correct verb forms (the simple present tense: *donate, ask*). Have students underline the cue word *(usually)* that specifies the verb form.

▶ Remind students that the verbs in the box are often linked with prepositions. For example, we *collect for* a cause, *talk to* someone, and *donate to* an organization.

▶ Have students work individually to complete the sentences and then check answers with a partner.

Workbook Link: Exercises 5, 6

(continued on p. 5)

Lesson Plan, Unit 1: Practical grammar (for Student pages 4-5)–*continued*

Non-action verbs

Content: non-action verbs used with the simple present tense

Procedure:
- Write the heading *Non-action verbs* on the board. Explain that these verbs often express mental or emotional states or refer to the senses.

- Ask students to read the verbs in the box and describe any patterns they notice. Elicit that some verbs relate to the senses (for example, *What do the words "hear, see, smell, sound," and "taste" have in common?*), some to emotions (for example, *What do the verbs "like, love," and "hate" have in common?*), and some to mental states (for example, *What about "think, understand," and "know"?*).

- Under the heading, write *senses, emotional states,* and *mental states* and list the verbs from the box that fit under each category. With students, create example sentences such as *She feels tired, I hate calls during dinner, They know the food pantry is a good cause.* Point out that non-action verbs often express situations that exist not only in the immediate present but were probably true yesterday and will be true tomorrow. Give example sentences such as *Matt has two sisters, We're not interested in phone offers.*

Option: Continue using the "Find someone who" activity from page T1. Put students in small groups to identify the verb form used in each clause in items 7 through 10. Ask them to answer these questions: *Which verb form—simple present tense or present continuous—is used? Why?* Elicit that the simple present tense is used with non-action verbs. Share the completed sentences as a class.

Note: For a more complete list of non-action verbs, refer students to page 145.

C. Complete the conversation...

- Have students complete the exercise individually. Remind them to check whether the verb is in the boxed list of non-action verbs and also to think about the other restrictions related to using the simple present tense and the present continuous.

- Students can read the conversation in pairs to check their answers.

Option: Brainstorm ways to correct a speaker's mistake in pronouncing or reading a name. Such a list might include *That's Malino, not Balino* or *My last name begins with an M, Malino* or *That's M, as in Mary–Malino.* Have students work in pairs with Student A acting as a caller who mispronounces Student B's name. Student B can practice politely correcting the caller's pronunciation or spelling.

If your students are ready ...

Language note: Although the general rule is not to use a continuous form with non-action, or stative, verbs, students may find evidence to the contrary. Some non-action verbs can be used in the present continuous because they have more than one meaning. For example, when *think* means believe, it is not used in the present continuous. However, when *think* refers to using your mind, it is used in the present continuous to emphasize that something is happening right now: *I am thinking about grammar.* Similarly, *have* is not used in the present continuous when it indicates possession, but it can be used in the present continuous in certain expressions: *She's having a baby, They're having a good time. Be* is used in the present continuous when it describes an action (*He's being difficult*) and not a state (*He's tired*).

Some non-action verbs can also be used in the present continuous to indicate a new development, something that is taking place now that wasn't happening before: *Now I'm remembering what happened that day.* Conversationally, some non-action verbs may be used in the present continuous to emphasize a temporary condition: *I'm loving this weather, They're looking good.*

Workbook Link: Exercises 7, 8, 9

▶ Do it yourself!

Procedure:
- Model the conversation with a more advanced student. Play the role of the caller in order to give the student an opportunity to respond appropriately to a telemarketer's offer.

- Remind students to choose the name of a company and of a product, service, or cause the telemarketer is selling or soliciting for.

- Working in pairs, students practice the telephone conversation, using as models Model 2 on page 3 and Exercise C on page 5.

- Have volunteers present the conversation in front of the class.

LESSON PLAN, UNIT 1: AUTHENTIC PRACTICE 1 & 2 (for Student pages 6-9)

Summary of Lesson Plan

▶ **PRESENTATION**
Authentic practice 1 & 2:
Listening (Student pages 6-9)
Suggested teaching time: 60 minutes
   includes Language Note
   and Cultural Discussion
Your actual teaching time: _____

▶ Authentic practice 1
(Student pages 6-7)

Suggested teaching time: 30 minutes
Your actual teaching time: _____

Volunteerism and charity

Procedure:

- ▶ Ask questions about the pictures, such as *Who's in the pictures?* (two women) *Where are they?* (in a restaurant) *What do you think they're talking about?* (a bake sale). Remind students that baking something for a bake sale is one of the ways to volunteer that they read about on page 2.

- ▶ To help students practice discrete listening skills, direct them to keep their books closed while they listen to the story. To focus their listening, ask questions before they listen: *What has the first woman volunteered to do?* (run a bake sale) *How can the second woman help?* (She can contribute a pie, make a cash contribution, or help work the booth.) *How is she going to contribute?* (She's going to write a check.)

- ▶ Play the cassette or read the picture story. After students have listened, elicit the responses to the focused listening questions. If students missed anything, let them listen again.

- ▶ Have students open their books and read the picture story silently.

- ▶ Point out the use of the present continuous in the first picture (*We're setting up a booth at the railroad station*) and in the second picture (*I'm going to be out of town for two days*). Note that the present continuous is often used to talk about future plans as well as actions in progress right now.

- ▶ Make sure students understand words or phrases that may be unfamiliar to them. In the first picture, the woman uses the expression *run a bake sale*. Elicit synonyms such as *operate, have,* or *hold.* In the second picture, the woman says *A million people always show up for that!* Ask students if they think she really means a million people. Elicit the response that she is speaking figuratively, not literally, using exaggeration for emphasis. Jane responds with *Actually, on second thought.* If necessary, point out that this expression is used to indicate that the person has reconsidered something. In the last picture, the woman says *Better come early!* Remind students that *Better* is a reduction of *You had better* and is used for a strong suggestion or warning. Ask students to rephrase her next statement *(We always run out of everything by two):* We have nothing left to sell by two.

A. Read the picture story again...

- ▶ To model the activity, write the first item on the board and ask volunteers to fill in the blank. Have students read the picture story again to find the answers to the rest of the items.

- ▶ After students complete Exercise A individually, correct as a group.

B. Listen...

- ▶ Tell students that they will listen to the tapescript or the cassette and then read aloud the responses from their text.

- ▶ Read each item in the tapescript out loud or play the cassette. Allow students to listen as many times as necessary to complete the exercise. If students have difficulty, prompt them by reading the response yourself.

Note: The speakers on the cassette for this exercise are different from those who recorded the text of the picture story. This has been done intentionally in order to give students the opportunity to hear a wide variety of voices.

Challenge: Use the prompts for Exercise B as a dictation. Have students listen to the questions and write what they hear. Allow students to listen as many times as necessary. Ask volunteers to write the questions on the board. Make corrections as a class. Students can then practice the prompts and responses with a partner.

(continued on p. 7)

Lesson Plan, Unit 1: Authentic practice 1 & 2 (for Student pages 6-9)–*continued*

Challenge: For an out-of-class assignment, ask students to find out the names of homeless shelters or food pantries in your community. Sources of information include religious organizations, social service agencies, and local newspapers or magazines. After the information has been collected, students can work in small groups to find out what services the organizations provide and what volunteer needs they have. The groups can generate questions, rehearse conversations, and actually call the organizations for information.

Tapescript

1. Would you be willing to contribute one of your wonderful pies?
2. Saturday's not great for me. But could I write you a check?

C. Vocabulary...

▶ Write *show up, make it out, stop by, pick up,* and *run out of* on the board. To review the meaning of these phrases in context, have students reread the speeches in pictures 2 and 4 on page 6.

▶ Explain that the meanings of these verb and preposition combinations cannot be figured out simply by pairing the definition of the verb with the definition of the preposition. They form units that must be considered together. If necessary, go over the meanings of these phrases with the class.

▶ Model item 1 by writing the sentence on the board with the two choices listed below the underlined phrase. Ask students for the correct choice and circle *arrived* on the board.

▶ Have students complete the exercise individually and then correct as a class.

D–E.

▶ Have students answer individually and then compare responses with a partner before reading aloud the items and responses.

Option: After both students in each pair have practiced reading the items and responses in Exercise D, have Partner B close his or her book. Partner A then reads an item and Partner B responds from memory.

Challenge: Have students create sentences or questions for Exercise D that would give rise to the alternate response. For example, the alternate response for item 1 is *Is this a sales call?* A statement that might produce this response could be *This is Mark Hibler of Vacations, Unlimited. How are you this evening?* Write all the students' ideas on the board. Students can vote for the ones they like best.

If your students are ready...

Language note: Verb and preposition combinations, called phrasal verbs, are often difficult for non-native speakers because meanings are not always obvious. Also, phrasal verbs can be separable or non-separable. Separable phrasal verbs allow or require an object between the verb and the preposition. So, for example, students may see the phrase *make out the check* or *make the check out*. Similarly, students may see the phrase *pick up cookies* or *pick cookies up*. In other combinations, the verb cannot be separated from the preposition, so the object comes after: *run out of everything*. As a class, list the phrasal verbs from the picture story on page 6 and give example sentences that show whether each verb is separable or not.

Workbook Link: Exercises 10, 11

▶ Do it yourself!

Procedure:

A. Write your own response...

▶ Working individually, students write responses to each question.

▶ Before students practice with a partner, have volunteers play the parts of the three speakers and read each speech balloon aloud. Answer each question yourself, giving students an opportunity to check the appropriateness of their own responses.

▶ Elicit examples of student responses and write them on the board. Answer any questions.

B. Discussion...

▶ Lead a class discussion about volunteering, using the questions in Exercise B as prompts. Additional prompts may include the following: *Did you volunteer here or in your home country? How do you feel about volunteering? What kinds of causes do you support? Do you support them with a check or cash, by volunteering at a booth, by baking something for a bake sale?*

(continued on p. 8)

Lesson Plan, Unit 1: Authentic practice 1 & 2 (for Student pages 6-9)–*continued*

Avoiding telemarketing fraud

Suggested teaching time: 30 minutes
Your actual teaching time: _____

Procedure:

A–B.
➤ To help students anticipate the topic, ask them to read the heading in the bar. Ask *What is fraud?* Elicit the response that it is a deception or trick intended to take money from someone.

➤ Have students look at the pictures. Ask *What do you see in the pictures?* (a man and a woman from a television news program; the woman pointing to tips for preventing fraud).

➤ Read the instructions for Exercise A and the question out loud. Then read the selection on the tapescript out loud or play the cassette. Allow students to listen as many times as necessary to complete the exercises.

➤ Working individually, students answer the question in Exercise A and then compare answers with a partner.

C. Listen again...
➤ Have students read the statements in Exercise C and check whether they are true or false. If they are unsure of the answers, let them listen again.

➤ Review answers as a class and elicit students' help in changing false answers to make them true.

Challenge: After deciding if the statements are true or false, students can listen to the report again and write down the exact wording that led them to their decision. For example, on a separate sheet of paper, students might write *1. telephone solicitation as a new and effective way to sell products and services.*

D. Answer the questions...
➤ Remind students that not all sales calls are fraudulent. They may report on a legitimate call.

➤ Students work individually to answer the questions. Tell students to be as precise and complete as possible since they will be using their answers in Exercise E on page 9.

Workbook Link: Exercises 12, 13

If your students are ready...

Culture / Civics note: The following tips are provided by the office of the Attorney General in Alaska. They may help your students avoid telemarketing fraud. For more information, refer students to this Web site:

www.law.state.ak.us/consumer_tips

A telemarketing sales pitch or charitable solicitation may be fraudulent if a telemarketer:

- says you've won a prize . . . .or that it is a "free" offer, but that you need to send money for fees, shipping, handling, insurance, etc.
- tells you that you have been pre-approved for anything that you have not requested yourself
- asks for your credit card number, bank account number, or social security number for any reason
- insists on an immediate decision to guarantee your participation in this wonderful opportunity or limited offer
- offers to have someone pick up your check at your home or office or requests that you use overnight mail. This can be a sign that the telemarketer wants to avoid inspection under the federal mail fraud law.
- confuses you with fast talk that he or she does not adequately explain
- keeps talking after you've said no

Tapescript
Man: And now we turn to Consumer Corner, a weekly feature of interest to consumers. Here's Julie Clark, our consumer reporter, with tonight's topic. Good evening, Julie. I know you have something very interesting for us tonight.

Woman: Good evening, Bill. Good evening, viewers. Can you name the number-one consumer complaint nationwide? If you said telemarketing, you're absolutely right. Just in case you don't know what telemarketing is, it's those annoying calls that arrive as soon as you've put dinner on the table or lowered yourself into a nice hot bath.

Man: What is telemarketing?

(Tapescript is continued on page 9.)

Lesson Plan, Unit 1: Authentic practice 2 (for Student pages 8-9)–continued

Tapescript (continued from page 8)

Woman: The term *telemarketing* was first used by telephone companies to promote telephone solicitation as a new and effective way to sell products and services. And although most telemarketers are honest, others are dishonest and take advantage of the situation, selling inferior products or—worse—collecting money and not delivering the merchandise ordered.
 Remember: Telemarketers who do this are con artists. And the product they sell is a fraud.

Man: What can we do to protect ourselves from telemarketing fraud?

Woman: Well, there are some important steps any consumer can take. First of all: The law says that telemarketers cannot call you before 8 a.m. or after 9 p.m.
 Next: Get the name and address of the company that is calling. Also, telemarketers have to tell you that they are selling something, that this is a sales call.
 Con artists pretend that they are taking a survey or offering you something for free. Before you know it, they're selling you something, trying to get you to give them your credit card number. That's fraud.

Man: Why is it such a bad idea to give them your credit card number?

Woman: Well, if the call is a fraud, and the con artist who's calling you has your name and your credit card number, he or she can use that information to charge things with your card. Your card has been stolen, but you don't even know it's been stolen.
 And finally: Before you pay for anything over the phone, ask the telemarketer to tell you the total cost of the goods you are buying.

Man: That's great advice. So you're saying (1) Get the name of the company. And (2) Get the total price before paying. That's great advice. It should go a long way toward preventing telemarketing fraud.

Woman: Oh, and one more thing. If you suspect fraud, or if the caller insists on continuing after you've said you're not interested, hang up the phone. *You're* not being rude. The caller is.

Man: As always, practical advice from Julie Clark. This is Bill Bell, with tonight's Consumer Corner report, thanking you for me and for Julie Clark. Good night.

E. True story...

▶ Model this activity by telling a true story about a sales call you received. Describe the call, covering all the questions given in Exercise D on page 8.

▶ After students practice telling their stories to a partner or a group, invite volunteers to share stories with the class.

▶ Elicit or point out any patterns in the calls, such as the types of businesses, the time of day, students' responses, their feelings about the calls.

FYI...

▶ Encourage students to investigate the FTC Web site. Depending on your students' previous experience using the Internet, you may need to help them with computer skills.

If your students are ready...

Culture / Civics note: In the United States and Canada, government and social service agencies often have a Web site, a place on the Internet where people can get information. People can access such Web sites by typing in the URL (Web site address) in the address box. A URL often begins with the letters http://www.

▶ Do it yourself!

Procedure:

A-B.

▶ Model the phone call with a student to show that the role play begins with the written conversation and then continues with the students' own words and ideas. Play the role of Partner B as a con artist or an honest salesperson. If necessary, repeat the conversation, making the other choice for the caller.

▶ Put students in pairs. Partner A answers the call. Partner B plays either a con artist or an honest salesperson. Have students continue the conversation and then switch roles.

▶ Lead a discussion about the role play. Read the questions from the book and extend the discussion by asking additional questions such as *Was it harder to play the role of a con artist or an honest salesperson? Why? Was it easier to respond to the con artist or the honest salesperson? What was the hardest thing to do on the phone? What consumer response was most effective against the con artist?*

Copyright © 2004 by Pearson Education, Inc.
All rights reserved.

LESSON PLAN, UNIT 1: AUTHENTIC PRACTICE 3 (for Student pages 10-11)

Summary of Lesson Plan

▶ **PRESENTATION**
Authentic practice 3:
Reading and critical thinking (Student pages 10-11)
Suggested teaching time: 60 minutes
  includes Language Note
Your actual teaching time: _____

▶ Authentic practice 3
(Student pages 10-11)

Suggested teaching time: 60 minutes
Your actual teaching time: _____

Volunteerism in the local community

Procedure:

A. Read and listen to the letters.

➤ Ask students if they have seen advice columns before. If possible, bring in advice columns from a local newspaper. Explain that people write when they have a problem and ask for advice or an opinion about what they should do. The columnist writes back, and the letters are published in the newspaper. Ask students if the newspapers in their countries have advice columns.

➤ Explain that *Ask Joan* is an advice column for people who are new to this country and have questions about cultural expectations.

➤ Play the cassette or read the letters. Students listen and read silently. Pause after Nero's letter and ask *What is the problem? What will Joan's advice be?* Encourage students to make predictions and then have them listen to the response. Ask *What was Joan's response?* Repeat for Grace's letter and the response.

Option: Have students close their books and list the volunteer opportunities they can remember from the letters. Brainstorm other volunteer opportunities such as clothing drives, toy collections, and blood drives.

B. Check . . .

➤ Allow students to listen to the letters again, if helpful, and then have them complete the exercise. Remind them to check the column marked with **?** if the letters do not give any information.

➤ As students compare answers with a partner, circulate to answer any questions.

Challenge: To help students practice discrete listening skills, pass out slips of paper on which you have written the following words: *junior, college, wonderful, participating, tradition, ambulance, food pantry, chores, homemaker, church, synagogue, mosque, soup kitchens, homeless shelters, donated goods, charitable contributions.* Give everyone at least one slip. Depending on the number of students, you may have to write down some phrases more than once. Tell students that they are going to hear the letters again. When they hear the word on the slip of paper, they should stand up. If students miss their cues, play the cassette or read the letters again.

Challenge: Have students listen to the letters for the rising or falling intonation of items in a list. First have them locate the lists (teenager volunteer activities, volunteer activities at the firehouse, religious organizations, non-religious institutions). Then play the cassette or read the letters again. Have students mark the intonation above the listed items and then practice reading the lists aloud with a partner. Invite volunteers to read for the class. Discuss the general pattern of intonation in a list (rising intonation at the end of each item and falling intonation at the end of the list) and ask students to create their own lists (for example, what they need at the store, chores they have to do) to read aloud.

If your students are ready . . .

Language note: In these letters, Joan lists options for both Nero and Grace. In writing, items in a list are usually separated by commas, with *and* or *or* before the last item (*a church, a synagogue, or a mosque*). In speaking, the speaker indicates a list by using rising intonation at the end of each item and falling intonation on the last item.

(continued on p. 11)

Lesson Plan, Unit 1: Authentic practice 3 (for Student pages 10-11)–*continued*

C. Discussion...

➤ After students answer the questions individually, have them discuss their answers in small groups.

FYI...

➤ Explain the difference between federal programs (those run by the U. S. government) and national programs (nonprofit groups that are found throughout the country). Ask what students know about the programs listed. Tell them, or have them find out, which organizations have a local branch in your city or town. With the class, add other volunteer opportunities to the lists, or make a third list of local programs on the board.

➤ Have students check the HUD Web site for more information on volunteerism. Students may also want to compare volunteering in the United States and Canada after accessing the Canadian Web site.

Option: Put students in small groups. Have each group choose a national volunteer program to research. Each group should first brainstorm questions they want answered about the volunteer program. They can look the organization up in the phone book to see if there is a local office. Students can then call the office or go online to find out the answers to their questions. Questions might include *What kind of work do volunteers do? Do they need experience? How much time is usually involved? Do you need volunteers now?*

Workbook Link: Exercises 14, 15, 16

➤ Do it yourself!

Procedure:

A–B.

➤ Put students in small groups of mixed nationalities and have them fill in the chart with information from group members.

➤ Lead a discussion about volunteering in different cultures. Copy the chart on the board to list the different ways people help each other.

Option: To extend the discussion, read the following statements. Ask groups to agree or disagree with each statement and defend their opinions. Have volunteers from each group share their opinions with the class.

1. Charity should be left up to the individual.
2. The government is responsible for making sure everyone has food and shelter.
3. To be a good citizen, you must give time and/or money to help others.
4. The needs of the poor are adequately met by government agencies.

Your notes

LESSON PLAN, UNIT 1: REVIEW (for Student pages 12-14)

Summary of Lesson Plan

➤ **Review (Student pages 12-14)**
Suggested teaching time: 60 minutes
Your actual teaching time: _____

➤ **UNIT REVIEW**
Includes expansion activities
role play
dialogues
writing
Workbook activities
outside reading
realia applications
math skills applications
civic lesson applications
Booster Pak activities

 Review (Student pages 12-14)

Suggested teaching time: 60 minutes
Your actual teaching time: _____

Procedure:

A. Pair work or group work.
➤ Have students take turns pointing to and naming as many things as they can in the picture.

Ask and answer questions.
➤ Ask the class *Who are the people?* (a family preparing for a bake sale and a used clothing sale and a telemarketer) *What are they doing?* (The father is collecting used clothing for the sale, the mother is baking for the bake sale, the daughter is making a sign for the sale, the son and the telemarketer are having a telephone conversation.)
➤ Point to one person in the picture and ask questions such as *Where is this person? What is this person wearing? How does this person feel? Why do you think so?*

Option: Working in pairs, students can write their own questions about the picture. Elicit example questions before they begin, such as *Where are they? What does the sign say?* Create a game by separating the students into two teams. Teams take turns asking the questions team members have created. Give points for each correct answer.

Create conversations.
➤ Ask the class to choose one of the two pairs of people with speech balloons in the picture. Have students label the person on the left A and the person on the right B. Write A: on the board and elicit the help of the class in creating the first line of a conversation between the people. Then write B: and elicit a response. Continue adding lines to the conversation as a class, encouraging students to say as much as they can.

➤ With a partner, have students role-play the parts of the other pair in the picture. Circulate and listen to the conversations. Use prompts if necessary to help students extend the conversation, such as *What company does the woman represent? What is she selling? Do you think she's a con artist or an honest salesperson? Why do you think so? What can the son say to discourage the telemarketer?* Review the different ways people can decline a telemarketer's offer.

Option: After students have created the conversations suggested by the picture, give them a new task. Have them imagine conversations between different pairs, this time including the young woman at the table, and having a family member accept the telemarketer's solicitation.

Tell a story.

Option: Ways to volunteer. Have students point to the members of the family and explain the way in which each is volunteering. Brainstorm other possible ways to volunteer.

Option: Would you be willing...? Imagine that a member of the family is making a telephone solicitation for donations for the sale. As a class, discuss possible questions the recipient might have, such as *Who did you say it was for? When is the sale? Where is it?*

Option: Right now! Have students summarize the activities in the picture. Encourage the use of the present continuous by asking such questions as *What is the young man doing right now? What is telemarketer saying right now?*

(continued on p. 13)

12   **Book 4 Lesson Plans**

Lesson Plan, Unit 1: Review (for Student pages 12-14)–*continued*

🎧 B. Listening comprehension...

➤ To set the scene, tell students they will hear a conversation between a telemarketer and the man who answers the call.

➤ Play the cassette or read the conversation out loud while students listen with books closed.

➤ Have students open their books. Read the instructions out loud. Emphasize that students will be deciding whether the statements are true or false, based on the conversation they hear.

➤ Play the cassette or read the conversation as many times as necessary for students to complete the exercise.

Option: Have students rewrite the false statements to make them true.

C. Complete the conversation...

➤ If necessary, review the restrictions on using the present continuous and the simple present tense, including the categories of non-action verbs: the senses, mental states, emotional states, possession.

➤ Have students check answers with a partner. Review answers as a class.

Option: Have partners read the conversation out loud, changing roles for further practice.

If your students are ready...

Culture / Civics note: International law defines refugees as people who are forced to flee their country. They have run away because they are afraid that they will be hurt or killed because of their race, religion, nationality, membership in a social group, or political opinion. They are afraid to return to their own country because they believe their government cannot protect them. Both the United States and Canada accept a limited number of refugees each year. Refugees are given money, medical treatment, English-language classes, job training, and other services to help them start a new life.

Tapescript

Man: Hello?

Woman: Good evening. How are you this evening?

Man: Fine, thanks. But we're having dinner right now, and the baby's crying. Is this a sales call?

Woman: Actually, no. I'm calling on behalf of the Institute for Better Parenting. Do you have a moment to answer some questions?

Man: What was the name of the institute?

Woman: The Institute for Better Parenting.

Man: Are you selling something?

Woman: Not really. But we *do* have a special one-time free offer for new subscribers to our magazine, *Parent and Child*. Have you had an opportunity to see *Parent and Child* on the newsstand?

Man: No, I never have, ... but as I said, we're having dinner right now, and ...

Woman: That's because it isn't sold on newsstands. But if it were, it would cost $36.00 a year. But because you're a new parent, we'd like to offer you a subscription to *Parent and Child*, absolutely free, with no obligation for three months. Then, after three months, if you're not absolutely thrilled with *Parent and Child*, just send back the last month's issue and we won't bill you for any issues you have received.

Man: I'm sorry, but we never accept offers over the phone. If you'd be kind enough to send us the offer in writing, we'd be glad to consider the offer.

Woman: Well, the problem is that this offer is only good until Tuesday. It's a one-time offer, and as I said, it's absolutely free and there's no obligation, and [click]

(continued on p. 14)

Lesson Plan, Unit 1: Review (for Student pages 12-14)–*continued*

D–F.

➤ Students work individually to complete the review exercises.

➤ Circulate to offer help as needed.

➤ Have students check answers with a partner. Review answers as a class.

➤ Identify any areas of difficulty that may require additional instruction and practice.

Option: Have students practice Exercise D in pairs. One person reads the statement or question and the other reads the response.

Option: Have students write definitions for the words or phrases that are not defined in Exercise E.

Option: Have students share the advice they wrote in Exercise F.

G. Composition ...

➤ Provide students with concrete approaches to writing about the picture on page 12. Use one of the following options, give students a choice of options, or assign options based on students' level of proficiency. Model what is expected of students for each option.

➤ Advise students to look back through the unit for help and ideas as they write.

➤ Circulate to offer help as needed.

Option: Have students choose one of the pairs of people who are talking to each other in the picture, label the people *A* and *B*, and write an extended conversation for them. Have students use the same format as the model conversations on pages 2 and 3. Students can later role-play their conversations for the class.

Option: Have students number the people in the picture and then write two sentences about each one. To reinforce the grammar points in the unit, one sentence can describe what the person is doing right now, and the other can discuss the person's activities using a non-action verb.

Option: Have students write a paragraph about a sales call they received at home. They should include answers to the questions in Exercise D on page 8. If they answered previously about a fraudulent call, this paragraph should be about a legitimate call, and vice versa.

Challenge: Ask students to exchange compositions. Partners will peer-edit the compositions.

Now I can

➤ Read the first item in the box out loud: *Now I can agree to contribute to a good cause.* Elicit from the class an example of how to agree to contribute to a good cause, such as *The homeless shelter is a good cause. I'd be happy to make a donation.*

➤ In pairs, students take turns reading each item in the box and giving an example of what they have learned. When students can provide an example, they should check that box. For the items students weren't able to check, they should look back through the unit for ideas.

➤ When students have finished reviewing with their partners, read each item out loud and elicit an example from the class.

➤ Students can add examples of other skills they acquired while working on this unit.

Oral test (optional)

You may want to use the *Now I can* box as an informal evaluation. While students are working on the *Composition* activity, you can call them up individually and check their ability with two or three objectives.

LESSON PLAN, UNIT 2: PREVIEW/PRACTICAL CONVERSATIONS (for Student pages 15-17)

Summary of Lesson Plan

▶ **Preview and Practical conversations** (Student pages 15-17)
Suggested teaching time: 60 minutes
includes Language Notes & Discussion
Your actual teaching time: _____

Preview and Practical conversations (Student pages 15-17)

Suggested teaching time: 60 minutes
Your actual teaching time: _____

Warm up. Look at this section of a lease. What is a lease for? Have you ever signed a lease?

Procedure:
- ▶ Ask students to stand and sort themselves into groups according to the type of housing they live in. When students are grouped—perhaps into *apartment, house, condo*—form new small groups consisting of a student from each type of housing.
- ▶ To access students' own experience, ask the small groups to answer questions such as *Where do you live now? Do you rent or do you own? What are some differences between buying a residence and renting or leasing one?* (When you buy a residence, you usually take out a mortgage, you have monthly payments, you gain equity over time, you are responsible for upkeep and repairs; when you lease, the landlord is responsible for at least some maintenance and repairs, you pay rent each month, you have responsibilities toward the property.) *What are some advantages of renting? Of owning?* One student from each group should be the recorder and one the reporter of the group's ideas.
- ▶ Write *Advantages of renting* and *Advantages of owning* on the board. Elicit students' ideas from the reporters in each group. Your lists might look like the following:

Advantages of renting	Advantages of owning
Less money up front	Mortgage payments are tax deductible
Landlord responsible for major repairs	It's an investment that you can then sell or rent
May be cheaper	
More available	More stable

- ▶ Ask students to look at the sections of the lease. To encourage reading strategies, ask *What are the headings in this section of the lease?* (pests, utilities)

  Remind students that headings help readers know what topics will be discussed.

- ▶ Check comprehension of terms. Ask *What are pests?* (bugs, rodents) *What are utilities?* (gas, electricity or power, cable, telephone) *Who is the lessee?* (the person renting) *Who is the lessor?* (the landlord or property owner).

- ▶ Have pairs of students read the sections of the lease and summarize the terms. Review the terms of the lease as a class, explaining difficult wording as necessary.

If your students are ready...

Language note: Tell students that they will see the *-or* (or *-er*) ending in *lessor* and the *-ee* ending in *lessee* attached to different base words. For example, elicit that an *employer* is the person who employs or hires (the boss) and that an *employee* is the person who gets employed or hired (the worker). Elicit that a *lessor* is the person who gives the lease, and the *lessee* is the person who receives the lease. Brainstorm other words with the same endings, such as *supervisor* and *supervisee*, and discuss the meanings of the words and the endings.

Unit 2 objectives

Procedure:
- ▶ Have students read the objectives. Ask them to put a check next to the objectives that they can do now and circle those they want to work on most.

- ▶ Ask students to underline any words they do not understand. Write any unfamiliar terms on the board. Some students may not be familiar with *tenant rights, the Fair Housing Act,* or *housing discrimination*. Give a quick explanation of these terms.

- ▶ Focus students' attention on the issues in the unit. Ask *What are housing emergencies?* (no heat, no hot water, a broken pipe) *What would you look for in a potential rental?* (safety features, evidence of good building maintenance, laundry facilities). Tell students they will learn more about these topics in the unit.

(continued on p. 2)

Book 4 Lesson Plans

Lesson Plan, Unit 2: Preview and practical conversations (for Student pages 15-17)–*continued*

Model 1

Content: asking for an emergency repair, talking about household emergencies

Procedure:

A. Listen and read.

➤ Direct students' attention to the picture. Set the scene by asking questions such as *Who are the people?* (a tenant and a building manager) *Where are they?* (outside the building manager's office) *How do you know?* (There's a sign on the manager's door, and he's got a name tag on his shirt.)

➤ After students have listened to the conversation, check for comprehension. Ask questions such as *What is A's problem?* (There's no heat in his apartment.) *When does B say he can look at it?* (tomorrow) *What is A's response?* (It's urgent, meaning that tomorrow is too late.)

➤ Point out that, in *A's* first line, *I've got* is not the present perfect. It's an expression that means I have.

➤ Explain that *A's* response *I'm sorry* is not an apology for something the speaker has done but an expression of disagreement. *A* does not agree with *B's* plan to take care of the problem with the heat tomorrow.

B. Pronunciation and intonation practice.

➤ Tell students that they will listen to the conversation again and have the opportunity to repeat each speaker's lines. Play the cassette or read the conversation again. Encourage students to imitate the rhythm, stress, and intonation of the conversation as closely as possible. Correct where necessary, helping students to pronounce the language clearly.

Option: Have the class read the conversation chorally, with half the class reading *A's* part and half reading *B's* part. Then have students switch parts. Or have the entire class read one part while you read the other.

Vocabulary

➤ Compare the household emergencies to those the students volunteered when they discussed the objectives on page 15. Brainstorm other household emergencies. Your list might include these problems: *The ceiling is leaking, the basement is flooded, there's no electricity.*

➤ Point out to students that the expression *There's no . . .* is the same as *There isn't any . . .* Have students rephrase *There's no heat, hot water, air conditioning* using *There isn't any.*

➤ Play the cassette or read the phrases and have students repeat the household emergencies.

Option: Put students in small groups to discuss household problems that they are responsible for fixing vs. those problems that they have to get help for. Have students consider how their responsibilities change depending on whether they are renters or owners.

C. Pair work . . .

➤ Model the conversation with a more advanced student. Play the role of Student A. Make sure students understand that they can use any of the household emergencies from the *Vocabulary* in the first slot.

➤ Repeat the conversation playing the role of Student B. Make sure that students understand that they must use a future time in Student B's first slot. You can exaggerate the manager's unwillingness to cooperate by responding *Well, I can't look at that until Thursday* in the last slot.

➤ Students practice the conversation with a partner, taking turns playing the roles of Student A and Student B. Circulate and offer help as needed.

If your students are ready . . .

Language note: Point out that the first emergency states that <u>A</u> pipe burst, whereas the next two emergencies state <u>The</u> lock is broken and <u>The</u> window is broken. Direct students' attention to the use of the indefinite article in one emergency and the use of the definite article in the other situations. If necessary, explain that in the case of the lock and the window, we are looking at one specific lock and one specific window. In the case of a pipe bursting, it could be any one of the many pipes that provide water to the household.

Workbook Link: Exercises 1, 5

(continued on p. 3)

Lesson Plan, Unit 2: Preview and practical conversations (for Student pages 15-17)–*continued*

Model 2

Content: extending a casual greeting, discussing an outage with another tenant, talking about utilities

Procedure:

A–B.

- Read the bar for Model 2. Explain that *an outage* is a way of saying that something electrical doesn't work.

- To set the scene for the conversation, direct students' attention to the photo. Ask questions such as *Who do you think the people are?* (tenants, neighbors) *Where are they?* (in an apartment building lobby) Have students look at the corner picture of the TV. Ask *What's the matter with the TV?* Elicit or state the phrase *bad reception* and ask students to think about why the reception might be bad.

- Draw on students' experience by asking *How many of your neighbors do you know by name? Speak to on a regular basis? Feel you can call on for help?*

- Play the cassette or read the conversation and then check comprehension. Ask questions such as *What is the man's name?* (Peter) *What is the problem?* (Their cable is out.) *What is the woman going to do?* (check her cable and let Peter know)

Vocabulary

- After students repeat the words, tell them that *power* is a synonym for *electricity*. We can say that *our power's out* or *our electricity's out*. We can also talk about *a power outage* although not *an electricity outage*.

- Relate to the students' experience by asking questions such as *Who has cable? Gas? Phones?* Explain that most people have electricity, but the other utilities may be less common. Ask whether students have satellite dishes rather than cable and cell phones rather than a land line.

C. Pair work ...

- Model the conversation with a more advanced student. Play the part of Student B to demonstrate a negative response to Student A's question and describe a problem. Note that Student B says *Our* (or *My*) *cable, power, gas is out* but *Our* (or *My*) *phones are out*. Students can use *my* or *our*.

- Have students practice the conversation in pairs, stating a variety of problems with their utilities.

Workbook Link: Exercises 2, 3, 4

➤ Do it yourself!

Procedure:

A. Pair work ...

- Direct students' attention to the picture on the right. Ask *What's the problem?* (There is a flood in the woman's kitchen.)

- Put students in pairs to create a conversation between the woman and the building manager. The woman reports the urgent problem and asks for help. Have pairs practice the conversation, switching roles for more practice.

B. Discussion ...

- Ask volunteers to read the speech balloons at the bottom of the page and match each solution to a household emergency or outage.

- Students may see the term *super* rather than *building manager*. Explain that *super* is a shortened form of *superintendent* and is common in urban areas. *Superintendent* and *building manager* are often used interchangeably.

Option: Create a chart on the board. Write the headings *Problem, Called the manager, Called the utility company, Called a specialist, Fixed it myself*. Ask students what household emergencies they have had. As they describe the problems, write them in the left-hand column under the heading *Problem*. When you have a list of problems, ask *How many people called the building manager for this problem? How many people called the utility company? How many people called a specialist such as an electrician or a plumber? How many people fixed the problem themselves?* As students raise their hands, put a tally mark in each column. You might have a chart like the one following:

Problem	Called the manager	Called the utility company	Called a specialist	Fixed it myself
A power outage	///	++++ ++++ //		
A broken pipe	////		//	/
A cable outage		////		
A broken lock	/		/	
A broken window	/			/

Copyright © 2004 by Pearson Education, Inc.
All rights reserved.

LESSON PLAN, UNIT 2: PRACTICAL GRAMMAR (for Student pages 18-19)

Summary of Lesson Plan

▶ **PRESENTATION**
Practical grammar (Student pages 18-19)
Suggested teaching time: 60 minutes
  includes Language Notes (10 minutes)
Your actual teaching time: _____

▶ Practical grammar
(Student pages 18-19)

Suggested teaching time: 60 minutes
Your actual teaching time: _____

The present perfect

Content: contrast between the use of the present perfect when an exact past time is not stated and the simple past tense when an exact past time is known

Procedure:
➤ Review the formation of the present perfect. Remind students that the past participle for regular verbs ends in *–ed*. They can refer to page 145 for the past participle of irregular verbs. If necessary, review the structure of negatives and questions in the present perfect.

➤ Have volunteers read the information in the box aloud. Make sure students understand the term *stated*. Ask students to circle the stated time in the last example sentence.

➤ Review the adverbs that indicate the use of the present perfect (*ever, never, still, yet, already*). Have students underline these adverbs in the first five example sentences.

➤ Remind students of the difference between the simple past tense (an action completed at a specific stated time in the past) and the present perfect (an action not completed, or one for which the past time is not known or not important).

A. Complete the paragraph ...

➤ Tell students that they can contract the subject pronoun *I* with *have* in each sentence: for example, *I've seen*.

➤ After the students have completed the exercise, correct as a class.

➤ Point out the adverbs that cued the use of the present perfect: *still* in item 5 and *yet* in item 8.

Option: Ask students to write their own paragraphs about trying to find a place to live, a school, or a job. Tell them to use the present perfect at least five times. When they are finished, ask them to exchange paragraphs with a partner to read and correct.

(continued on p. 5)

Your notes

Lesson Plan, Unit 2: Practical grammar (for Student pages 18-19)–*continued*

B. Complete each sentence...

➤ To model item 1, write down the sentence with each possible answer inserted. Have students choose the correct sentence. Point out that the phrase *on Monday* states a specific time in the past and therefore requires the simple past tense.

➤ Have students complete the exercise individually and then check answers with a partner. Review as a class.

Option: To reinforce the use of the present perfect in questions with *ever*, play *Have you ever...?* Ask students to write five questions that begin with *Have you ever*. The questions should be about things that most people have done, such as *Have you ever eaten fast food?* Have students sit in chairs arranged in a circle. One student stands in the middle of the circle and asks one of his or her questions. Students who can answer *yes* to the question must stand up and find a new place to sit. The student in the middle also tries to find a place to sit. The student left standing goes to the middle and asks a question. Play the game long enough so that most students have a chance to ask a question.

Workbook Link: Exercise 6

For and *since*

Procedure:
➤ Write example sentences on the board, underlining *for* and *since*. Use these sentences or create your own: *I've lived here for a long time, I've lived in my apartment for 10 years, I've had this VCR for three years, I've had my TV since 2000, I've worked at my current job since 1998.* Elicit the use of the present perfect with *for* and *since* to talk about actions that began in the past and that continue in the present.

➤ Review the use of *for* with numbers and intervals of time (for example, *for five years*) and *since* with a specific point in time (*since last Monday*). Write examples such as the following and ask students to add *for* or *since*: (for) three weeks, (since) yesterday, (since) 2:30, (for) a month, (since) December.

➤ Tell students that with *for* and *since* certain verbs (*work, live, study, teach*) have the same meaning in the present perfect continuous as in the present perfect. Read the pair of example sentences in the box and create other pairs with the class.

➤ Brainstorm with the class the non-action verbs that they remember from Unit 1. Tell students that non-action verbs take the present perfect rather than the present perfect continuous for actions that began in the past and continue to the present. Read aloud the example sentence in the box: *Ms. Drake has been our landlord for ten years.*

➤ Have students read the rules and the example sentences in the box silently.

C. Complete the paragraph...

➤ Have students complete the paragraph and compare answers with a partner. Review as a class.

Option: Have students interview a partner, using these questions as a guideline: *How long have you lived at your present address? How long have you lived in this city? How long have you worked at your present job? How long have you studied at this school?* Students can then write a paragraph or report to a group about their partners.

Workbook Link: Exercises 7, 8

➤ Do it yourself!

Procedure:

A–B.

➤ Ask students to explain why the simple past tense is used for the last question on the form. ("Before that" is a "stated" time.)

➤ After students have completed the form, put them in small groups to brainstorm questions that a rental agent might ask.

➤ Write students' ideas on the board. Questions might include the following: *How long have you lived at your current address? Where did you live before that? What kind of work do you do? How long have you worked there? How many people are in your household? What size apartment are you looking for?*

➤ Have students work in pairs and role-play a conversation between a rental agent and a prospective tenant, using the information in their housing history forms and providing additional personal information as necessary. Have students switch roles for more practice.

Workbook Link: Exercises 9, 10

LESSON PLAN, UNIT 2: AUTHENTIC PRACTICE 1 & 2 (for Student pages 20-23)

Summary of Lesson Plan

▶ **PRESENTATION**
Authentic practice 1 & 2:
Listening (Student pages 20-23)
Suggested teaching time: 60 minutes
Your actual teaching time: _____

Authentic practice 1
(Student pages 20-21)

Suggested teaching time: 30 minutes
Your actual teaching time: _____

Renting a house or apartment

Procedure:

➤ To set the scene for the picture story, ask questions about the pictures, such as *Who's in the pictures?* (a man and a woman) *Where are they?* (in a rental office) *What do you think they are talking about?* (the lease; renting an apartment)

➤ Play the cassette or read the picture story. With books open, students read along silently.

➤ Check for comprehension by asking questions such as *Who is having the conversation?* (a rental agent and a prospective tenant) *Does the tenant have to pay for repairs?* (only if the tenant is at fault, or has done something that caused the damage) *What does the tenant want to do with his apartment this summer?* (rent it to his uncle)

➤ Students may see some terms that are unfamiliar but whose meaning can be inferred from context: *at fault, fair enough, not off the top of my head, get back to you, take your time.* If necessary, explain.

Option: Have students read the speech balloons again. Ask *What questions does the man ask?* (Who's responsible for repairs? What do you mean, "at fault"? Is that a problem? Does that include cable? Do you mind if I take the lease home and get back to you tomorrow?) Have volunteers read the man's questions and the agent's answers.

A. Read the picture story...

➤ Have students read the statements and then reread the picture story.

➤ Have students individually check *True* or *False* and then compare answers with a partner. Students should be prepared to support their answers with direct quotations from the picture story.

Option: Students rewrite each false statement to make it true (for example, *Landlords are responsible for repairs unless the tenant is at fault*).

B. Listen...

➤ Tell students that they will listen to the tapescript or the cassette and read aloud the responses in their text.

➤ Read each item in the tapescript out loud or play the cassette. Allow students to listen as many times as necessary to complete the exercise. If students have difficulty, prompt them by reading the response yourself.

Challenge: Use the prompts for Exercise B as a dictation. Have students listen to the questions and write what they hear. Allow students to listen as many times as necessary. Ask volunteers to write the questions on the board. Make corrections as a class. Students can then practice the prompts and responses with a partner.

Tapescript

1. Have you had a chance to look over the lease?

2. Do you mind if I take the lease home and get back to you tomorrow?

(continued on p. 7)

Book 4 Lesson Plans

Lesson Plan, Unit 2: Authentic practice 1 & 2 (for Student pages 20-23)–*continued*

C. Vocabulary...

➤ Have students complete the exercise. If necessary, let them refer to the picture story to use the context to infer meaning.

Challenge: Put students in pairs to write definitions for the words that were not used to complete the sentences. In item 1, for example, students write a definition for *leasing*: paying money to a landlord for the use of an apartment for a certain period of time. Encourage students to use dictionaries. As a variation, students can form two teams to write the definitions of the unused words. Each team can challenge the other to provide the word that matches their definition.

D–E.

➤ Have students answer the questions in Exercise D individually and then compare responses with a partner before reading aloud the items and responses.

Option: After both students have practiced reading the items and responses in Exercise D, have Partner B in each pair close his or her book. Partner A then reads the item, and Partner B responds from memory.

Challenge: Have pairs of students work together to write a statement or a question for each unused response in Exercise D. For example, in item 1, a statement that could elicit the response *Fair enough* might be *If you break it, you fix it*. Have students take turns reading the new items and responses.

Workbook Link: Exercises 11, 12

➤ Do it yourself!

Procedure:

➤ Tell students to imagine that this rental agent is discussing their new lease with them. Have students write their own responses.

➤ Before students practice with a partner, have a volunteer play the part of the rental agent and read each speech balloon aloud. Respond to each statement or question for yourself, giving students an opportunity to check the appropriateness of their responses.

➤ Have students interview each other in pairs to check their responses.

(continued on p. 8)

Your notes

Lesson Plan, Unit 2: Authentic practice 1 & 2 (for Student pages 20-23)–*continued*

Authentic practice 2
(Student pages 22-23)

Tips for apartment hunters

Suggested teaching time: 30 minutes
Your actual teaching time: _____

Procedure:

🎧 A. Listening comprehension ...

➤ To help students attend to important information in the listening, ask them to read the bar above the pictures.

➤ To set the scene for the listening, ask students about the picture on the left: *Who do you think the man is?* (someone on the radio, a talk show host) Have students look at the pictures on the right and repeat the captions after you. Make sure students understand what each item is used for.

➤ Ask students to predict what the tips will be about. Elicit the topics *pests, security,* and *electrical concerns.* Brainstorm other issues that might be important to apartment hunters: *appliances, general maintenance, cleanliness, facilities on site.* Write students' ideas on the board.

➤ Tell students that the caller on the radio show is going to take notes about the tips and that they should too. To practice the important academic skill of note taking, ask students to write down the topics and then add details under these headings.

➤ Sequential connectors are important cues. To help students follow the listening and take good notes, brainstorm words and phrases that give the order of information (*first, second, third, next, then, finally*). Tell students to listen for these words.

➤ Read the instructions for Exercise A out loud. Then read the selection or play the cassette through once and have the students write down the main topics using the sequencing connectors. They should note nine points (*the neighborhood at night, security, emergency exits, plumbing, appliances, electrical problems, pest infestation, maintenance, laundry facilities*). Read the selection out loud or play the cassette again so students can write down supporting details. Have students compare notes with a partner.

Option: Have volunteers come up to the board and write down their notes for each of the nine points mentioned in the selection.

B–C.

➤ After students answer the questions individually, have them compare answers with a partner.

Option: In preparation for a class discussion, have students list reasons for their answer to item 3 and discuss the topic with their partners. Ask the class which piece of advice they thought was most important. Write students' reasons on the board. After the discussion, have students vote on the most important piece of advice.

🎧 D. Which subjects ...

➤ Have students read the list of subjects.

➤ Let students listen to the selection again and then check the appropriate boxes.

➤ Have students check their answers with a partner, and then review as a class.

E. Vocabulary ...

➤ Tell students to go over the notes they took in Exercise A. Reading the main topics and the details will help them do the matching vocabulary exercise.

➤ Read the first item in column A and the related item in column B. Make sure students understand that they are to write the letter of the term in column B. Ask students if they noted any other terms under the topic *Security* (window locks).

➤ After students match the terms in column A with those in column B, have them compare answers with a partner. Review as a class. Ask if reviewing the notes helped them complete this exercise.

Tapescript

Jack: This is Jack Mee at "Rent Talk," W-A-L-K's call-in show with tips for tenants. Our number's 1-800-TENANTS, that's 1-800-836-2687. Let's go to our phones. Irene in Moline. Speak to me.

Irene: Jack?

Jack: Yes, Irene. You're on the air.

Irene: Thank you for taking my call. I was recently separated from my husband, and I'm looking for my own place. Tomorrow I'm going to see a bunch of apartments, and I don't know what to look for.

Jack: Do you live alone, Irene?

Irene: Well, I have a ten-year-old daughter.

Jack: OK. Let me make a few suggestions. Do you have a pencil and paper for a few tips? You might want to jot them down. They'll save you a lot of grief down the line.

Irene: OK, Jack. I'm ready.

Jack: First: Check the neighborhood at night. Does it feel safe? If you came home late with your daughter, would you feel frightened? If you took a

(Tapescript is continued on page 9.)

Lesson Plan, Unit 2: Authentic practice 1 & 2 (for Student pages 20-23)–continued

Tapescript (continued from page 8)
bus, could you walk from the bus stop without looking over your shoulder?
Irene: [writing] Hmm. Check the neighborhood at night. That *is* a good idea.
Jack: Second: Still thinking about security, check the doors and windows. Are there dead-bolt locks on the front and back doors? Do the windows lock?
Irene: [writing] Dead-bolt locks.
Jack: Third: And this might seem unnecessary, but check the emergency exits, fire stairs, and fire escapes, and see that there are smoke detectors. Fire code violations are common, especially if you're renting an apartment in a smaller building or a private home. Better safe than sorry.
  Fourth: Check the plumbing. Look for leaks, drips, and evidence of past damage. You don't want to deal with burst pipes and ruined possessions.
Irene: You can say *that* again.
Jack: Fifth: Check the appliances. For example, turn on the stove. Raise and lower the oven temperature. Turn on the broiler. Turn on all the burners to make sure they all work.
Irene: That's a good idea.
Jack: Sixth: Look for electrical problems—frayed wires, blown fuses or tripped circuit breakers, missing switches, and the like.
  Seventh: Look for evidence of pest infestation: roaches and other insects, mice, or worse, rats. Are there bait traps or sprays around, in cabinets and under sinks? You know where to check!
  Eighth: Check the maintenance of the common areas: stairs, halls, basement, elevators. Is there trash or other evidence of neglect?
  Ninth: Check laundry facilities. If there are no washers and dryers in the building, is there a laundromat in the neighborhood? And while you're at it, look for other facilities in the neighborhood: a supermarket, dry cleaner's, etc. Did you get all that?
Irene: I hope so! Those are good tips. Thanks, Jack. If I could ask you one more question.
Jack: I'm sorry. I've got another call waiting. Give us a call back and let us know how it goes. [click] This is Jack Mee at "Rent Talk," 1-800 T-E-N-A-N-T-S. Nathan, what's on *your* mind?

F–G.

▶ Have students work individually to complete the self-test.

▶ Model the activity in Exercise G by telling the class about your neighborhood and home. Give your answers from the self-test and add any other details.

Challenge: Tally the results for each question. Questions are worded so that a *no* answer indicates a potential problem. Put students in small groups to problem-solve the issues. Ask groups to fill in a chart like the one following. Planning action is important to getting students to be more proactive.

Problem	Possible solutions	Action steps
Don't feel safe in neighborhood.	Get to know neighbors, form a neighborhood watch.	Organize a meeting to discuss safety with neighbors.

Challenge: Ask students to write a composition based on one of the problems identified in the chart. Students can discuss a course of action for dealing with the problem using sequential or chronological connectors, just as Jack Mee did in the listening comprehension exercise on page 22. For example: *If you don't feel safe in your neighborhood, you should take action. First, call a meeting with your neighbors. Second . . .*

FYI . . .

▶ Read the list of other places to look for apartments. Ask students to raise their hands if they used any of these ways to find their apartment.

▶ Make sure students know what *word of mouth* is. Brainstorm people whose word-of-mouth recommendations students would trust.

▶ Have students investigate the Web site and report their findings. Ask questions such as *Would you use this Web site? Why? Why not?*

▶ Do it yourself!

Procedure:

A. Write a list . . .

▶ Remind students of the issues discussed in the listening comprehension selection and in the other exercises in this *Authentic practice* section.

▶ Have students in pairs or small groups brainstorm a list of questions to ask a rental agent.

B. Pair work . . .

▶ Model the role play with a more advanced student. Have the student use his or her own questions to play the role of the prospective tenant while you play the rental agent.

▶ Tell students they can use their own house or apartment as the model on which to base the answers to the questions the "tenant" asks.

▶ Ask volunteers to present their role play.

Workbook Link: Exercises 13, 14

LESSON PLAN, UNIT 2: AUTHENTIC PRACTICE 3 (for Student pages 24-25)

Summary of Lesson Plan

▶ **PRESENTATION**
Authentic practice 3:
Reading and critical thinking (Student pages 24-25)
Suggested teaching time: 60 minutes
  includes Cultural Discussion
Your actual teaching time: _____

Authentic practice 3
(Student pages 24-25)

Suggested teaching time: 60 minutes
Your actual teaching time: _____

Fair housing and equal opportunity

Procedure:

A. Read about...

➤ Have students read the information on the Fair Housing Act. Ask them to focus on identifying the seven factors that cannot be used as a basis for discrimination and the four actions that are specifically prohibited.

➤ Make sure students understand the meaning of *race, national origin, sex, familial status, color, religion,* and *handicap*. Put each word or phrase on the board and ask the class for examples for each category.

➤ With students, discuss the meaning of the actions that are prohibited. Have students reword these actions to make sure they understand the meaning. Be sure students understand the difference between *renting* and *selling*.

➤ To demonstrate the relevance of the Fair Housing Act to the students, ask them to look at the seven factors again and identify those that apply to them.

Option: Coming up with strategies to remember key information is an important academic skill. Brainstorm with the class strategies that could help them remember the information in the reading. Write the strategies on the board. Ideas might include *remembering the first initials, creating a mental picture, linking the concepts to something already known.*

Challenge: Have students access the Web site whose address is given at the top of the monitor screen. Ask them to summarize the additional information they read about the Fair Housing Act.

B. Vocabulary...

➤ Have volunteers read the eight definitions aloud. Discuss and reword as necessary to make sure students understand the terms and definitions. Ask students for examples of each term and together create example sentences.

➤ Brainstorm other disabilities. Write them on the board.

➤ Point out that some of the terms (*an act, refuse, a complaint*) have other definitions. Elicit these other meanings and remind students to use the context to determine the specific meaning.

➤ Have students complete the sentences. Then correct as a class.

Challenge: All of the words in the *Vocabulary* belong to word families, words that are different parts of speech but have the same base. Have students work in pairs to identify nouns and verbs with the same base. The list may include *act, action; prohibit, prohibition; refuse, refusal; disability, disable; discrimination, discriminate; complaint, complain; dwelling, dwell.*

Workbook Link: Exercises 15, 16

(continued on p. 11)

Lesson Plan, Unit 2: Authentic practice 3 (for Student pages 24-25)–*continued*

C–D.

- ➤ Put students in pairs or small groups to read the case studies and then discuss whether the landlord has committed a violation of the Fair Housing Act in refusing to rent to the person.

- ➤ Have students give advice about how to handle the situation to each person.

Option: Assign one case study to each pair of students. Give students about 10 minutes to prepare a role play between the prospective tenant and the landlord that presents the issues. After students have presented their role play, ask the class to identify the issues and vote on whether the landlord committed a violation of the Fair Housing Act.

Option: Print out the complaint form from HUD and give a copy to each group. Ask students to fill out the form based on the situation in one of the case studies. Circulate and offer help as needed.

Option: Refer students to the picture story on page 20. Point out that the prospective tenant has a disability and is in a wheelchair. Ask *Is the rental agent discriminating against the man because of his handicap? How can you tell?* Have students suggest how landlords can encourage or discourage tenants with disabilities. If necessary, suggest that a building may or may not have wheelchair access, doors that are wide enough to accommodate wheelchairs, or bathrooms that can accommodate wheelchairs.

Workbook Link: Exercises 17, 18

➤ Do it yourself!

Procedure:

A. Discussion...

- ➤ If your students come from different countries, put them in small groups according to home country.

- ➤ Ask them to discuss the three questions according to practices in their country. Tell students to be prepared to offer specific examples to support their discussion.

B. Culture talk...

- ➤ Explain that students will now be "ambassadors" to a new group to whom they will explain housing rights in their home country.

- ➤ Form new groups of students consisting of "ambassadors" from different home countries.

- ➤ Have groups discuss the differences and similarities between their countries in terms of housing rights and discrimination.

- ➤ Lead a class discussion about housing rights in various countries. Be sure to include whether discrimination occurs, what factors affect discrimination, and what tenants do about suspected discrimination.

Your notes

LESSON PLAN, UNIT 2: REVIEW (for Student pages 26-28)

Summary of Lesson Plan

➤ **Review (Student pages 26-28)**
   Suggested teaching time: 60 minutes
   Your actual teaching time: _____

➤ **UNIT REVIEW**
   Includes expansion activities
      role play
      dialogues
      writing
      Workbook activities
      outside reading
      realia applications
      math skills applications
      civic lesson applications
      Booster Pak activities

 Review (Student pages 26-28)

Suggested teaching time: 60 minutes
Your actual teaching time: _____

Procedure:

A. Pair work or group work.
➤ Have students take turns pointing to and naming as many things as they can in the picture.

Ask and answer questions.
➤ Point out the two questions asked in the directions. Point to one of the three numbered buildings on High Street. Ask *What are the people doing?* (301: repairing a problem with the cable; 303: talking about renting one of the three available apartments; 305: The tenant is complaining to the building manager.) Ask *What is the problem?* (301: The cable is out; 303: There may be discrimination against the family because of their children, pets, color, religion, or national origin; 305: There's a flood in the kitchen.)

Option: Working in pairs, students can write their own questions about the picture. Elicit example questions before they begin, such as *Who is the man in the apartment at 301 High Street? What does the sign in the window of 303 High Street say?*) Create a game by separating the students into two teams. Teams take turns asking the questions team members have created. Give points for each correct answer.

Option: Give students one minute to study the picture, trying to remember all they can about it. Remind them of some of the memory strategies you discussed earlier. Then have students close their books and form small groups. Ask questions about the picture and keep a record of the correct answers. After each question, allow the groups time to discuss and record the group's answer on a sheet of paper. Possible questions include *How many people are walking on the other side of the street?* (two) *How many dogs are in the picture?* (two) *What street are the three apartment buildings on?* (High Street) *Who is crossing the street?* (a woman pushing a child in a stroller) *Is there a parking lot in the picture?* (yes)

Create conversations.
➤ Hold up the book and point to the tenant and the manager in the lobby of 305 High Street. Play the role of the tenant and say *I've got an emergency in my apartment.* Elicit from the class an appropriate response for the manager, such as *What's the problem?* Respond, and then elicit an appropriate next line for the manager. Continue playing the role of the tenant and eliciting responses for the manager from the class.

➤ Put students in pairs and have them choose two people in the picture and create a conversation for them. Ask volunteers to role-play their conversations for the class.

Option: After students have created the conversations suggested by the picture, give them a new task. Have them imagine conversations between different pairs, such as the two tenants in the lobby of 305 High Street, or the parents of the family in front of 303 High Street.

Tell a story.
Option: Create a character. Point to one person in the picture and relate the details or his or her life. For example, for the woman crossing the street with a child in the stroller, say *Her name is Maria Arenas. She's from Chile. She's been living in the neighborhood for five years. She's been studying English since 2001 ...* Then have students tell the story of at least one person in the picture to a partner. Explain that they will need to make up the information they relate.

(continued on p. 13)

Lesson Plan, Unit 2: Review (for Student pages 26-28)–*continued*

Option: Describe the family. Have students describe the family members in front of 303 High Street. Students should include details such as a description of their clothing, their ages, and how long they have been looking for an apartment. They will need to make up some of the information.

Option: How's it going? Point to one person in the picture and give his or her extended response to the question. For example, for the tenant getting her mail at 305 High Street, say *Not so hot. My air conditioning's out again. And I've had a problem with my phone for a week . . .* Circulate through the room, encouraging students to make up as much as possible about each person's situation.

B. Listening comprehension...

➤ Tell students they are going to listen to five different conversations, one corresponding to each number in Exercise B. The task is to decide which problem is being discussed and fill in the oval.

➤ Ask students to read the options for item 1. Brainstorm terms related to an electrical problem that they might listen for, such as *outage, circuit, fuse, wire*.

➤ Read the first conversation or play the cassette.

➤ To model item 1, write out the two choices and have students choose the correct problem. Model how to select an answer by filling in the oval with the correct answer.

➤ Have students read the options for items 2 through 5.

➤ Read conversations 2 through 5 or play the cassette. Students fill in the correct ovals according to what they hear.

➤ Have students check answers with a partner. Then review as a class.

C. Read each sentence...

➤ Students work individually to complete the exercise.

➤ Have students check answers with a partner. Review answers as a class.

Challenge: Have partners create a statement or question that would require the alternate response. For example, for item 1, a student might write *The landlord wouldn't rent to me because I'm in a wheelchair.* This sentence might lead to the response *That's a violation of the Fair Housing Act!*

Tapescript

Conversation 1
A: Oh, no! Not again.
B: What?
A: I blew a fuse. It's this ridiculous hair dryer.
B: Better get a new one. Meanwhile, I'll call the super.

Conversation 2
A: Hello?
B: Hello, Mr. Cramden? This is Mrs. Norton in 3B. There's no hot water. And the cold water is dark brown.
A: You're kidding. I'll be right up to have a look.

Conversation 3
A: I can't believe the cable's out. I wanted to see the fight tonight.
B: Maybe it'll be back on by then. Did you call?
A: Sure. But it always takes a day or two until they get out to *this* neighborhood.

Conversation 4
A: Let's check the cabinets under the sink before we sign the lease.
B: Good idea. Hey, what's *this*?
A: What?
B: These boxes with blue stuff . . . I don't know what it is . . . Oh. Rat Resort? What???
A: Well, that's that. They've had rats. Forget this dump!

Conversation 5
A: We're here to see the apartment.
B: Certainly, Mr. . . . ?
A: Sirinivatsu.
B: Serina-who?
A: Sirinivatsu. It's a Chappaquakian name. We're from Chappaqua.
B: I see . . . Oh, your wife has a wheelchair? Well, I think you'd be happier in a different building. This apartment is in the basement.

(continued on p. 14)

Lesson Plan, Unit 2: Review (for Student pages 26-28)–*continued*

D–E.

➤ Students work individually to complete the review exercises.

➤ Circulate to offer help as needed.

➤ Have students check answers with a partner. Review answers as a class.

➤ Identify any areas of difficulty that may require additional instruction and practice.

Option: Review the vocabulary from the unit. You should include the terms for housing emergencies on page 16, utilities on page 17, the vocabulary items from Exercise E on page 22 and from Exercise B on page 24. Divide the class into two teams. Ask the members of Team A to define the first word. Give students a couple of minutes to prepare their definition. Teams get 1 point for each correct definition. If a team can't give an acceptable definition, the other team can try. Ask Team B to define the second word. Continue playing until all the words have been defined.

F. Composition...

➤ Provide students with concrete approaches to writing about the picture on page 26. Use one of the following options, give students a choice of options, or assign options based on students' level of proficiency. Model what is expected of students for each option.

➤ Advise students to look back through the unit for help and ideas as they write.

➤ Circulate to offer help as needed.

Option: Have students choose one of the pairs of people who are talking to each other in the picture, label them *A* and *B,* and write an extended conversation for them. Students can later role-play their conversations for the class.

Option: Have students number the people in the picture and then write two sentences about each one. To reinforce the grammar points in the unit, one sentence can tell something about the person using the present perfect with *for* or *since*. For example, for the cable repairperson, students might write *He's been repairing the cable since 2:00, He's been working for an hour.*

Option: Have students use sequential or chronological connectors to write a story about a situation in the picture. They should write each sentence on a different line and skip lines between sentences. Then ask students to cut up their papers so that each sentence is on a different strip. Have students scramble the strips and exchange them with a partner to reorder. Students can read aloud the reordered story to a group or the class.

Now I can

➤ Read the first item in the box out loud: *Now I can describe a housing emergency.* Elicit from the class an example of a housing emergency, such as *A broken pipe is a housing emergency.*

➤ In pairs, students take turns reading each item in the box and giving an example of what they have learned. When students can provide an example, they should check that box. For the items students weren't able to check, they should look back through the unit for ideas.

➤ When students have finished reviewing with their partners, read each item out loud and elicit an example from the class.

Oral test (optional)

You may want to use the *Now I can* box as an informal evaluation. While students are working on the *Composition* activity, you can call them up individually and check their ability with two or three objectives.

LESSON PLAN, UNIT 3: PREVIEW/PRACTICAL CONVERSATIONS (for Student pages 29-31)

Summary of Lesson Plan

▶ **Preview and Practical conversations (Student pages 29-31)**
Suggested teaching time: 60 minutes
includes Language Notes
Your actual teaching time: _____

 Preview and Practical conversations (Student pages 29-31)

Suggested teaching time: 60 minutes
Your actual teaching time: _____

Warm up. Do you have all the "should haves" in your car? Have you ever needed to use this equipment?

Procedure:
▶ Ask students to read the title of the magazine article: "The Responsible Driver." Have them close their books. Put them in small groups to discuss what being a responsible driver means.

▶ Ask for students' reactions and write their ideas on the board. The list may include *having a driver's license, registration, and insurance; obeying the traffic laws; not drinking and driving; being considerate of other drivers; maintaining the car properly; having the proper safety equipment.* If students have not included proper safety or emergency equipment, elicit by asking *What should a responsible driver do in an emergency? If the car breaks down?* Keep the students' list on the board.

▶ Tell students that scanning is a necessary academic skill. Remind them that scanning involves reading quickly to find specific information. Ask students to open their books and scan the article to find the five pieces of equipment that they should have in their car (a flashlight, a spare tire, a jack, flares, jumper cables). If necessary, remind students that formatting—headings, subheadings, boldfaced words, bullets, check boxes, pictures, etc.—can help with scanning.

▶ Some terms in the article may be unfamiliar to students. If necessary, review the meanings of *a moment's notice, better safe than sorry, ASAP, common sense, spare.* Point out that *spare* can be both a noun (*a spare*) and an adjective (*a spare tire, a spare battery*).

▶ Have students read the article silently. Ask questions such as *Can we plan for emergencies?* (No, but we can be equipped to handle them.) *When do drivers need these five pieces of equipment?* (in a breakdown or to help other drivers) *Why should drivers keep a jack in their car?* (to change a flat tire)

▶ Point out the use of exclamation marks in the article. Exclamation marks are used to emphasize a particular point or to convey emotion. Exclamation marks also make written text seem more like spoken English. Have students find the phrases that end with exclamation marks (*Better safe than sorry! keep some spares!*) and repeat them after you for proper emphasis and intonation.

Unit 3 objectives
Procedure:
▶ Have students read the objectives. Ask them to put a check next to the objectives that they can do now and circle those they want to work on most.

▶ Ask students to underline any words they do not understand. Write any unfamiliar terms on the board. Some students may not be familiar with the terms *road rage* and *Golden Rule.* Give a quick explanation of these terms. Students will find out more about road rage in the listening comprehension exercise on page 36. Students will read about driving by the Golden Rule in the advice column on page 38.

▶ Focus students' attention on the issues in the unit. Ask *Have you ever been stopped by a police officer because of a traffic violation? Have you ever been in a traffic accident?* Have students share their experiences. Tell students they will learn more about these topics in the unit.

▶ Refer to the students' list on the board about responsible driving. If the students listed anything that now appears in the objectives, put a check mark next to it. Point out that meeting these objectives will help students be more responsible drivers.

(continued on p. 2)

Book 4 Lesson Plans

Lesson Plan, Unit 3: Preview and practical conversations (for Student pages 29-31)–*continued*

Model 1

Content: responding appropriately in a traffic stop, apologizing for a traffic violation, traffic violations, gerunds

Procedure:

🎧 A–B.

➤ To set the scene for the conversation, ask questions about the photo and the inset, such as *Who is in the picture?* (a police officer and a driver) *What is happening?* (The police officer has stopped the driver, and the driver is giving her his license.) *What documents are in the inset?* (a car registration, a driver's license)

➤ Ask students about their own experiences with questions such as *Have you ever been stopped by a police officer while driving? How does an officer stop a motorist? What did you do when the officer flashed the lights?*

➤ After students listen to the conversation, check comprehension by asking questions such as *What was the traffic violation?* (speeding) *What does the driver say when the officer tells him that he is getting a ticket for speeding?* (You're right. I'm sorry.) *What documents does the officer ask for?* (the driver's license and registration)

➤ Play the cassette or read the conversation again. Encourage students to imitate the rhythm, stress, and intonation of the conversation as closely as possible. Correct where necessary.

Option: Play the role of the police officer and have the class respond chorally as the driver. Tell students that it is important to show the correct attitude through their voices, so they should be serious and respectful.

🎧 Vocabulary

➤ Play the cassette or read the traffic violations. Ask students to point to each picture as the caption is read.

➤ Call students' attention to the form of the verb in each violation. Tell students that the *-ing* form is called a gerund. Point out that the negative form of a gerund is *not* in front of the gerund.

➤ Play the cassette or read the traffic violations again and have students repeat.

➤ Ask questions about the pictures, such as *How fast is the driver going?* (70 mph) *What does the abbreviation "mph" mean?* (miles per hour) *What is the speed limit?* (55 miles per hour) *In the second picture, why is the pedestrian upset?* (Not stopping at a stop sign is dangerous, could cause an accident, is illegal.)

Option: Ask pairs of students to write descriptions or definitions to clarify each violation. For instance, *Speeding is going faster than the speed limit. Tailgating is following another car very closely.* Ask each pair to join another pair and compare explanations. Share explanations as a class to make sure students understand all the terms.

Option: Tell students that talking on a hand-held cell phone while driving is illegal in some states. Even if it is not a violation, it can be dangerous to talk on cell phones while driving. Tell students or elicit information about cell phone regulations in your state. Ask *Do you think talking on a cell phone should be a traffic violation? Why or why not?*

C. Pair work...

➤ Before students practice the conversation, direct their attention to B's second response, *Here you go.* Ask students to brainstorm other possible responses: *Here they are; Here; OK; I have them here.* Direct attention to B's last response. Make sure students understand that they must give an affirmative response such as *Yes, officer; Sure; Of course.*

➤ Model the conversation with a more advanced student. Play the role of Student A to demonstrate substituting a traffic violation from the *Vocabulary* box for *speeding*.

➤ Have students practice the conversation in pairs, using different violations from the *Vocabulary* box and switching roles so each student plays the part of the driver.

If your students are ready...

Culture / Civics note: In this culture, a traffic stop can sometimes lead to misunderstandings. It is important for drivers to stay in the car until told otherwise and to let the officer begin the interaction. Drivers should not do anything that the officer has not asked for, including taking out their license or registration. Sudden moves may be interpreted by the officer as threatening. If a driver receives a ticket, he or she must either pay it by the date specified or go to court to challenge the ticket. Failure to do either of these things can lead to more serious charges.

(continued on p. 3)

Lesson Plan, Unit 3: Preview and practical conversations (for Student pages 29-31)–*continued*

Model 2

Content: describing an accident, reactions to accidents, car accidents

Procedure:

A. Listen and read.

➤ Set the scene for the conversation by asking questions about the photo, such as *Who do you see in the picture?* (a man and a woman, a husband and wife) *Where do you think they are?* (at home) Have students look at the man's expression and speculate about how he feels and what problem he has.

➤ After students listen to the conversation, check comprehension by asking questions such as *What happened?* (The man had a car accident.) *Was anyone hurt?* (no) *Was the accident serious?* (No, it was just a fender bender.) *How will he pay for the car repair?* (The insurance will cover it.)

➤ Explain that a *fender bender* is an accident that causes minor damage. A fender is the part of a car that covers the wheels. A fender bender is a collision that bends or dents the fender but doesn't damage the rest of the car.

➤ After students listen to *Reactions to accidents*, direct their attention to the conjunctions *but* and *and* used in the two sentences. Ask the students how the two conjunctions are used. Elicit or point out that *and* is used to add information that is similar, and *but* is used to add information that is contradictory. The first sentence presents two pieces of information: the damage is minor, the driver is upset. We expect the driver not to be upset about minor damage, so *but* is used to add information that contradicts our expectation.

B. Pronunciation and intonation practice.

Option: Play the cassette or read the conversation again, stopping after the formulaic expressions that indicate emotion: *Oh, no; thank goodness; take it easy.* Ask students to repeat just these expressions.

Vocabulary

➤ Play the cassette or read the captions, and have students repeat the different car accidents.

➤ Explain that *sideswipe* means to brush or swipe against the side of another car. Sideswiping usually scratches or dents the side panels of one or both cars.

Option: Point out the verb forms in the second and fourth sentences. The past continuous (*was following, wasn't paying attention*) is used to describe a past action in progress, and the simple past tense (*rear-ended, hit*) is used to describe a past action that interrupted the action in progress.

Challenge: Brainstorm other car accidents (*bumped into another car, hit a sign, scratched the door*). Begin sentences in the past continuous and have students describe car accidents in the simple past: *I was following too closely, and I bumped into another car; I wasn't paying attention, and I hit a stop sign.*

Workbook Link: Exercises 1, 2

C. Pair work . . .

➤ Ask students what information should go in the first slot (a type of car accident) and in the second (a reaction to the accident).

➤ Brainstorm other sympathetic responses for Student B if Student A says *But there was a lot of damage, and I'm really upset.* Responses might include *That's really too bad, I'm so sorry to hear that, Don't worry.*

➤ Model the conversation with a more advanced student. Play the role of Student A to demonstrate substituting a car accident from the *Vocabulary* box and a reaction.

Workbook Link: Exercises 3, 4

➤ Do it yourself!

Procedure:

A–B.

➤ Have students read the example in the chart. Ask them to complete the second line of the chart with their own information. Prompt students by asking *Have you been in an accident recently? Has anyone you know been in an accident recently? What caused it?*

➤ Pair students to talk about the information in their charts.

C. Discussion . . .

➤ If you or the students have brought in articles about traffic accidents, have students take them out. On the board, write the following questions: *What type of accident was it? What was the cause? What happened? Was anyone hurt?* Working individually, students scan the article and underline the answers to the questions on the board.

➤ Put students in small groups to discuss the accidents. Have them report the answers they underlined as well as any other important details.

LESSON PLAN, UNIT 3: PRACTICAL GRAMMAR (for Student pages 32-33)

Summary of Lesson Plan

▶ **PRESENTATION**
Practical grammar (Student pages 32-33)
Suggested teaching time: 60 minutes
   includes Language Notes (10 minutes)
Your actual teaching time: _____

▶ Practical grammar
(Student pages 32-33)

Suggested teaching time: 60 minutes
Your actual teaching time: _____

Using gerunds

Procedure:
▶ Write three sentences on the board:
1. She is smiling.
2. She is the smiling woman.
3. Smiling is a sign of friendliness.

▶ Ask the students which word is repeated in all three sentences (smiling). Tell them that this –ing word has a different use in each sentence. In one, it is an adjective; in another, it is a noun; and in the other, it is part of the verb. Ask students to tell you how this –ing word is used in each sentence. Elicit that it is part of the verb in sentence 1, an adjective in 2, and a noun in 3.

▶ Tell students that, in this section, they will be focusing on –ing words when they act as nouns. Mention that these –ing words are called gerunds. This term was introduced earlier in the Vocabulary section on page 30.

▶ Direct students' attention to the box. Have volunteers read the information aloud. Make sure that students know what a complement is (it completes sentences that have linking verbs such as the verb be).

Option: Point out the gerund (speeding) in the model conversation on page 30. Note that all the traffic violations in the *Vocabulary* box are gerunds.

Option: To help students practice using gerunds as objects of verbs or prepositions and as complements, have them play a game. Read aloud the following

incomplete sentences or create your own. Students should complete each sentence with a single word—a gerund. Model the activity by completing the first two sentences yourself. Brainstorm gerunds for the third sentence to make sure students understand that they should use a gerund and not another kind of noun. Move up and down the rows, reading the incomplete sentences and having students answer. Change the sentence frequently.

1. I really enjoy ___.
2. I don't like ___.
3. I appreciate ___.
4. I am afraid of ___.
5. I am excited about ___.
6. My favorite activity is ___.
7. One thing that really annoys me is ___.
8. Most people are worried about ___.
9. Everyone is hurt by ___.
10. Police will stop you for ___.

A. Complete the sentences ...
▶ Model the activity by writing the sentence on the board. Point to the word *stop* below the line. Ask students to supply the correct verb form and write it in the blank.

▶ Review the spelling rules for gerunds. Remind students to double the last consonant in one-syllable verbs that end in a consonant-vowel-consonant pattern (stop ➡ stopping), and to drop the –e from the simple form before adding –ing (hope ➡ hoping). Refer to page 147 for additional rules.

▶ After students have completed the sentences individually, have them compare answers, including spellings, with a partner. Review as a class.

▶ The word *rotary* in item 3 may be unfamiliar to students. In some areas it is called a circle, a traffic circle, or a roundabout. If necessary, draw a picture on the board.

Challenge: Ask students how the gerund is used in each sentence—as subject (s), object of a verb (ov), object of a preposition (op), or complement (c). Elicit the following: 1 (op); 2 (s); 3 (op); 4 (s); 5 (op); 6 (op); 7 (c); 8 (s); 9 (op), (ov); 10 (op,) (ov).

Workbook Link: Exercise 5

(continued on p. 5)

Lesson Plan, Unit 3: Practical grammar (for Student pages 32-33)–*continued*

Infinitives of purpose

Procedure:

- Ask a series of *why* questions like the ones following, or create your own. Answer the first two questions yourself to demonstrate the use of the infinitive. *Why did you turn on the TV?* (to watch the news) *Why did you buy the newspaper?* (to read the news) *Why did you go to the supermarket?* (to buy bread) *Why did you go to the drugstore?* (to buy aspirin) *Why did you go to the post office?* (to buy a money order) Write down the infinitives that students use in their answers.

- Remind students that *to* plus the simple form of the verb is an infinitive. Refer to the list of infinitives on the board and add the heading *Infinitives*.

- Tell students that, like gerunds, infinitives are used in several ways. Explain that infinitives of purpose often answer the question *why*.

- Create a series of example sentences on the board that show the use of infinitives after the verbs *forget, need, plan,* and *want*. Use the following sentences or create your own. Ask volunteers for additional sentences that follow the pattern. *I forgot to stop at the stop sign, He needs batteries, She didn't plan to total the car, The officer wanted to see my license and registration.* Tell students that another use of infinitives is after certain verbs.

- Have students read the information in the grammar box. Point out that a list of verbs followed by infinitives appears on page 146.

B. Read...

- Ask students if they ever make "to-do" lists, lists of chores or errands that they need to accomplish on a certain day or at a certain time. Elicit examples of what kinds of things they write on their lists. Write a few items on the board, beginning each one with the simple form of the verb. For example, students may say *do the laundry, buy pet food, pay the car insurance bill.*

- Have students read Dr. Jamie Greene's "to-do" list. Students then answer the questions individually. Correct as a class.

- Point out that students have to convert the wording of some of the tasks in their answers. For example, the list says *renew my driver's license,* but the answer for item 1 is *her driver's license*. In item 4, students have to change *pay my parking ticket* to *her* (or *a* or *the*) *parking ticket*.

Option: On a separate sheet of paper, students write their own "to-do" lists with at least five items. Have students exchange lists with a partner and make up an appropriate *why* question for each item. The writer of the list then answers, using an infinitive of purpose. The task, question, and answer might look like this: *do the laundry. Why did you go to the laundromat? to do the laundry*

C. Complete each answer...

- Model the exercise by writing the question on the board. Write the first part of the answer, *They stop speeders,* and ask the class for possible answers. List students' suggestions on the board, using an infinitive of purpose for each idea.

- Students work individually to answer the questions and then compare answers with a partner.

If your students are ready...

Language note: The verbs *remember* and *forget* can be followed by either an infinitive or a gerund, but each choice produces a very different meaning. *I remembered to get new tires* means that I didn't forget, I accomplished my task. *I remembered getting new tires* means I have a memory of doing it. *I forgot to get new tires* means I didn't accomplish my task, whereas *I forgot getting new tires* means that I bought the tires, but I forgot that I did so. Refer students to the list of verbs that are followed by gerunds or infinitives on page 146.

Workbook Link: Exercises 6, 7, 8

► Do it yourself!

Procedure:

A. Make a list...

- Direct students' attention to the example and ask *Why did I go to the ATM yesterday?* (to get money for groceries)

- Have students write down one activity they did yesterday and the purpose of the activity. On a separate sheet of paper, have students write down three or four more actions they completed yesterday with the purpose for each one.

B. Pair work...

- Put students in pairs. Student A says where he or she went yesterday, and Student B asks why. Student A answers with an infinitive of purpose. Students take turns reading their activities until all the items on their lists have been discussed.

Workbook Link: Exercise 9

LESSON PLAN, UNIT 3: AUTHENTIC PRACTICE 1 & 2 (for Student pages 34-37)

Summary of Lesson Plan

▶ **PRESENTATION**
Authentic practice 1 & 2:
Listening (Student pages 34-37)
Suggested teaching time: 60 minutes
   includes Cultural Discussion
Your actual teaching time: _____

▶ Authentic practice 1
(Student pages 34-35)

Suggested teaching time: 30 minutes
Your actual teaching time: _____

Appropriate behavior with a police officer

Procedure:

🎧

▶ To set the scene, have students look at the picture story. Ask *Who are the people in the story?* (a police officer and a driver) *What are they doing?* (talking) *What does the sign say?* (Speed Limit 65) *What do you think their conversation is about?* (how fast the man was driving)

▶ Have students listen with their books closed for answers to the following questions: *Why did the police officer stop the driver? What explanation does the driver give?*

▶ After students have listened to the picture story once, ask *Why did the police officer stop the driver?* (He was speeding.) *Why was the driver speeding?* (to get to the bank before it closed)

▶ Have students open their books and read along as you read the picture story or play the cassette again.

▶ Ask comprehension questions such as *How fast was the driver going?* (74 miles per hour) *How fast does he think he was going?* (about 65, maybe 70) *Why is it a good idea to leave yourself a little extra time?* (to avoid having to speed) *What will happen the next time the driver speeds?* (He'll get a ticket and points.)

▶ Some terms may be unfamiliar to students but can be inferred from the context. Make sure they understand the meanings of *hand over, pull over, clocked, a big hurry, let off,* and *pull out*. Point out that the speed limit is given in miles on the sign. The officer and the driver also discuss how fast the driver was going in miles. Give the speeds in kilometers if necessary (65 mph = 105 kilometers; 70 mph = 113 kilometers; 74 mph = 119 kilometers).

▶ Ask the students to describe the driver's behavior and give supporting examples from the story. If necessary, prompt with questions such as *Why does the driver say "Yes, officer" and "Thank you very much, officer"? What does the sentence "I'll be more careful in the future" express about the driver's attitude?* You may want to discuss whether students think the driver's behavior and attitude are appropriate.

Option: In pairs, students read the picture story, playing the roles of the police officer and the driver.

A. Read the picture story again...

▶ Point out that item 1 is a *why* question. Write the question on the board and ask students for possible answers. Model the answer *(to give the driver a warning about his speeding)* to demonstrate the use of an infinitive of purpose and write it on the board.

▶ Have students complete the exercise individually and then check answers with a partner. Review as a class.

B. Vocabulary...

▶ Working individually, students complete the sentences and check answers with a partner.

▶ Review the answers as a class before having students read their completed sentences out loud.

▶ Discuss the choices in item 2 and elicit or point out that *cop* and *officer* have the same meaning but are very different in tone. Make sure students understand that *cop* is an informal term. It is not appropriate to address a police officer as *cop*.

Challenge: Assign one sentence to each pair of students. Have partners work together to create a conversation that contains that sentence. Ask volunteers to read their conversations in front of the class.

Challenge: Ask pairs of students to create sentences for each of the unused phrases or words. Have them share their sentences with another pair or small group.

(continued on p. 7)

Lesson Plan, Unit 3: Authentic practice 1 & 2 (for Student pages 34-37)—continued

> **If your students are ready...**
> **Culture / Civics note:** In some areas, drivers who commit moving violations earn points. In a point system, each moving violation is assigned a certain number of points. If a driver gets more than a certain number of points in a given time (typically eight to twelve points over three years), the driver's license is suspended for a period of time. Moving violations are assigned different numbers of points, depending on the severity of the violation. Students need to be aware of how moving violations can result in the loss of their licenses. If appropriate, help students get information from your state's Department of Motor Vehicles.

Procedure:

C. Listen...
- Read each item in the tapescript out loud or play the cassette as many times as necessary for students to complete the exercise. If students have difficulty, prompt them by reading the response yourself.
- Review the answers before having students read their responses out loud.

Challenge: Use the items in the tapescript as a dictation. Have students listen to the items and write what they hear. Allow students to listen as many times as necessary. Ask volunteers to write the questions on the board. Make corrections as a class. Students can then practice the prompts and responses with a partner.

D–E.
- Students complete the exercise individually and then compare responses with a partner.
- Partners read the items and responses, switching roles for more practice.

Option: After both students have practiced reading the items and responses in Exercise D, have Partner B in each pair close his or her book. Partner A then reads each item, and Partner B responds from memory.

Challenge: Have pairs of students work together to write a statement or a question for each unused response in Exercise D. For example, in item 2, a question that could elicit the response *To get to the bank* might be *Why were you speeding?* Have students take turns reading their new items and responses.

Workbook Link: Exercises 10, 11

▶ Do it yourself!

Procedure:

A. Write your own response...
- Tell students to imagine that the police officer in the pictures has just pulled them over for a traffic violation. Have students read the speech balloons and write an appropriate response to each one.
- Remind students that they can refer to the model conversation on page 30 or to the picture story on page 34 for help in responding.
- Before students practice with a partner, have a volunteer play the part of the police officer and read each speech balloon aloud. Respond to each statement for yourself, giving students an opportunity to check the appropriateness of their responses. Remind students of the importance of appropriate, respectful behavior in a traffic stop.
- Have students interview each other in pairs to check their responses.

B. Culture talk...
- Put students in small groups, trying to include people from different cultures in each group.
- Ask one student in each group to be the facilitator, one to be the recorder, and one to be the reporter. Elicit or tell students what each role involves: the facilitator asks questions and encourages everyone to talk, the recorder takes notes of the group's discussion, and the reporter tells the class about the discussion. When students have an active role in the discussion, they are more likely to be involved.
- Circulate and offer help as necessary.
- Have reporters tell the class about the discussions.

Option: Write the names of the countries represented in the class across the top of the board. Down the left side write *traffic violations, penalties, appropriate responses*. Have one student from each group fill in the columns on the board. You may have a chart like this one following:

	Mexico	Somalia	Vietnam	Russia
Traffic violations				
Penalties				
Appropriate responses				

> **Tapescript**
> **1.** Hand over your license and registration, please.
> **2.** Are you aware how fast you were going?
> **3.** Are you in a big hurry to get somewhere?
> **4.** I'll let you off easy with just a warning this time. Next time it's a ticket and points.

(continued on p. 8)

Lesson Plan, Unit 3: Authentic practice 1 & 2 (for Student pages 34-37)–*continued*

Authentic practice 2
(Student pages 36-37)

Aggressive driving and road rage

Suggested teaching time: 30 minutes
Your actual teaching time: _____

Note: For the *Discussion* on page 31, have students bring in articles from the newspaper about traffic accidents.

Procedure:

➤ Have students read the bar. Brainstorm ideas about the two terms. Write ideas on the board.

➤ Lead a discussion about the students' experiences with aggressive driving and/or road rage by asking questions such as *Have you ever been in a situation where another driver did something that made you angry? What did the other driver do? How did you respond?*

A–B.

➤ Have students read the question.

➤ Read the tapescript out loud or play the cassette as many times as necessary for students to complete the exercise.

➤ Students work individually to write an answer to the question. When students have finished, elicit the difference between the two terms according to the selection. (*Aggressive driving* is cutting other drivers off, excessive honking, and other behaviors that can be dangerous. *Road rage* is a driver's behavior that purposely results in injury to another driver, to a pedestrian, or to another driver's car.)

➤ Refer to the list of students' ideas about the two terms that you wrote on the board earlier. Check how closely their ideas resemble the descriptions in the selection.

C. Listen to the panel discussion ...

➤ Read the six pieces of advice. Tell students to listen to the advice the panel gives and check the advice the panelists offer.

➤ Read the tapescript or play the cassette again so students can check the advice as they hear it.

➤ Read the tapescript or play the cassette again so students can confirm their responses. Have students compare answers with a partner.

D. Look at the examples ...
Vocabulary

➤ Put students in pairs or small groups. Make sure they know the examples of aggressive driving given in the panel discussion. Brainstorm other examples and write them on the board.

➤ Read the examples of aggressive driving or play the cassette, and ask students to point to the pictures.

➤ Read the examples or play the cassette again and have students repeat the phrases.

➤ Refer to the list of examples students brainstormed earlier and check those that are included in the *Vocabulary*.

Option: To review gerunds as subjects and as objects of verbs, ask students to use the examples of aggressive driving in the *Vocabulary* box to complete these sentences.

1. _____ really annoys me.
2. I really hate _____.

Ask volunteers to share their sentences with the class.

E. Discussion ...

➤ If necessary, review the examples of aggressive driving given in the panel discussion, in the list on the board, and in the *Vocabulary*. Ask students which of the speakers at the bottom of the page best express their own reactions.

➤ Have students discuss their reactions with a partner or a group. Students can use these questions as discussion starters: *Which behavior makes you angry? How do you respond?*

(continued on p. 9)

Lesson Plan, Unit 3: Authentic practice 1 & 2 (for Student pages 34-37)–continued

Tapescript

Jessica: This is Jessica Mondale. Welcome to "Driving Smart." Today's segment deals with a serious subject that many of us have to confront on a daily basis: Aggressive driving and road rage. Today's panel of experts includes Dr. James Levin, senior administrator of the Behavior Management Institute. The institute specializes in teaching drivers to stay cool when traffic gets hot. Welcome, Dr. Levin.

Levin: Thanks, Jessica.

Jessica: Next is Jane Taylor, author of *When Good Drivers Go Bad*, a self-help encyclopedia of coping skills for driving in heavy traffic. Hello, Jane.

Jane: Hello, Jessica.

Jessica: And our third expert today is Detective Clarence Breen of the Rapid City Traffic Enforcement Department. Welcome to all of you. Let's start with Detective Breen. Detective Breen, has Rapid City been experiencing a rise in aggressive driving incidents recently? It seems that everyone has a terrible story to tell.

Breen: Yes, Jessica, I'm afraid so. Just yesterday, we had two complaints, one quite serious, that I would describe more as road rage than as aggressive driving.

Tapescript (*continued from page T36*)

Jessica: What exactly is the difference between aggressive driving and road rage?

Breen: Aggressive driving is just that: cutting other drivers off, excessive honking, pulling out in front of another driver, cutting into a lane too close to the front of another car, et cetera. Aggressive driving is also the cause of a lot of accidents. Aggressive drivers get too close to other drivers, *and* they're unpredictable. Especially in heavy, fast traffic, the consequences of aggressive driving can be catastrophic.

Jessica: And road rage? Dr. Levin, I'll let you tackle that one.

Levin: Road rage describes a driver's behavior that purposely results in injury to another driver, to a pedestrian, or to another driver's car. These are the cases we read about in the newspaper and see on the nightly news. A driver gets angry at another driver or a pedestrian for some real or imagined cause and then yells, or worse, purposely slams into the other driver's back bumper. There's actually been a case of an argument between two drivers leading to one driver's running over another driver. We've even heard of shootings and stabbings. People need to step back from their anger and control themselves.

Jessica: Ms. Taylor, what can drivers do to avoid getting carried away with their anger when faced with other drivers who are aggressive or incompetent?

Taylor: I'm glad you asked me that question, Jessica, since that's the subject of my book, *When Good Drivers Go Bad*, published by Lyman and Bluster, and which you can receive by calling 1-800-DRIVERS, and …

Jessica: Ms. Taylor. What can an angry driver do to calm down?

Taylor: Yes, of course. Well, in my book, I have a three-step program for avoiding the road rage trap.
   First: Recognize that you have no control over other drivers, only over yourself.
   Second: Don't take others' driving personally. They don't even know who you are.
   Third: Get a life. Driving is not life: It's just a way to get somewhere.

Breen: And if I might break in—don't forget the serious legal consequences of road rage. Assault is a felony, and the law takes it very seriously.

Jessica: That's very good advice. And that's all for today's segment of "Driving Smart." This is Jessica Mondale, wishing you happy driving and saying thank you to today's panelists. Until next week!

Workbook Link: Exercises 12, 13

(*continued on p. 10*)

Lesson Plan, Unit 3: Authentic practice 1 & 2 (for Student pages 34-37)–*continued*

➤ Do it yourself!

Procedure:

A–B.

➤ Have students read the survey introduction and directions silently. Ask volunteers to read each of the 12 "hot-button" behaviors aloud. Explain *"hot-button" behaviors* and any other unfamiliar terms.

➤ Model the activity by writing the first item on the board, followed by numbers 1, 2, 3. Read the item aloud and circle the number that corresponds to your reaction: 1 for not bothered, 2 for annoyed, 3 for very angry. Tell students *Tailgating to make others go faster or get out of the way doesn't bother me (or annoys me or makes me very angry)*.

➤ Students work individually to complete the survey about their attitudes. If students are not drivers, let them answer as passengers. Have students total their score.

➤ Write the numbers 12 through 36 on the board. Beginning with 12, read each number out loud. Ask students to raise their hands when they hear the number that represents their score. Put the corresponding tally mark or marks next to each number. Group the scores into three categories (12–23, 24–29, 30–36).

➤ Have students read the box at the bottom of the page. Make sure students understand the expression *cool as a cucumber*. Ask which students are "cool as a cucumber," "let others have power," or need to "calm down."

Note: The list of commonly misspelled words on page 144 warns students not to make the word *behavior* plural. This word is rarely seen in the plural. It is almost always used as a non-count noun.

C. Culture talk...

➤ Put students in small groups to answer the questions. Try to have students from different cultures in each group.

Option: Call a local police station and ask if a community or public relations officer is available to talk to your class about driving issues. Have pairs or groups of students prepare questions in advance and take notes during the officer's visit.

Workbook Link: Exercises 14, 15

Your notes

Summary of Lesson Plan

▶ **PRESENTATION**
Authentic practice 3:
Reading and critical thinking (Student pages 38-39)
Suggested teaching time: 60 minutes
includes Cultural Discussion
Your actual teaching time: _____

➤ Authentic practice 3
(Student pages 38-39)

Suggested teaching time: 60 minutes
Your actual teaching time: _____

Driving by the Golden Rule

Procedure:

🎧 A–B.

➤ Have students read along silently while you read the letters or play the cassette.

➤ Some words and phrases may be unfamiliar to students: *I'm with your wife, over and above, put yourself in the shoes, let this be a lesson to you, common sense, Golden Rule*. Make sure students understand how these expressions are used.

➤ Working individually, students answer the questions and then compare answers with a partner.

Option: Have students practice focused listening by doing this activity. Write the following list of words from the advice letters on the board: *baby, parking lot, court, bottle, bumped, threw, leave, scratch, dent, damage, wife, law, shoes, shoulder, passenger, family, life, advice, phone, doctor, reached, think, understand, stop, help, behave, sick*. Draw a four by four grid and tell students to create their own grids on a separate sheet of paper. Ask students to choose 16 words from the list and write one word in each of the 16 boxes in their grid, in any order they choose. Tell students that they will not use every word. Have students listen to the letters with books closed. Every time they hear a word in their grid, they should put a check in that box. The goal is to check all of their boxes. After students have listened to the letters once, find out who checked the most boxes.

Option: To boost academic skills, have students express Joan's advice in their own words.

C. Pair work...

➤ Have students read the speech balloons and work individually to write advice.

➤ Put students in pairs and ask them to take turns reading the speech balloons and responding with their advice.

➤ Circulate and offer help as needed. If students are having trouble, model the exercise with a student. The student reads the driver's speech balloon and you give the driver advice.

➤ Have volunteers read their advice aloud. Ask the class which advice is best and why.

Workbook Link: Exercise 16

(continued on p. 12)

Book 4 Lesson Plans

Lesson Plan, Unit 3: Authentic practice 3 (for Student pages 38-39)–*continued*

D. Read...

➤ Remind students of the magazine article they read at the beginning of the unit. Review the equipment responsible drivers should have in the car (a flashlight with working batteries, a spare tire, a jack, flares, jumper cables).

➤ Elicit from students the other items that they now know they should have in the car. If necessary, prompt by asking *What do you need to show if you are stopped by a police officer?* (the car registration, your driver's license) *What else do you need if you have an accident?* (an insurance card)

➤ Have students open their books and read the entire article, paying special attention to the section headed "Must haves." Explain that *damages* is a legal term meaning an amount of money. It is not used here as an ordinary non-count noun. Tell students that they already know the information presented in the article.

➤ Be sure students observe the infinitives of purpose in the "should haves" and "must haves" sections of the article.

Challenge: Discuss the difference between *should* (advisable, a good idea) and *must* (necessary, a requirement). Ask students to make a chart of things they should do and things they must do as good drivers or responsible community members. Have them explain why they must do these things using an infinitive of purpose. Their chart may look like the following:

I should	(because)	I must	(because)
pay my bills on time	to avoid a late fee.	get a driver's license	to drive here legally.

When students have completed their charts, have them read their sentences to a partner.

E. Critical thinking...

➤ Students should first identify the objects in each trunk and then decide what equipment is missing based on the "should haves" self-check in the article in Exercise D. Then have them work individually and write the missing equipment on the line.

➤ Put students in pairs to compare answers and make sure that each list includes all five "should have" items mentioned in the article. If any items are still missing, have students scan the article again.

Workbook Link: Exercise 17

➤ Do it yourself!

Procedure:

A–B.

➤ Have students read the list of topics and choose one that they would like to talk about.

➤ Put students in small groups. Tell them to make sure their true stories include answers to the questions *What was the problem? What happened? What was the solution?* Give them a few minutes to plan what they're going to say. Encourage them to make notes of specific details they want to include.

➤ Circulate and offer help as needed. If students are having difficulty, you may want to model the activity by telling a true car story of your own.

Challenge: Have students write their true car story. They should explain the problem and what happened but not write the solution. Students exchange papers with a partner who then writes advice about how to solve the problem.

LESSON PLAN: UNIT 3: REVIEW (for Student pages 40-42)

Summary of Lesson Plan

➤ **Review (Student pages 40-42)**
Suggested teaching time: 60 minutes
Your actual teaching time: _____

➤ **UNIT REVIEW**
Includes expansion activities
   role play
   dialogues
   writing
   Workbook activities
   outside reading
   realia applications
   math skills applications
   civic lesson applications
   Booster Pak activities

➤ **Review (Student pages 40-42)**

Suggested teaching time: 60 minutes
Your actual teaching time: _____

Procedure:

A. Pair work or group work.

Ask and answer questions.
➤ Ask general questions about the picture, such as *What is the police officer doing?* (writing a ticket) *What is the driver doing?* (giving the officer her license and registration) *What's the problem with the yellow car on the left?* (a flat tire, no spare tire or jack)

➤ Ask *What examples of aggressive driving do you see in the picture?* (flashing lights, weaving, honking, gesturing, using a cell phone while driving, tailgating)

Option: Have students write a question about the picture and its answer on two separate slips of paper. Collect all the slips and distribute either a question or an answer to each student. Have students walk around the room, asking and answering questions until they have their match.

Create conversations.
➤ Have the students look at the two people in the traffic stop at the top of the page. Play the role of the police officer and have a more advanced student come to the front of the class and play the role of the driver. Initiate a conversation; for example, say *I'm going to have to give you a ticket for not stopping at a stop sign.* If necessary, the class can help the student playing the role of the driver to respond. Continue the conversation as long as possible, with each of you making a tally mark on the board every time you speak. When finished, count the marks.

➤ In pairs, have students create conversations for the people with a flat tire and keep track of how many times they speak. Explain that the goal is to say as much as they can. Have pairs count their tally marks and report how many times they spoke.

Option: Have pairs create a third conversation between one of the drivers in the picture and a friend. In the conversation, the driver should tell the friend about a problem they had on the road. The friend should ask questions, express concern, and give advice.

Tell a story.
➤ Have a student time you while you talk about the picture for one minute. Then, put students in pairs or small groups and have each student talk about the picture for one minute. Encourage students to describe each of the scenes in the picture and to say as much as they can. Tell students to continue talking until you say *Stop*, indicating that the minute is up.

(continued on p. 14)

Book 4 Lesson Plans

Lesson Plan, Unit 3: Review (for Student pages 40-42)–*continued*

🎧 B. Listening comprehension...

➤ Tell students that they are going to hear a conversation between a father and his teenage daughter. Have students read the list of equipment and identify the "should have" items (items 4 through 8). Ask students to speculate which items they think the daughter's car has and which she needs.

➤ After students listen to the conversation the first time, ask questions such as *Where is the daughter going?* (to a concert) *Does the daughter have a spare tire?* (no) *Why doesn't she have a spare?* (The tires are new, nothing's going to happen to them.) *Why does she carry jumper cables?* (One of her friends always needs a jump.)

➤ Have students read the list of equipment and listen again to complete the exercise. Discuss whether students' speculations were accurate.

Challenge: Divide the class into two teams. Ask the teams to listen to the conversation again and then to create comprehension questions. The two teams alternate asking and answering questions. Keep score on the board of the correct answers for each team.

C–D.

➤ Students work individually to complete the review exercises.

➤ Circulate to offer help as needed.

➤ Have students check answers with a partner. Review answers as a class.

➤ Identify any areas of difficulty that may require additional instruction and practice.

Tapescript

Father: I don't believe you're going to drive all the way to the concert in this car!

Daughter: What's wrong?

Father: What's wrong? What *isn't* wrong? Didn't you take driver's ed? Didn't you pass the driver's test? Doesn't it occur to you that something can go wrong? You're just looking for trouble.

Daughter: Calm down. You're ridiculous. What's going to go wrong?

Father: Did you ever hear of a flat tire?

Daughter: But these tires are brand new. Nothing's going to happen to them!

Father: It's just common sense to have a spare. And what about a jack? Of course, if you have no tire, you certainly don't need a jack.

Daughter: You are *so* ridiculous. Nothing's going to go wrong. Take it easy!

Father: You wait until you have children. Then you'll understand. Let's go through the checklist.

Daughter: Oh, come *on*. I've got to go.

Father: Young lady, you're not going anywhere until I'm sure you have the minimum of equipment in case there's a problem. Ready?

Daughter: Oh, all right.

Father: License?

Daughter: Yup.

Father: Registration and insurance card?

Daughter: Yup, yup.

Father: Spare tire? Get that from the garage, ASAP. And we have a spare jack in Mom's car. Get that too.

Daughter: Yes, *sir*.

[pause, door slamming]

Daughter: OK. Bye, Dad. See you on Sunday.

Father: What about a flashlight?

Daughter: Yes.

Father: Flares?

Daughter: You are paranoid. You need help.

Father: Flares?

Daughter: Yes. What else? I'm going to be late.

Father: I saw the jumper cables. Congratulations!

Daughter: Yeah. Well, one of my friends always needs a jump.

(continued on p. 15)

Lesson Plan, Unit 3: Review (for Student pages 40-42)–*continued*

E–F.
🎧Vocabulary

➤ Read aloud the items in *Vocabulary* box or play the cassette. Have students repeat each item.

➤ Model item 1 in Exercise E to demonstrate that students will have to modify the phrases in the *Vocabulary* when they write infinitives of purpose, changing the pronoun *you* to *me*. Write on the board *I have a flashlight* and ask students what purposes it might serve. Answers may include *to read a map, to look in the glove compartment, to find something under the seat*. List the answers on the board, underlining the infinitives of purpose. Complete item 1: *to help me look under the hood in the dark.*

➤ Students work individually to complete the review exercises.

➤ Circulate to offer help as needed.

➤ Have students check answers with a partner. Review answers as a class.

➤ Identify any areas of difficulty that may require additional instruction and practice.

G. Composition...

➤ Provide students with concrete approaches to writing about the picture on page 40. Use one of the options that follow, give students a choice of options, or assign options based on students' levels of proficiency. Model what is expected of students for each option.

➤ Advise students to look back through the unit for help and ideas as they write.

➤ Circulate to offer help as needed.

Option: Have students choose one of the pairs of people who are talking to each other in the picture, label them *A* and *B*, and write an extended conversation for them. Students can later role-play their conversations for the class.

Option: Have students look at the traffic violations in the picture and then write two sentences about each driver's dangerous behavior. To reinforce the grammar in the unit, one sentence should tell something about the violation using a gerund.

Option: Tell students to focus on the equipment shown in the scenes with the police officer and the flat tire. Have them create a car safety equipment checklist and add any missing equipment. To reinforce the grammar in the unit, have students write about car equipment using infinitives of purpose.

Challenge: Have students write an *Ask Joan* letter from the driver receiving the ticket. Advise students to include the driver's name, length of time in this country, the reason for the traffic stop, and how drivers would respond to such a traffic stop in their home countries.

Now I can

➤ Read the first item in the box out loud: *Now I can respond appropriately to a police officer in a traffic stop.* Elicit from the class an example of how to respond appropriately; for example, a student could say *I should be polite and apologize for my mistake.*

➤ Put students in pairs and have them take turns reading each item in the box and giving an example of what they have learned. When students can provide an example, they should check that box. For the items students weren't able to check, they should look back through the unit for ideas.

➤ When students are finished reviewing with their partners, read each item out loud and elicit an example from the class.

Oral test (optional)

You may want to use the *Now I can box* as an informal evaluation. While students are working on the *Composition* activity, you can call them up individually and check their ability with two or three objectives.

LESSON PLAN, UNIT 4: PREVIEW/PRACTICAL CONVERSATIONS (for Student pages 43-45)

Summary of Lesson Plan

➤ **Preview and Practical conversations (Student pages 43-45)**
Suggested teaching time: 60 minutes
includes Language Note
Your actual teaching time: _____

➤ Preview and Practical conversations (Student pages 43-45)

Suggested teaching time: 60 minutes
Your actual teaching time: _____

Warm up. Do you believe this offer is true? Explain your answer.

Procedure:

➤ Direct students' attention to the illustration and encourage critical thinking by asking questions such as *Is the envelope sent by a business or an individual?* (business) *How can you tell?* (There is a printed message in the return address space, the postage is metered, the envelope has an address window.) *What is the letter about?* (a dream vacation) *How does the letter get people interested in the offer?* (by saying the recipient has been specially selected, by promising a spectacular luxury vacation)

➤ Point out that offers for vacation packages often use exaggerated adjectives such as *spectacular*.

➤ Ask students if they think the offer is true. Have them explain their reasoning in small groups.

➤ Access students' experience by asking *Have you ever received an offer like this one?* Ask students to use their personal experience in their answer to the *Warm up* question.

Option: Point out the ways this vacation offer tries to capture the consumer's interest. The flyer uses all capital letters and an exclamation mark to emphasize the message. The picture is designed to make the recipient think of a luxurious pampered vacation. In small groups, have students discuss ways that a flyer can attract business. Then have students draft the text for a special vacation offer and think of an appropriate picture.

Option: Working in pairs, students sort pairs of adjectives into two classes, plain and more exaggerated. Use this list or create your own: *funny, hilarious; interesting, exciting; great, stupendous; unusual, phenomenal; big, gigantic; happy, ecstatic; unexpected, incredible*. Ask what kind of adjectives they used in their group's vacation offer and why.

Unit 4 objectives

Procedure:

➤ Read the objectives. Discuss any unfamiliar vocabulary.

➤ Point out the word *service* in the first two objectives. Ask students *What is service?* (doing something to help others) *What are some service industries?* (hospitality, food, health care, retail) *Do any of you work in service industries? What kinds of qualities are necessary in a service worker?* (courtesy, responsibility, people skills, attention to detail, trying to please the customer)

➤ Have students read the objectives again. Ask *What service industry do you think this unit will focus on?* (hospitality, hotel, travel) Ask students to put a check next to the objectives that they can do now and circle those they want to work on most.

(continued on p. 2)

Lesson Plan, Unit 4: Preview and practical conversations (for Student pages 43-45)–*continued*

Model 1

Content: asking for service, responding to a request, hotel room amenities, *some* to describe an indefinite number

Procedure:

A–B.

➤ To set the scene for the conversation, direct students' attention to the split photo on the right and ask questions such as *Who do you see in the picture?* (a man and a woman on the phone, a hotel worker and a hotel guest on the phone) *Who is the hotel employee? How do you know?* (the woman, she is wearing a uniform and a name plate) *What is her expression?* (She is smiling.)

➤ After students listen to the conversation, check comprehension by asking *What is the guest's name?* (Mr. Hasan) *What does he need?* (an ironing board and some extra towels) *What are some expressions of politeness and helpfulness that the hotel employee uses?* (May I help you? Absolutely. Right away. Is there anything else? Sure, no problem.)

➤ Point out that *extra* means additional. The ironing board is not extra because there is none in the room.

Option: Tell students that intonation is very important in conveying meaning and emotion. Read the hotel employee's first line to convey polite helpfulness, as it was said on the cassette. Then read it again in a bored, monotonous way. Put students in pairs to read the conversation again, with each student alternating in the role of the employee. The first time, students should read in a bored, monotonous tone. The second time, they should read with expression. Have them exaggerate both styles. Ask volunteers to read in front of the class.

Vocabulary

➤ After students listen to and repeat the hotel room amenities, explain *skirt hangers*, if necessary.

➤ Brainstorm other amenities found in a hotel room or offered at the front desk, such as *a hairdryer, toothpaste, an ice bucket, paper, a pen, a toothbrush, a razor, tea bags*. Write students' ideas on the board.

C. Pair work...

➤ Have students read the items in the box. Remind them of the list of other amenities on the board.

➤ Model the conversation with a more advanced student. Play the role of Student B to demonstrate substituting any of the items in the box or on the board for *an ironing board* and *some extra towels*.

➤ Have students practice the conversation in pairs, using any of the items in B's two requests.

If your students are ready ...

Language note: The words *may* and *can* are often used interchangeably when offering help: *May I help you? Can I help you?*, although *may* is perhaps seen as a little more polite. We also use both *may* and *can* in making requests: *Can I have some more towels? May I have some more towels?* The most formal way to make a request is *Would it be possible to have some more towels?*

(continued on p. 3)

Your notes

Lesson Plan, Unit 4: Preview and practical conversations (for Student pages 43-45)—*continued*

Model 2

Content: complaining about service, responding to complaints about service, hotel services

Procedure:

🎧 A–B.

➤ To set the scene for the conversation, point to the picture and ask questions such as *Who is in this picture?* (a hotel desk clerk and a guest) *Look at the guest's expression. How do you think she is feeling?* (not happy, mad, upset)

➤ After students listen to the conversation, check comprehension by asking questions such as *What is the guest's complaint?* (Her breakfast never came.) *What does the guest want the hotel to do?* (make sure the breakfast doesn't appear on her bill) *What does the hotel employee do?* (apologize)

➤ Note that hotel employees may say *Please accept our apologies* because they are speaking on behalf of the hotel staff. If necessary, explain the meaning of the expression *make that up to you* (repair the damage, set something right).

🎧 Vocabulary

➤ Ask students why people go to hotels. Elicit examples such as *for lodging on trips, for meetings or conferences, for special events, to go out to eat*. In small groups, have students discuss the features that might be important for each function. Have them create a chart like the one following.

Note: This discussion can serve as an introduction to the *Do it yourself!* activity, or it can take place later as part of that activity.

Lodging	Meetings	Special events	Dining
Comfortable beds	Good equipment	Large rooms	Good food

➤ Play the cassette or read the hotel services and have students repeat the items.

➤ If students are unfamiliar with the audiovisual equipment, explain as necessary.

C. Pair work...

➤ Have students read the hotel departments in the box. Brainstorm some service that is provided by each department, such as extra blankets from the housekeeping department. Point out the use of the article with hotel departments: *the gift shop, the front desk*, but *room service* (no article).

➤ Ask students to work in pairs to create sentences with complaints like the one in the conversation; for example, *I ordered a newspaper from the gift shop, and it wasn't delivered*. Review the sentences and ask volunteers to put examples on the board.

➤ Still in pairs, students create a resolution for their complaint sentences; for example, *Please make sure I get one tomorrow*. Elicit resolutions and write them on the board next to the complaints.

➤ Model the conversation with a more advanced student. Play the role of Student A to demonstrate how to complain about a problem and suggest a resolution.

➤ Have students practice the conversation in pairs. Refer them to the complaints and resolutions on the board.

Workbook Link: Exercises 1, 2, 3, 4

➤ Do it yourself!

Procedure:

A–B.

➤ Ask students to identify their reason for going to a hotel. (Refer to the discussion and chart in the *Vocabulary* section above.)

➤ Read the list of variables. Make sure students understand that a rating of 1 means that the item is least important to them, while a rating of 5 means it's most important. It is possible for students to give the same rating to more than one variable. Model the activity and give your own rating for each item.

➤ Read aloud the speech balloon. Point out that the man stresses *location* and explains why it's important to him.

➤ Put students in pairs to discuss their ratings and explain their opinions.

Challenge: To review infinitives of purpose (Unit 3), ask students to hold the following conversation. First have Student A tell which factor is most important in choosing a hotel. Student B then asks why, and Student A responds with an infinitive of purpose. Note that students may have to use their ingenuity to find an appropriate infinitive of purpose. Students' conversations may look like the following:

A: I choose a hotel based on its <u>price</u>.
B: Why?
A: <u>To save money</u>.

Workbook Link: Exercise 5

LESSON PLAN, UNIT 4: PRACTICAL GRAMMAR (for Student pages 46-47)

Summary of Lesson Plan

▶ **PRESENTATION**
Practical grammar (Student pages 46-47)
Suggested teaching time: 60 minutes
  includes Language Notes (10 minutes)
Your actual teaching time: _____

▶ **Practical grammar**
(Student pages 46-47)

Suggested teaching time: 60 minutes
Your actual teaching time: _____

Some and any

Procedure:

▶ Write on the board *The housekeeping department brought us some extra towels.* Brainstorm other hotel amenities that the housekeeping department might supply, such as *some extra soap, lotion, conditioner; some extra pillows, blankets, glasses.* Write the examples on the board in two lists, one using *some* with non-count nouns and one with count nouns. Underline the word *some* in each sentence.

▶ Ask *How many towels are "some towels"? How much soap is "some soap"?* Elicit or point out that *some* describes an indefinite amount or number. The exact amount or number is not known.

▶ Put the following sentences on the board: *I don't need any lotion, No one has any shampoo, I never use any conditioner, We don't have any towels.* Underline the word *any* in each sentence. Point to the sentences on the board with the word *some*. Elicit from the class or tell students that *some* is used in affirmative statements and *any* is used in negative statements.

▶ Read the information in the box. Have volunteers read the example sentences. Stress that *any* is used with negatives (*not, no one, never*).

Option: Note that *some* and *any* are used with both count and non-count nouns. Have students change the first example sentence in the box to a sentence using a count noun. Refer to the list of hotel amenities generated above.

A. Rewrite the affirmative sentences...

▶ If necessary, review the formation of the negative in the simple present tense and the simple past tense. Practice with the verb *to be* and other verbs. Make sure students use *do / does / did* where necessary.

▶ Model item 1 of the exercise. Write on the board *There is some ice in the bucket.* Elicit the negative statement and write it on the board: *There isn't any ice in the bucket.* Note that some students will produce *There's no ice in the bucket.* That's also acceptable.

▶ Have students complete the exercise individually and then check answers with a partner. Review as a class and ask volunteers to write the sentences on the board.

Option: Review how to express a polite complaint in a hotel. Write on the board *This is _____ in Room _____ and I don't have any _____.* Play the role of a front desk clerk and say *Front desk. May I help you?* Call on individual students to respond with the completed sentence.

Challenge: Practice the use of *some* and *any* by playing a riddle game. Tell students that they should think of something and give clues about its identity using only sentences with *some* or *any*. Model the activity by describing something yourself: *It has some keys, but it doesn't have any wheels. It has some letters, but it doesn't have any mail. It has some pictures, but it doesn't have any paper. It has some memory, but it doesn't have any feelings.* Have students guess: *a computer.* Give students a few minutes to think of their own object and create *some* and *any* statements, and then ask volunteers to present their riddles to the class.

Workbook Link: Exercises 6, 7

(continued on p. 5)

Lesson Plan, Unit 4: Practical grammar (for Student pages 46-47)–*continued*

B. Complete each statement ...

➤ Have pairs of students read each statement in the exercise and decide if it is affirmative or negative. Ask them to write *A* for affirmative or *N* for negative next to each item.

➤ Elicit from the students or remind the class to use *some* in affirmative statements and *any* in negative statements. Review that questions such as item 5 can use either *some* or *any*.

➤ Have the pairs complete the exercise and then review as a class.

Challenge: In pairs, students create mini-conversations using the items from the exercise as responses or prompts. For example, item 1 could be the response to the question *Would you like some more coffee?* Remind students to use *some* or *any* in their questions. Have volunteers perform their conversations for the class.

C. Write *yes-no* questions ...

➤ Model the first item. Write the sentence elements on the board and elicit the *yes-no* question from the class. Write *Is there some / any cold food on the menu?*

➤ Have students work individually to complete the exercise and check questions with a partner.

➤ After you review the questions as a class, have volunteers write them on the board.

Option: Have partners take turns reading the questions and answering them.

Challenge: Play the game "Create a character." Ask pairs of students to create a character and imagine a monologue that might end with one of the questions in Exercise C. Model this activity with a character and monologue of your own: *I am an elderly man, and what teeth I have left are very sensitive. I cannot eat any warm or hot food. If I eat hot food, I get a terrific pain in my tooth that shoots up into my head, and I have to lie down. So what I'm asking is* ... Stop and elicit the question in item 1: *Is there some / any cold food on the menu?* Encourage students to create an interesting character and a detailed monologue. Have students read their characters' monologues and ask the rest of the class to fill in the appropriate question from the exercise.

Workbook Link: Exercises 8, 9

➤ Do it yourself!

Procedure:

➤ Working individually, students look at the picture and create questions using *Is there*, *Are there*, and *some* and *any*. Tell students that their questions can elicit *yes* or *no* answers. Give them one minute.

➤ Ask students to close their books. Put students in pairs and have them take turns asking and answering their questions.

Option: Have pairs write all their *yes* answers as a connected paragraph describing the picture. Pairs can then exchange paragraphs and see which pair has included the most details.

Option: After students have created questions and committed the picture to memory, divide the class into two teams. A member of Team A asks a question of a member of Team B. The game continues, with teams alternating questions. A correct answer earns a point for that team.

LESSON PLAN, UNIT 4: AUTHENTIC PRACTICE 1 & 2 *(for Student pages 48–51)*

Summary of Lesson Plan

▶ **PRESENTATION**
Authentic practice 1 & 2:
Listening (Student pages 48–51)
Suggested teaching time: 60 minutes
  includes Cultural Discussion
Your actual teaching time: _____

▶ **Authentic practice 1**
(Student pages 48–49)

Suggested teaching time: 30 minutes
Your actual teaching time: _____

The hotel check-in

Procedure:

🎧

▶ To activate students' prior knowledge, ask *What happens when you check in at a hotel?* Write students' answers on the board. They may include what the clerk does (checks the reservation, asks about room preference, asks about length of stay, asks about the number in the party) and what the guest does (gives his or her name, gets keys, gets help with baggage, asks about check-out time and airport shuttle service).

▶ After students have read and listened to the picture story, have volunteers come to the board and put a check mark next to each item that was actually covered in the story. Have students add any activities in the story that are not written on the board.

▶ Some words or expressions may be unfamiliar to students. Check for understanding of *imprint, mini-bar, bellman, stay*. Point out that the gender-neutral term *bellhop* is often preferred to *bellman*. Other gender-neutral terms in current use include *police officer* (not *policeman*), *fire fighter* (not *fireman*), and *chairperson* (not *chairman*). Ask students if they can add any others.

▶ Remind students that some expressions are used frequently in service industries because they demonstrate politeness. Ask them to identify such phrases in the picture story: *Certainly, Is that satisfactory?, That's no problem at all, Will you be needing any...?* Write these expressions on the board and ask students to express them in more casual speech: *Sure, Is that OK?, No problem, Do you need any...?*

▶ Point out that the question in picture 5, *Will you be needing any assistance with your luggage?*, conflicts with the rule presented in Unit 1 not to use the present continuous with non-action verbs. This regionalism is gaining acceptance, however, and students may hear non-action verbs used with continuous forms.

A–B.

▶ Working individually, students complete the exercises and then check answers with a partner.

▶ Note that it is sometimes difficult to tell the difference between requesting and confirming. For example, when the clerk says *I see you'll be with us for three nights, checking out on Saturday*, he is confirming information he already has.

Option: Have pairs of students make up additional *true-false* questions. They can then take turns asking and answering questions with another pair.

🎧 C. Listen...

▶ Read each item in the tapescript out loud or play the cassette as many times as necessary for students to complete the exercise. If students have difficulty, prompt them by reading the response yourself.

▶ Review the answers before having students read their responses out loud.

Challenge: Use the items in the tapescript as a dictation. Have students listen to the items and write what they hear. Allow students to listen as many times as necessary. Ask volunteers to write the questions on the board. Make corrections as a class. Students can then practice the prompts and responses with a partner.

If your students are ready...

Culture / Civics note: It is common to tip for services provided in the hospitality industry. Such services include serving in a restaurant, room cleaning, and carrying a guest's luggage to the room. In a restaurant, customers usually tip between 15 percent and 20 percent. The amount given to the housekeeping staff depends on the guest's length of stay and is usually from $1 to $2 per day. Bellmen usually receive from $1 to $2 per bag. Anyone who provides a special service—for example, a room-service waiter who brings breakfast or a member of the housekeeping staff who brings extra pillows—usually receives a 15-percent tip.

(continued on p. 7)

Book 4 Lesson Plans

Lesson Plan, Unit 4: Authentic practice 1 & 2 (for Student pages 48-51)–*continued*

Tapescript

1. Good afternoon. Are you checking in?
2. I see you'll be with us for three nights, checking out on Saturday.
3. Can I make an imprint of your credit card?
4. Will you be needing any assistance with your luggage?
5. Let me call the bellman for you.

Workbook Link: Exercises 10, 11

D. Vocabulary...

➤ Have students work individually to complete the exercise. If necessary, let them refer to the picture story to use the context to infer meaning.

➤ Have students check answers with a partner, and then review as a class.

Option: Put students in pairs to create sentences that use the words not selected in the exercise (*imprint, available, bellmen, single*). Have volunteers read their sentences aloud.

E–F.

➤ Remind students of the punctuation mark used for questions. Looking for question marks will help them scan the picture story and locate the questions.

➤ Have volunteers present their role plays to the class.

Option: To give students additional ideas for the hotel clerk's questions, create a list of appropriate topics and write it on the board. Look at the hotel reservations form on page 50 for ideas. Your list might include the guest's name and address, the guest's date of departure, the number of people checking in, the guest's preference in room type and bed size, the name of the guest's credit card. You may also want to refer to the answers generated in the discussion before the first reading of the picture story.

G. Reread the picture story...

➤ Tell students that sometimes information is stated directly and sometimes it is implied. Making correct inferences about implied information is an important academic skill.

➤ Put a chart on the board like the one following. Ask students first to write down what they know about Ms. Thompson. Then, in either the column headed *Direct* or the one headed *Implied*, have them write down the quotation from the picture story that supplies the information. Students' charts may include the following:

What is known	Direct	Implied
She's married.	"My husband will be joining me tomorrow."	
She doesn't smoke.	"I need to be certain that's a non-smoking room."	
She arrives on Wednesday.		"...three nights, checking out on Saturday."

➤ Do it yourself!

Procedure:

A. Read...

➤ Point out that there are three speakers and, therefore, three separate conversations. Have three volunteers each read aloud one of the speech balloons. Ask *Who are the speakers?* (hotel guests) *What do their statements have in common?* (The guests all have problems that need resolution.)

➤ If necessary, review bed sizes (single or twin, double, queen, king). You may want to refer to hotel room features in the *Vocabulary* on page 51.

➤ Tell students to imagine that they are hotel employees responding to the hotel guests. They should propose a solution to each problem and apologize when appropriate.

➤ Remind students that they can refer to the model conversations on pages 44 and 45 or to the picture story on page 48 for help in responding.

➤ Before students practice with a partner, have volunteers read each speech balloon aloud. Respond to each statement yourself, giving students an opportunity to check the appropriateness of their responses. Remind students of the importance of polite behavior toward hotel guests.

➤ Have students practice the conversations in pairs to check their responses. Ask volunteers to read their responses to the class.

B. Discussion...

➤ Brainstorm problems that the front desk can help resolve. Write students' ideas on the board. Problems may include needing local transportation, wanting a restaurant recommendation, needing a rollaway bed, having to replace forgotten toiletries, needing the address of a 24-hour pharmacy.

➤ Put students in small groups to discuss the problems and think of new problems to share with the class.

(continued on p. 8)

Lesson Plan, Unit 4: Authentic practice 1 & 2 (for Student pages 48-51)—*continued*

Authentic practice 2
(Student pages 50-51)

Suggested teaching time: 30 minutes
Your actual teaching time: _____

Note: For the activity on page 51, students should bring in phone books and travel ads. If possible, you should also bring in travel ads.

Procedure:

Reserving a hotel room

A–B.

➤ To set the scene for the conversation, have students read the bar. Then direct their attention to the pictures and ask questions such as *Who do you see on the left?* (a hotel clerk) *Who is on the right?* (a man calling the hotel) *Why do you think he is calling?* (to make a hotel reservation)

➤ Read the tapescript out loud or play the cassette.

➤ Before students listen again, have them read the questions. Read the tapescript or play the cassette again and have students answer the questions individually.

➤ Review answers as a class.

Option: Discuss when it's OK to give your credit card information over the phone and when it isn't. Elicit from students or tell them that it's OK if it's a real place and you make the call.

C. Look at the hotel reservations form...

➤ Have students look at the reservations form, and then ask them what information is required. Elicit *arrival date, departure date, occupancy, room type, bed size, traveler's name and address, payment information*. Tell students to listen for this information and write it on the reservations form as they listen to the conversation again.

➤ Have students check their information with a partner, and then review as a class.

Challenge: Have students listen to the conversation a third time and create their own questions. If necessary, you may want to suggest questions such as *Who answers the phone?* (Lauren) *Where does the man want a room?* (on a high floor, on the quieter side of the hotel) *Who will be traveling with him?* (his wife) *What time does their flight arrive?* (5:15 p.m.) Have students write the questions on slips of paper and take turns asking and answering questions with a partner. Or collect the slips and read the questions to the class, calling on individuals to answer.

Workbook Link: Exercise 12

Tapescript

A, female: Skyview Suites Conference Center. This is Lauren. How may I direct your call?

B, male: I'm calling to make a reservation.

A: Certainly. Let me put you through to our reservations department.

B: Thanks.

[Recorded music]

C, female: Reservations. Melanie speaking. Can I assist you with a reservation?

B: Yes, thanks. I need a reservation for two nights, arriving on September 5th.

C: Let me confirm those dates for you, sir. Night of the 5th, departing on the 7th.

B: Yes, that's right.

C: And what type of accommodations will you be needing?

B: I'd like a double room, non-smoking, on a high floor, on the quieter side of the hotel, that is, if there's a lot of street noise.

C: Double, non-smoking, quiet.

B: And on a high floor.

C: Right . . . Will you be traveling alone?

B: No, actually, my wife will be traveling with me.

C: And would you prefer a king-size bed or two queens?

B: We'll take the queens.

C: OK. I'll check availability for you. Just one moment, please.

[Recorded music]

C: Good. I can confirm that for you. Can you please give me your name and address?

B: Adam Stern, 10 Bank Street, White Lanes, Louisiana 70822.

C: Let me see if I've got that right: Adam Stern, 10 Bank Street, White Lanes, Louisiana, zip 70822. Would you like to guarantee that for late arrival, Mr. Stern?

B: What do you mean?

C: Ordinarily, if you don't arrive by 6 p.m., we give your room away. But if you'd like to protect your reservation in case your flight is delayed, or if you just come in after 6, we'll hold the room for you. Of course, if you don't arrive at all, we'll charge your credit card for one night.

B: Actually, that sounds like a good idea. Our flight isn't coming in until 5:15. We might not get there until after 6. What do you need to guarantee the room?

C: A major credit card will be fine.

(Tapescript is continued on page 9.)

Lesson Plan, Unit 4: Authentic practice 1 & 2 (for Student pages 48–51) – *continued*

> **Tapescript** (continued from page 8)
>
> **B:** OK. Just a minute while I get my card. [pause] Here you go: It's the MultiCard, number 1242-5674-3200-081.
>
> **C:** And the expiration date?
>
> **B:** 4/6/05.
>
> **C:** And is the card in your name, Mr. Stern?
>
> **B:** Yes. Adam J. Stern.
>
> **C:** Let me give you a reservation number, just in case you need to change your reservation. We require 48 hours notice. Do you have a pen?
>
> **B:** Yes.
>
> **C:** It's 2345 J, as in "John."
>
> **B:** Thanks.
>
> **C:** Good-bye, Mr. Stern. See you on the 5th.

➤ Do it yourself!

Procedure:

- ➤ Make sure you have phone books and/or travel ads for this activity. Have pairs of students choose the name of a hotel to use in their role play.

- ➤ After students listen to and repeat the hotel room features, have them point to the pictures as you read the items in random order.

- ➤ Read the directions for the hotel guest and the reservations clerk. Make sure students understand that Student A will play the reservations clerk and use the questions in the box as a guide. Student B will play the role of a hotel guest making a reservation. Before students begin their conversation, the guest must decide when he or she is arriving and departing, who is in the party, what type of bed is needed, and what other features he or she desires.

- ➤ Model the role play with a more advanced student. Play the role of Student B to demonstrate appropriate answers to the clerk's questions.

- ➤ Have students practice their role play, switching roles for more practice.

Option: Before pairs practice their conversations, divide the class in half. Have one half play the role of the reservations clerk and read the questions in the box together. Ask individual volunteers from the other half to answer the questions.

Option: Tell students to draw a line across the last picture in the *Vocabulary* box to separate the TV and fax machine from the mini-bar and safe. They now have a "Bingo" board with nine spaces. The object of this game is to mark off all nine spaces. As you read the following story, students mark off each space when you mention one of the hotel room features. At the end of the story, ask how many students marked all the spaces.

Optional read-aloud story

I worked a double shift yesterday. What a nightmare! I had several guests make complaints about their reservations. Mr. Stern had requested a double room, but he ended up with a king. That was a problem because he said he and his wife needed separate beds. Well, I found a room with two queens, but it was a smoking room, so I couldn't really make him happy. He decided to stay in the king but asked for a rollaway too. I wonder who ended up in which bed! Then Ms. Thompson came down. She said the key to the mini-bar didn't work. I finally had to go up to her room myself to show her how the key worked. Her husband was trying to get some work done, but he complained that the fax machine and the data port weren't working properly. The problem is that guests in the double rooms can't use the fax and the data port at the same time, so I had to switch the Thompsons to a suite. The suites have a much better setup for business work. Then it turned out that Ms. Thompson's co-worker arrived at the last minute to bring some papers for her big presentation tomorrow. Fortunately, we had a single room left—the last one—so I got that problem solved.

Workbook Link: Exercise 13

LESSON PLAN, UNIT 4: AUTHENTIC PRACTICE 3 *(for Student pages 52-53)*

Summary of Lesson Plan

▶ **PRESENTATION**
Authentic practice 3:
Reading and critical thinking (Student pages 52-53)
Suggested teaching time: 60 minutes
    includes Cultural Discussion
Your actual teaching time: _____

▶ **Authentic practice 3**
(Student pages 52-53)

Suggested teaching time: 60 minutes
Your actual teaching time: _____

Vacations

Procedure:

🎧 **A. Read and listen to the letters.**

▶ Play the cassette or read the letters. Students listen and read silently. Pause after Edward's letter and make sure students know what an *HMO* is (health maintenance organization). Explain as necessary *better safe than sorry* and *surf*, which refers to researching on the Internet.

▶ Have students continue to listen and read silently. After Joan's letter to Gus, check comprehension of the following terms: *overnight, too good to be true, red flag, scams,* and *nightmares*. Note that *overnight* is used as a verb meaning to send overnight. Tell students that the saying *There's no such thing as a free lunch* means that all offers come with conditions or obligations. We don't get anything without paying for it in some way.

▶ Check comprehension with questions such as *What does Edward want to do?* (take a wonderful driving trip with his family) *What three pieces of advice does Joan give?* (plan ahead, be cash smart, shop around) *What offer did Gus get over the phone?* (a free vacation) *What does Gus have to do to get this "free" vacation?* (overnight a cash deposit and pay for the hotel) *What is a warning sign that an offer might not be legitimate?* (pressuring the person to send cash)

Option: Summarizing is an important academic skill. Have pairs of students work together to summarize Joan's advice to Edward.

Option: Ask students if there is an expression in their language similar to *There's no such thing as a free lunch*. Write any such expressions on the board and discuss. Ask students to give their reasons for agreeing or disagreeing with the expression.

Challenge: Have students do the following sentence completion task as a dictation. Before students read and listen to the letters, write these incomplete sentences on the board:

1. I would like to plan _____.
2. Congratulations on _____!
3. Surf the travel sites for _____.
4. That free vacation offer _____.
5. There's no such thing _____.

Play the cassette or read the letters and have students complete the sentences according to what they hear. Let students listen several times if necessary. Have pairs of students check their answers by comparing their sentences with the sentences in the text.

B. Choose an answer...

▶ Students complete the exercise individually and then compare answers with a partner.

▶ To practice scanning for information, students can underline the sentences in the text where they found the answers.

If your students are ready...

Culture / Civics note: In North America, full-time employees usually get a paid vacation as one of their benefits. This paid vacation time is usually two weeks. In some workplaces, the amount of paid vacation leave increases with the length of time the person is employed by the company.

Workbook Link: Exercise 14

(continued on p. 11)

Lesson Plan, Unit 4: Authentic practice 3 (for Student pages 52-53)–*continued*

C. Read the information...

➤ Review the terms of Gus's "free" vacation offer (He had to overnight a deposit in cash, pay for the hotel, decide quickly) and Joan's advice (Get details in writing). Tell students to keep this information in mind as they read about travel fraud. Ask them to look for information that is similar to Gus's situation and to Joan's response.

➤ Check comprehension and encourage key reading skills by asking questions such as *What is the topic of this reading?* (protecting yourself against travel fraud, vacation scams) *How many tips does the Web site give?* (five) *What's a good way to locate these tips?* (look at the bullets)

➤ Make sure students understand *unsolicited fax, legitimate businesses, a scam operator* or *artist*. Explain the meaning of *snap decisions* by snapping your fingers to indicate speed.

➤ Note that quotation marks are used in two ways in this reading: to indicate actual speech (say "no") and to suggest that a term is being used in an unusual or deceptive way (a "free" trip). Have students find additional terms that are used in deceptive ways and explain their meaning ("trip trap," "won").

➤ Direct students' attention to the Hello message at the top of the screen. Ask them to find the three adjectives that describe the vacation (spectacular, luxury, dream). Tell them that these exaggerated adjectives can be a clue that the offer is a scam.

➤ Remind students that they saw this message in the unit preview on page 43. Ask the *Warm up* question again: *Do you believe this offer is true?*

Option: On the board, create a chart of do's and don'ts. Ask students to divide the tips they read into these two categories. Write their suggestions on the board. Your list should include the following:

Do's	Don'ts
• Be careful.	• Be pressured into buying.
• Ask detailed questions.	• Give your credit card number over the phone.
• Say "no" if you have any doubt.	• Send money by messenger.

D. Warn this consumer...

➤ Have students look at the picture and read the letter that the woman received. Ask *What has the woman won?* (a vacation prize, a space at a timeshare) *Look at the woman's expression. How do you think she feels?* (surprised, excited, pleased) *Which exaggerated adjectives are used in the letter?* (all inclusive, exclusive) *What other words are red flags?* (extravaganza, hurry, limited)

➤ Ask students what problems they can identify in this situation. Remind students to think about the lists of do's and don'ts they prepared. They can also reread Joan's advice to Gus on page 52.

➤ Model the activity. On the board, write a warning to the woman, such as *Be careful. The vacation you've "won" probably isn't "free."* Brainstorm other warnings.

➤ Have students complete the activity individually. In pairs, students compare warnings.

Workbook Link: Exercises 15, 16

➤ Do it yourself!

Procedure:

A. True story...

➤ Model the activity for the class. Choose one of the three topics and tell a true story of your own. Include details about transportation, accommodations, and travel companions, and add two to three additional sentences. Focus students' attention on the verb forms you use.

➤ Brainstorm other details students could include in their stories in addition to information about transportation, accommodations, and travel companions. Write students' suggestions on the board to be used for additional prompts.

➤ Put students in pairs. To practice the simple past tense, ask them to talk about their best or worst vacations. They can use these questions as prompts: *What kind(s) of transportation did you take? What kind of accommodations did you have? Who did you travel with? What made the vacation memorable?* Have students add details based on the suggestions on the board. Tell students to try to talk for one minute.

➤ To practice future and conditional forms, partners can talk about a vacation they would like to take. They can use these questions as prompts: *Where would you like to go? Why? What kind of transportation will you use? What kind of accommodations do you want? Who will you travel with?*

B. Culture talk...

➤ Ask each pair of students to join another pair to create small groups of four. Have them discuss travel destinations and travel dangers in their home countries.

➤ Lead a class discussion. Explore common patterns by asking *What are some of the dangers or difficulties that tourists face? What are some of the warnings you might give a tourist?*

Copyright © 2004 by Pearson Education, Inc.
All rights reserved.

LESSON PLAN: UNIT 4: REVIEW (for Student pages 54-56)

Summary of Lesson Plan

➤ **Review (Student pages 54-56)**
Suggested teaching time: 60 minutes
Your actual teaching time: _____

➤ **UNIT REVIEW**
Includes expansion activities
role play
dialogues
writing
Workbook activities
outside reading
realia applications
math skills applications
civic lesson applications
Booster Pak activities

➤ **Review (Student pages 54-56)**

Suggested teaching time: 60 minutes
Your actual teaching time: _____

Procedure:

A. Pair work or group work.

Option: Create questions. Put students in pairs. Ask them to create questions about the pictures. Questions for scene 4, for example, might include *Who is going to help with their luggage?* (the bellman) *What do you think the clerk is giving the woman?* (the room key, the mini-bar key, a voucher for a free breakfast) Pairs then exchange questions with another pair and take turns answering them.

Ask and answer questions.

➤ Ask general questions about the picture, such as *Who are the people in these scenes?* (a husband and wife, hotel employees) *What is this picture about?* (a couple going on a trip) *Where do they go?* (New Orleans, the New Orleans Farley Hotel) *What does the woman request from the front desk?* (some hangers and towels)

➤ Have pairs of students take turns pointing to and describing different events in the story.

Create conversations.

➤ Point to the first scene. Play the role of the husband and say *You know, I'd really like to go to Paris. This brochure looks great.* Elicit the wife's possible responses: *That sounds wonderful, but too expensive, Let's go somewhere closer to home, Here's an ad for a hotel in New Orleans.* Put students in pairs to finish the conversation.

➤ Have pairs of students choose one of the four other scenes and create an extended conversation for the speakers. Remind students to refer to the conversation on page 44 for help and ideas.

➤ Have pairs number the speech balloons and, on a separate sheet of paper, write one line of conversation for each person in the picture.

Tell a story.

Option: One-minute stories. Have a student time you while you model the activity and talk about the picture for one minute. Then, in pairs or small groups, each student talks about the picture for one minute. Encourage students to describe each of the five scenes and to say as much as they can. Tell students to continue talking until you say *Stop*, indicating that the minute is up.

Option: Chronological order. Write the following sentences on the board. Have students rewrite them, putting them in chronological order. Have students check the order with a partner (4, 1, 8, 3, 2, 6, 5, 7).

- "Would you like to guarantee your room for late arrival?"
- Last May, Mr. and Mrs. Swenson talked about going on a trip.
- "Absolutely. I'll send them right up," the clerk replied.
- Mr. Swenson called the hotel and made a reservation.
- About a week later, Mrs. Swenson received an offer in the mail for a travel discount package.
- The bellman helped them with their luggage.
- They checked in at the Farley Hotel before dinner.
- Mrs. Swenson called the front desk to ask for some hangers and towels.

(continued on p. 13)

Lesson Plan, Unit 4: Review (for Student pages 54-56)–*continued*

Option: Travel warnings. Have students look at scene 2. They should then imagine a conversation between the husband or wife and a friend. The friend gives warnings about the travel offer the wife received. The friend's warnings might include *Don't overnight any money, Ask for details in writing, What's "free"?*

Option: Newspaper articles. Pairs of students choose one of the headlines in scene 2 and create the rest of the article. Volunteers can read their articles to the class.

Challenge: When journalists report a story, they write a very brief summary in the headline. A headline usually focuses on nouns and verbs and leaves out articles and adjectives. Ask students to write headlines for each scene. Headlines for scene 1 might include *Man reads travel brochure, Wife sees hotel ad.* Elicit examples and write them on the board. Ask students to judge the headlines based on length, accuracy, and active language.

B–C.

➤ Play the cassette or read the conversation out loud while students listen with books closed.

➤ Have students open their books. Read the questions in Exercise B out loud. Play the cassette or read the conversation again. Have students complete the exercise.

➤ Ask students to read the room service order slip in Exercise C. Play the cassette or read the conversation as many times as necessary for students to complete the exercise.

➤ Have students check Exercises B and C with a partner. Review as a class.

Challenge: After students have completed Exercise C, put students in pairs. Students should create the room service person's questions that elicited the filled-out order slip. For example, the room service person might ask *Would you like to start with a shrimp cocktail? How many? Small or jumbo?* Have students practice the conversation, playing the roles of the order taker and the guest in Room 306. Then have students switch roles for more practice.

D. Read each sentence or question ...

➤ Students work individually to complete the review exercise.

➤ Have students check responses with a partner. Review as a class.

Challenge: Pairs of students create extended conversations that include each item and its response.

Tapescript

Male: Claire? Could you check the other closet? There aren't any hangers in this one.

Female: Sure. Just a minute. Here you go. They must have put them all in here. I've got a ton of them. Are these enough?

Male: Yeah. That's great. [pause] What's this? Oh, no. Can you believe it? There are three ironing boards in this closet. No wonder there wasn't any room for hangers! . . . You know what? Let's order room service.

Female: But room service is so expensive.

Male: I know. But it's our anniversary. Let's make this like a second honeymoon. [pause] Hello. Room service? I'd like to order dinner. I'm in Room 306. For two people. [pause] Excuse me? How long did you say? Claire, he says it'll be forty-five minutes to an hour. Can you hold out?

Female: Well, actually, I'm not that hungry. It's only 5 o'clock. It isn't any problem for me. What about you?

Male: I'm OK. That'll give us a little time to finish unpacking. Why don't I just order for both of us? [pause] Room service? That'll be OK. We're not in a hurry. . . . We'll start with two jumbo shrimp cocktails. Then we'll have one broiled chicken with a salad and one steak. Medium. Do you have any fresh vegetables? Good. I'll have some broccoli with that steak. [pause] Dressing? Just a minute. Claire, any dressing with your salad?

Female: Yes. Italian, please.

Male: That'll be Italian dressing on the salad. Thanks.

Female: Mmm. Sounds great!

(continued on p. 14)

Lesson Plan, Unit 4: Review (for Student pages 54-56)–*continued*

E–F.
➤ Students work individually to complete the review exercises.

➤ Circulate to offer help as needed.

➤ Have students check answers with a partner. Review answers as a class.

➤ Identify any areas of difficulty that may require additional instruction and practice.

G. Composition...
➤ Provide students with concrete approaches to writing about the picture on page 54. Use one of the options that follow, give students a choice of options, or assign options based on students' levels of proficiency. Model what is expected of students for each option.

➤ Advise students to look back through the unit for help and ideas as they write.

➤ Circulate to offer help as needed.

Option: Have students write an extended conversation for one of the pairs in the picture. Students can later role-play their conversations for the class.

Option: Have students number the different people in the picture and then write two sentences about each one.

Option: Have students write a letter to the manager of the Farley Hotel, complaining about the service.

Now I can
➤ Read the first item in the box out loud: *Now I can request service and respond to requests for service.* Elicit from the class an example of how to request and respond to service, such as *Would it be possible to get more hangers?* and *Of course. How many would you like?*

➤ Put students in pairs. Tell the students to take turns reading each item in the box and giving an example of what they have learned. When students can provide an example, they should check that box. If there are items students aren't able to check, have them look back through the unit for ideas.

➤ When students are finished reviewing with their partners, read each item out loud and elicit an example from the class.

Oral test (optional)

You may want to use the *Now I can* box as an informal evaluation. While students are working on the *Composition* activity, you can call them up individually and check their ability with two or three objectives.

Your notes

LESSON PLAN, UNIT 5: PREVIEW/PRACTICAL CONVERSATIONS (for Student pages 57-59)

Summary of Lesson Plan

▶ **Preview and Practical conversations** (Student pages 57-59)
Suggested teaching time: 60 minutes
includes Cultural Notes & Discussion
Your actual teaching time: _____

▶ Preview and Practical conversations (Student pages 57-59)

Suggested teaching time: 60 minutes
Your actual teaching time: _____

Note: For the plan-ahead project on page 67, divide the students into four topic groups: registering a child at a day-care center, voter registration, community college registration, and immunizations for schoolchildren. Students should get information about deadlines for each topic. Assist students by giving them the names of local day-care centers and community colleges. The number of the central office of the public school system can be found in the telephone book. Libraries and the League of Women Voters are good sources of information about voter registration. Provide local phone books for reference.

Warm up. What do these documents have in common?
Procedure:
▶ Ask *What documents do you see?* (a computer-generated "card" for a library book, a driver's license, information about voter registration) *What information is circled on each document?* (the due date, the expiration date, the dates by which voter registration requirements must be met) Elicit that these are all deadlines. If necessary, clarify the meaning of *deadline*: the time by which you must finish something.

▶ Elicit students' experience by asking questions such as *Is anyone registered to vote? Who has a library card? What materials can you borrow with your library card? How long can you check materials out? Who has a driver's license for this state? How often do licenses have to be renewed?*

▶ Note that Joan Manners's driver's license expires on her birthday. Many states match the license expiration date with a driver's birthday.

▶ Ask *What is the difference between a due date and an expiration date?* Elicit that a *due date* is a date on which something must be returned or paid. Sometimes a late fee is charged if a payment or return is late. An *expiration date* is the date after which something is no longer good, or effective.

▶ Write *Due date* and *Expiration date* on the board. Brainstorm things that have due dates or expiration dates and write them under the appropriate heading. Your list may include the following items:

Due date	Expiration date
Library books	Licenses
Videos from the video store	Parking permits
Bills	Student IDs

Option: Ask additional questions related to voter registration: *Do you have to be a citizen to vote? Is anyone in the class a citizen? What do you have to do to become a citizen?* Broaden the discussion by asking *Why is it important to vote? What are other ways of being a good citizen or community member?*

Option: Elicit information about your local library's policy on length of loans and amount of fines. Write this information on the board. Your list may look like the one following:

Material	Length of loan	Late fine per day
Book	Three weeks	$.15
Cassette	Three weeks	$.15
Video or DVD	Two days	$1.00

Unit 5 objectives
Procedure:
▶ Have students read the objectives. Ask them to put a check next to the objectives that they can do now and circle those they want to work on.

▶ Ask students to underline any words they do not understand. Define any words that are unfamiliar, such as *prioritize* (to put in order of importance).

▶ As a class, choose one of the objectives. Find out what related information students already know. For the objective *Manage time*, for example, ask *What does "manage" mean?* (direct, handle, control) *Can we really control time?* (no) Point out that when we talk about managing time, we really mean using our own time with positive results. Then brainstorm questions students have related to the objective. These may include *How can I do my job and also take care of my family? I can't get used to the attitude that people in this country have about time. What can I do? How can I do things at the time people in this country want them done?* Write the questions on a large sheet of paper for students to answer at the end of the unit.

(continued on p. 2)

Lesson Plan, Unit 5: Preview and practical conversations (for Student pages 57-59)–*continued*

Model 1

Content: expressing dismay, offering advice, consequences of missing a deadline

Procedure:

🎧 A–B.

▶ To set the scene for the conversation, ask questions about the photo, such as *Who do you think the people are?* (friends or family) *Why do you think so?* (They're informally dressed, sitting at a table together.) *What is their mood?* (serious, upset)

▶ After students listen to the conversation, check comprehension by asking questions such as *What was the young woman supposed to do?* (return the books by the 14th) *What is the consequence of returning the books late?* (She'll have to pay a fine.) *What advice does the man give?* (Write everything down so you won't forget.)

▶ Point out that the young woman says *the 14th*. Remind students that we use ordinal numbers when talking about dates.

▶ Note that the young woman says *by the 14th*. Point out that the preposition *by*, not *on*, is used with deadlines, since we have the opportunity to pay a bill or return a library book up until the deadline.

Option: If necessary, review ordinal numbers and the abbreviations (first) *-st*, (second) *-nd*, (third) *-rd*, (fourth through ninth) *-th*. Have students stand and form a line. Have them use ordinal numbers to give their position on line. Model by standing at the front of the line and saying *I'm first*. Give additional examples by changing your place in line and saying *I'm fourth, I'm ninth,* and so on. Ask questions such as *When is Independence Day? Christmas?* Write students' answers on the board and underline the ordinal numbers: July <u>4th</u>, December <u>25th</u>. Have the class repeat the dates. For more practice, draw or tape a large calendar for the current month on the board. Tell students that if we are talking about a date in the current month, we can just say *the [10]th*, without the month. Ask questions such as *When is our next class? When does the weekend begin? When do we return to school?* Make sure students answer with *the* + an ordinal number.

🎧 Vocabulary

▶ Point out that this *Vocabulary* section includes obligations that must be met by a certain deadline and the consequences of missing that deadline. For example, in the first item, the obligation is to pay a credit card bill by a certain deadline. The consequence of missing that deadline is "You'll have to pay a late fee and interest."

▶ Note that there is a deadline printed on the credit card bill, the library slip, the Board of Elections envelope, and the driver's license. The information circled in red has been enlarged to make it easier to read the deadline.

▶ Have students listen to and repeat the obligations and the consequences of missing a deadline.

Option: Write the heading *Obligation* on the board. Brainstorm other obligations that involve deadlines and write them under the heading. In pairs, students predict the consequences of not meeting the deadlines. Elicit students' ideas and write them on the board. Your list may look like this one:

Obligation	Consequences of missing a deadline
renew a visa	You'll have to leave the country.
pay a utility bill	Your phone service will be cut off.
pay the rent	You'll be charged a late fee.
file tax returns	You'll have to pay a fine.

C. Pair work ...

▶ Point out that the consequences expressed in the *Vocabulary* are addressed to the reader: *You'll*. In the *Pair work*, students will have to say *I'll*, as in *I'll get a ticket*.

▶ Direct students' attention to Student A's second line. Point out that Student A must first state a missed obligation and a date: for example, *I was supposed to <u>renew my driver's license by the 23rd</u>*. The consequence of missing the deadline goes in the next slot: *I'll <u>get a ticket</u>*.

▶ Model the conversation with a more advanced student. Play the role of Student A to demonstrate choosing an obligation, stating the date of the deadline, and expressing the consequence of missing the deadline.

▶ Have students practice the conversation in pairs, using the *Vocabulary* or the ideas on the board for obligations and consequences.

Challenge: If appropriate for your class and community, assign students to interview someone outside the class about work deadlines. As a class, brainstorm possible interview questions: *What kind of work do you do? What happens if you miss a deadline?* Students report their findings about deadlines to the class.

Workbook Link: Exercises 1, 2, 3

(continued on p. 3)

Lesson Plan, Unit 5: Preview and practical conversations (for Student pages 57-59)—*continued*

Model 2

Content: notifying someone about missing an appointment, apologizing for missing an appointment, asking about rescheduling, agreeing to reschedule, types of appointments

Procedure:

🎧 A–B.

➤ To set the scene for the conversation, point to the photos and ask *Who is on the left?* (a woman on the phone) *How do you think she is feeling?* (upset) Point to the inset and ask *What is this?* (a schedule of appointments) *Who do you think is on the right?* (a receptionist in an office, a woman who is reading the schedule)

➤ After students read and listen to the conversation, check comprehension by asking questions such as *Who calls Mrs. Martin?* (Paula in Dr. Paine's office) *Why is she calling?* (to tell Mrs. Martin she missed an appointment and to reschedule) *Is Mrs. Martin surprised that she missed the appointment?* (yes) *How do you know?* (She is upset, she says "Oh, no! You're right!")

➤ Practice choral reading of the conversation. Play the role of Student A, Mrs. Martin, and have the class play the role of Student B, the receptionist Paula. Read Student A's second and third lines with exaggeration, emphasizing Mrs. Martin's dismay (*Oh, no! You're right!*) and then her apology (*I'm so sorry*). Switch roles. Remind students to exaggerate their dismay and apology.

🎧 Vocabulary

➤ After students listen to and repeat the appointments, brainstorm other appointments that they might have. Suggestions may include a meeting at a child's school, a job interview, a business meeting. Write the appointments on the board and have students repeat them after you.

C. Pair work...

➤ Model the conversation with a more advanced student. Play the role of Student B, demonstrating how to notify someone of a missed appointment. To complete Student B's line, *This is _____,* give both your name and location; for example, *This is Max at Grove Street Auto* or *This is Ms. Perry at Ridge Elementary School.*

➤ Before students practice the conversation in pairs, remind them to choose a name for Student A, a name and location for Student B, and to decide what kind of appointment Student A has missed.

If your students are ready...

Culture / Civics notes: Note that the receptionist in Dr. Paine's office calls the patient Mrs. Martin. According to current social usage, a woman is usually addressed as Ms. rather than Mrs., even if the speaker knows she is married. Note too that the caller identifies herself by her first name, Paula, rather than as Ms. plus her last name. It is common for a receptionist to use only his or her first name.

Workbook Link: Exercises 4, 5

➤ Do it yourself!

Procedure:

A. Write your appointments...

➤ On the board, make a chart like the one on page 59. Model the activity by writing your own appointment and a consequence for missing it in the Monday slot; for example, *a haircut appointment / I'll have to reschedule for sometime later in the week.* Point out the use of the future *will* to express the consequence. Fill in the rest of the chart with appointments and consequences suggested by volunteers.

➤ Tell students to open their books and complete the charts for themselves. They should write down at least one appointment or deadline for each weekday next week. Have them write down a consequence of missing the appointment or deadline in the column on the right.

➤ Remind students to use the future *will* or *won't* to express the consequence.

➤ Have students share their schedules in pairs.

B. Discussion...

➤ Put the following questions on the board: *What appointment or deadline did you miss? Why did you miss it? What was the consequence of missing it? Did you reschedule?*

➤ Model the activity by telling about an appointment or deadline you missed in the past. Refer to the questions on the board and include the reason for missing the appointment and the consequence. Tell students whether you rescheduled.

➤ In pairs or small groups, students tell about their own missed appointments.

Copyright © 2004 by Pearson Education, Inc.
All rights reserved.

LESSON PLAN, UNIT 5: PRACTICAL GRAMMAR (for Student pages 60-61)

Summary of Lesson Plan

▶ **PRESENTATION**
Practical grammar (Student pages 60-61)
Suggested teaching time: 60 minutes
Your actual teaching time: _____

▶ Practical grammar
(Student pages 60-61)

Suggested teaching time: 60 minutes
Your actual teaching time: _____

Conditional sentences

Procedure:
- Review the consequences of missing a deadline from the *Vocabulary* box on page 58. Ask students questions using *if* and have them respond with the quoted statements from the text; for example, *What happens if you pay a credit card bill late?* (You'll have to pay a late fee and interest.) Write the questions and answers on the board as conditional sentences: *If you return a library book late, you'll have to pay a fine.* Underline the *if* clauses.
- Tell students that the sentences on the board represent real possibilities: If you miss a deadline, certain consequences are likely to occur. A sentence with an *if* clause and a consequence, or a result clause, is called a conditional sentence.
- Write on the board *If I paid my bills on time, I wouldn't have to pay interest.* Underline the *if* clause. Write a series of unreal conditions on the board; for example, *If I were you, If I wanted to save money.* Brainstorm result clauses and write students' ideas on the board, making sure to use *would*. Ask *Are these real situations?* (no) Tell students that unreal conditional sentences express hypothetical or imaginary situations.
- Have students read the information in the box. Answer any questions.

A. Read the conditional sentences...
- Model item 1. Write the sentence and the check box on the board, and underline the *if* clause. Ask *Is this a real situation?* (yes) Continue with item 2. Ask *Does Carl take music lessons?* (no) *Is this a real situation?* (no) Put a check in the box.

- Tell students to look at the *if* clauses in the remaining sentences and ask themselves if they describe real or unreal conditions. Working individually, students check the boxes next to unreal conditions.

Option: After the class has reviewed Exercise A, read the *if* clauses out loud in random order and call on individual students to respond with the consequences in the result clauses.

Workbook Link: Exercise 6

Verb forms in conditional sentences

Procedure:
- Write on the board the first example sentence from the box. Include the blue brackets and labels. Ask *Does this sentence describe a real condition or an unreal condition?* (real, it represents a real possibility) *How many clauses are there in this conditional sentence?* (two) *What are they?* (the *if* clause, the result clause) Have volunteers read aloud the two clauses.
- Remind students that an *if* clause states a condition that leads to the consequence in the result clause. Tell students that we use *if* and the simple present tense to state a real condition. We can use the simple present tense or the future in the result clause. Illustrate the correct use of verb forms in several examples. Write on the board items 1, 3, 4, and 5 from Exercise A or your own examples. Point to each verb form and elicit what it is.
- Write on the board the first unreal conditional sentence from the box and add blue brackets and the labels *if clause* and *result clause*. Ask *Does this sentence describe a real condition or an unreal condition?* (unreal, Paul doesn't wear his glasses) *How many clauses are there in this conditional sentence?* (two) *What are they?* (the *if* clause, the result clause) Read aloud the two clauses.
- Tell students we use *if* and the simple past tense to state an unreal condition. We can also state unreal conditions using *if* and *were*. We use *would* or *could* + the base form of the verb in the result clause. Illustrate the correct use of verb forms in several examples. Write on the board items 2, 6, 7, and 8 from Exercise A or your own examples. Point to each verb form and elicit what it is.
- Have students read the information in the box. Direct attention to the unreal conditions and ask questions such as *Does Paul wear his glasses?* (no) *Is she a doctor?* (no). Answer any questions and give additional examples if necessary.

(continued on p. 5)

Lesson Plan, Unit 5: Practical grammar (for Student pages 60-61)–*continued*

Challenge: Give students an example of a possible condition (you pay the phone bill early) and an obviously imaginary one (you won a million dollars). Working in pairs, students create a list of five possible conditions and five imaginary or impossible ones. Students use their lists to write real and unreal *if* clauses. Have pairs exchange their lists and add a result clause to each one to form complete sentences (If you pay the phone bill early, you won't have to pay a fine. If you won a million dollars, you could travel).

Order of clauses in conditional sentences

Procedure:

➤ On the board, write pairs of conditional sentences. In the first sentence of each pair, write the *if* clause first and circle the comma. In the second sentence, write the result clause first. You can use the example sentences from the grammar boxes on page 60 or your own sentences. If necessary, remind students that *I'd* is a contraction for *I would*.

➤ Read the sentence pairs out loud. Ask *Is there any difference in meaning between the two sentences?* (no) Ask *What is different in the two sentences?* Elicit the response that there is a comma between the two clauses in the first sentence. Tell students that when the *if* clause comes first, there is a comma before the result clause.

B. First complete...

➤ Focus students' attention on item 1. Read the first sentence aloud. Ask *Is this a real or an unreal condition?* (real) *How can you tell?* Elicit or tell students that the use of the future and the simple present tense provides a clue. Read the second sentence aloud. Ask *Is this a real or an unreal condition?* (unreal) *How can you tell?* Elicit or tell students that the use of *would* and the simple past tense provides a clue.

➤ Working individually, students complete the exercise.

➤ Students compare answers with a partner.

➤ Have volunteers write their pairs of sentences on the board.

Option: If possible, bring in the children's book *If You Give a Mouse a Cookie*. Read it aloud to provide extended examples of real conditions. (Other related books by author Laura Nemeroff are *If You Give a Moose a Muffin, If You Take a Mouse to School, If You Take a Mouse to the Movies, If You Give a Pig a Pancake.*)

Challenge. Tell students that you are going to tell a group story. Each person will contribute an unreal conditional sentence. Begin the story with an idea of your own or use this one: *If I were a movie star, I would live in Hollywood.* The next person must continue *If I lived in Hollywood, I would or could....* If necessary, prompt students with the correct beginning.

Workbook Link: Exercises 7, 8

➤ Do it yourself!

Procedure:

A–B.

➤ On the board, write a chart like the one on page 61 but with several more rows. Read aloud the heading in the first column *If I had more time,* and point out the comma. Fill in the first row for yourself; for example, *I could read more.* Write *What could you do if you had more time?* on the board and underline the word *could* to remind students to use it in their answer. Ask several students the question and write their responses in the first column.

➤ Read aloud the heading in the second column *If I had more money,* and fill in the first row for yourself. Continue, following the same procedure as before.

➤ Put students in small groups to compile their ideas. Elicit any new examples from the class. Make sure students are using *would* or *could* with the base form of the verb.

Workbook Link: Exercise 9

LESSON PLAN, UNIT 5: AUTHENTIC PRACTICE 1 & 2 (for Student pages 62-65)

Summary of Lesson Plan

▶ **PRESENTATION**
Authentic practice 1 & 2:
Listening (Student pages 62-65)
Suggested teaching time: 60 minutes
    includes Cultural Discussion
Your actual teaching time: _____

▶ **Authentic practice 1**
(Student pages 62-63)

Suggested teaching time: 30 minutes
Your actual teaching time: _____

Juggle commitments

Procedure:

🎧
▶ Point to the sign on the wall in the second picture. Ask *Where do you usually see this sign?* (at a doctor's or dentist's office) *How else can you tell this is a doctor's or dentist's office?* (The receptionist or nurse is wearing a white uniform.) *Why do you think the woman with the baby is here?* (She has an appointment.)

▶ Read the conversation out loud or play the cassette. With books open, students read and listen. Then ask students to underline all the idioms in the picture story: *juggle* (handle, balance), *have a lot on your plate* (have too many things to do), *I'm on total overload* (I'm overwhelmed, dealing with too much), *it's no picnic* (it's not easy), *make ends meet* (have enough money to pay for expenses), *if I were in your shoes* (if I were in your situation), *better late than never* (even if it is late to get started, it's a good idea to do it). Make sure students understand the meanings.

▶ Note that *better late than never* is similar in structure to another expression students know: *better safe than sorry.*

▶ Have students talk about the pressures and responsibilities that Mrs. Gebert is handling right now. Elicit examples: *her husband went back to school, she's on total overload, she's working, she has a young child.*

▶ Then have students find and circle two pieces of advice that Ms. Fun gives Mrs. Gebert (write everything down in one place, make a habit of checking the list every morning).

A. Read the picture story again...

▶ Working individually, students answer the questions and then compare answers with a partner. Review answers as a class.

▶ To support their answers, have students underline the appropriate lines in the text.

Option: In pairs, have students offer additional advice to Mrs. Gebert.

B. Vocabulary...

▶ Students read the items in the box and then find and circle each one in the picture story. To reinforce context as a way of getting meaning, have students reread the speech balloons in which the items occur.

▶ Note that the exercise continues on page 63. Have students complete the entire exercise individually. Then review the five sentences as a class.

Challenge: After reviewing the answers, have students use each idiom in an original sentence. Have students check their sentences with a partner before reading them aloud.

If your students are ready...

Culture / Civics note: Many of your students may come from cultures where extended families are the norm. Our North American culture is a mobile one, and often nuclear families are separated geographically from grandparents, aunts and uncles and cousins, and other family members. Mrs. Gebert is fortunate to have her mother close by to help her. Many families in this culture turn to social service agencies or private organizations for help in difficult times. These may include day-care arrangements, federal food stamp programs, and government loans to students.

Workbook Link: Exercises 10, 11

(continued on p. 7)

Lesson Plan, Unit 5: Authentic practice 1 & 2 (for Student pages 62-65)–*continued*

C. Listen...

- Students listen to two statements and read the correct responses from the picture story. If students have difficulty, prompt them by reading the response yourself.

- Review the answers before having students read their responses out loud.

Challenge: Use the items in the tapescript as a dictation. Have students listen to the statements and write what they hear. Allow students to listen as many times as necessary. Ask volunteers to write the questions on the board. Make corrections as a class. Students can then practice the prompts and responses with a partner.

D–E.

- Students complete the exercise individually and then compare responses with a partner.

- Partners read the items and responses, switching roles for more practice.

Option: After both students have practiced reading the items and responses in Exercise D, have Partner B in each pair close his or her book. Partner A then reads the item, and Partner B responds from memory.

Option: After students have practiced reading the items and responses, have them close their books. They then respond chorally when you read the items in random order.

Challenge: Have pairs of students work together to write a statement or a question for each unused response in Exercise D. For example, in item 1, a statement that could elicit the response *I don't believe it!* might be *You missed another appointment.* Have students take turns reading their new items and responses.

➤ Do it yourself!

Procedure:

A. Write your own response...

- Students read each speech balloon and speculate who the person might be. (a close friend or colleague, a family member)

- Model this activity with a more advanced student. Ask the student to read the first speech balloon so that you can demonstrate an appropriate response. Note that there are three different speakers, so the conversations do not have to be linked.

- Students read the speech balloons and complete the activity individually.

- Review as a class. Have a volunteer read each speech balloon and elicit a variety of appropriate responses.

- Students read their conversations out loud with a partner and then change roles to practice both parts.

B. Culture talk...

Option: Put students in groups. Ask them to create a Venn diagram illustrating the similarities and differences between their home cultures and this culture. Prompt them with questions such as *What stresses did you have in your home country? What stresses do you have here? What stresses are the same in both cultures?* Elicit some examples and model a Venn diagram on the board.

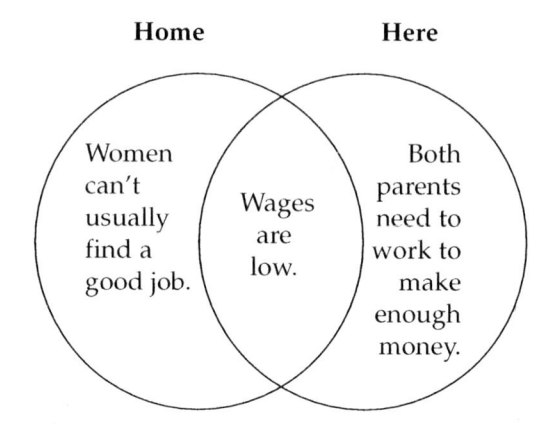

Home   Here

- Women can't usually find a good job.
- Wages are low.
- Both parents need to work to make enough money.

Tapescript

1. Please accept my apology again about the last appointment. I can't believe I missed it.
2. Let me give you a little tip. If I were in your shoes, I'd write everything down—in one place. And make a habit of checking the list every morning.

(continued on p. 8)

Lesson Plan, Unit 5: Authentic practice 1 & 2 (for Student pages 62-65)–*continued*

Authentic practice 2
(Student pages 64-65)

Suggested teaching time: 30 minutes
Your actual teaching time: _____

Time management

Procedure:

A. Listening comprehension...

➤ Ask students to read the bar. Check understanding of the term *time management.* Elicit that it means using our time effectively to get done what we need to do.

➤ Read the directions and brainstorm possible time management tips. Based on the picture story, answers may include *Ask someone to help out, write all obligations down in one place.* Tell students that in this selection they will hear some additional suggestions to help them manage time.

➤ Tell students that they should first listen for the main ideas of the lecture. Play the cassette or read the tapescript.

➤ Write on the board *perfectionism, procrastination, prioritization.* Elicit brief definitions based on the information in the selection.

➤ Understanding a lecture and taking notes are important academic skills. Tell students to take notes as they listen a second time.

Option: Using a graphic organizer can help with taking notes. Put the following outline on the board, and ask students to complete it in their notebook.

Time Management Problems

A. Causes
1.
   Explanation:
2.
   Explanation:

B. Remedy
1.
   Explanation:

B-C.

➤ Working individually, students complete the exercises. Have them refer to their notes.

➤ In pairs, students compare answers. Check exercises as a class and have volunteers read their answers to Exercise B aloud.

Option: Is your class full of perfectionists, procrastinators, or prioritizers? Have students rate their perfectionism, procrastinating, and prioritizing on a scale of 1 (least) to 5 (most). For example, someone who is content with things that are less than perfect might be rated as a 1 on perfectionism. Someone who is not happy unless everything is done absolutely perfectly might be rated as a 5. A person who never procrastinates, who always does things on time or ahead of time would get a 1 rating on procrastination. Tally the results on the board.

D. Read about...

➤ Note that this exercise continues on page 65.

➤ Ask students to quickly read Ramon Cruz's and Wendy Del Aguila's time management problems. Make sure students understand the following terms: *bit off more than she can chew, Girl Scouts, den mother, carpools.*

➤ Read the list of possible advice aloud.

➤ Put students in groups of three. Designate one member in each group as reader, one as facilitator, and another as reporter. The reader reads both time management problems to the group, the facilitator encourages everyone to contribute advice, and the reporter tells the group's ideas to the class.

➤ When the small groups are finished, elicit their advice for Ramon and for Wendy.

Tapescript

Woman: This is Business Today, a service of KKCC Radio, Kalamazoo Public Radio, being brought to you today direct from the business management school of Kalamazoo Community College. This lecture was recorded on September 12 and is replayed here for our radio audience. [pause]
   Good morning. Today's lecture is on time management. Our guest lecturer is Professor Heinz Gutentag, visiting KCC from the University of Gutenberg. Professor Gutentag, good day.

Man: Good day to you and to the listeners. Today I'd like to discuss the two most important causes of time management problems and offer a simple, effective solution.
   First: Perfectionism. Now, no human being can be perfect. In today's busy world, almost everybody has too much to do and not enough time to do it in. And somewhere in our childhood, we are given the message that we have to do everything perfectly.
   Take a moment to step back from your commitments and evaluate whether it's realistic to try to accomplish them all. You may have bitten off more than you can chew. But, if you need two jobs to make ends meet, if you want to go back to school to train for a better job, if you have children who need your care and a house that needs keeping, you may have no choice. If that's the case, then forgive yourself for your mistakes, for the work undone, for the occasional missed appointment and deadline. If you forgive yourself, then others will too.

(Tapescript is continued on page 9.)

Lesson Plan, Unit 5: Authentic practice 1 & 2 (for Student pages 62-65)–*continued*

Tapescript (continued from page 8)

The second major contributor to time management problems is procrastination. When we have too much to do, and when we are perfectionistic, we tend to procrastinate. Procrastination is putting off until tomorrow what we should do today. Sometimes we procrastinate because we're afraid that if we don't have enough time to do something, we won't do it well. But when you're on overload, you just have to roll up your sleeves, put one foot in front of the other, and forgive yourself if what you do isn't perfect. Others will forgive you too.

Now for the remedy. Since most people are perfectionistic, and most people procrastinate, the solution is to prioritize. Prioritization is deciding which of your responsibilities are essential and which are not essential. Make a list of the things you absolutely have to do. Call that list the A list.

Next, make another list of what you'd like to do if you had enough time. Call that list the B list.

Finally, make a list of things you don't really have to do or that you can get someone <u>else</u> to do. Call that the C list. Then put your day in order. Don't spend time on tasks from the B and C lists until you're sure the A list is taken care of. Another way to say this is don't procrastinate on the A list.

A final thought: Some lives are just too difficult to prioritize. Sometimes the only way to manage a busy life is to learn to say no. If someone asks you to work the booth at the school book fair and you've promised yourself you would pay all your bills on time, just say no . . . politely.

So, to review. We all have too much to do and too little time. This causes unhappiness because we cling to the idea that we must do everything perfectly, with no mistakes. We procrastinate and make the problem worse by putting things off. We can help ourselves by prioritizing our tasks. And, when all else fails, we can learn to politely say no.

Option: Draw a blank "to-do" list for the next week on the board. Ask students to complete a list for Ramon and one for Wendy. The list for Ramon might include the following items:

Ramon's "to-do" list

Monday	Tuesday	Wednesday	Thursday	Friday
Work until 5:00	3:30: Take son to soccer practice			

Note: Keep the list on the board as a reference for the *Do it yourself!* activity on this page.

E. Discussion ...

➤ In pairs or small groups, students list the week's responsibilities for Ramon and for Wendy. Next to each responsibility, they write a consequence of missing the appointment, deadline, or obligation. Ramon's list might include the following:

Responsibility	Consequence of missing it
• Return library books	• Pay a fine
• Help at voter registration	• They'll have to get someone else

➤ Have groups share the consequences of each missed deadline.

Workbook Link: Exercise 12

➤ Do it yourself!

Procedure:

A–C.

➤ Working individually, students make "to-do" lists for themselves including their obligations and responsibilities for tomorrow or for the week. Refer students to Ramon's "to-do" list that they completed in the Option for Exercise D above.

➤ To help students understand how to prioritize their lists, ask *What should you write A next to?* (the most essential things, things they have to do no matter what) Elicit examples such as go to work and take care of the children. Ask *What items are B items?* (things they might do, things they'll do if they have time) Elicit examples such as go to the library and drop clothes off at the cleaners. Finally ask *What items on your list can be classified as C?* (least essential things, things they don't have to do or that someone else can do) Elicit examples such as help with the bake sale and go to the movies with a friend.

➤ Students write A, B, or C next to each item on their list and then explain to a partner the reasons for their prioritization.

Workbook Link: Exercise 13

LESSON PLAN, UNIT 5: AUTHENTIC PRACTICE 3 (for Student pages 66-67)

Summary of Lesson Plan

▶ **PRESENTATION**
Authentic practice 3:
Reading and critical thinking (Student pages 66-67)
Suggested teaching time: 60 minutes
  includes Cultural Discussion
Your actual teaching time: _____

▶ **Authentic practice 3**
(Student pages 66-67)

Suggested teaching time: 60 minutes
Your actual teaching time: _____

The importance of time sensitivity

Procedure:

🎧 **A. Read and listen to the letters.**

➤ Before playing the cassette or reading the letters... ask *How important is being on time at work? How important is being on time for social activities?*

➤ As students listen to and read the letters, pause at the end of each paragraph and ask volunteers to retell the main information in their own words.

Option: Have students find and underline all the conditional sentences in the letters. Remind students to look for the word *if* as they scan the letters. Have students determine which sentences express real conditions and which unreal conditions.

Option: After students have read and listened to the letters, have students close their books. Write the following sentences on the board. Ask students to number the sentences from 1 to 6, according to their order in the letters. Let the students listen again so they can check their answers (4, 1, 5, 3, 2, 6).

_____ It's very hard to explain why one culture has one idea and another culture sees things differently.

_____ I think people here are very nervous about time.

_____ I'm sure you don't like to wait a long time when you have an appointment to see a doctor or a dentist.

_____ I think it's very unfriendly.

_____ Sometimes it takes a little longer to finish the book.

_____ People all over the world are basically the same: friendly, fun-loving, hard-working.

Challenge: Joan tries to respond to Deborah's argument point by point. Have pairs of students find Joan's answer to each of Deborah's concerns. They can also add their own answers.

1. I think people here are very nervous about time.
2. What would the big deal be if (something) were late?
3. I think (being crazy about schedules and time) is unfriendly.

B. Culture talk...

➤ Read the questions aloud and elicit examples from the class. Write them on the board.

➤ Remind students that generalizations and stereotypes are often unfair to individuals. Encourage students to talk about other cultures with respect.

Workbook Link: Exercises 14, 15

(continued on p. 11)

Lesson Plan, Unit 5: Authentic practice 3 (for Student pages 66-67)–*continued*

C. Collaborative activity...

▶ Put students in groups of four. Tell students that when completing a group project, it is often a good idea to divide up the tasks. To register Grace for kindergarten, the group must first understand the document. Each student should take one of the bulleted items and read the document to find information that relates to the item: *If you don't have a family doctor you can go to a clinic; Grace can get the booster at one of the clinics; she is eligible for kindergarten this year;* and *Grafton School registers students on Tuesday, May 7*. Students report their findings to their group.

▶ The groups create two lists: documents to prepare and things to do. The list of things to do should be chronological, beginning with tasks that must take place early in the process and ending with the deadline of kindergarten registration. Suggest that students work backwards from the registration date. Ask questions such as *What day will Grace register?* (Tuesday, May 7) *What immunizations does she need to have to register?* Elicit that she needs a polio booster. *How can she get the booster?* (by going to one of the Clark County Health Department clinics)

▶ Remind students to read the entire document carefully to create their lists.

▶ While groups are working on their lists, circulate and offer help as necessary.

Option: Have the groups create calendars that begin with April 1 and run through May 7. Note that the document states that May 7 is a Tuesday. Students can use that information to write in the dates. Have students decide when they will do each task and write it on the calendar. For example, students might write "Pick up registration packet at Grafton School Office" in the calendar box for Tuesday, April 9.

Challenge: Ask students to write 10 *if* statements using the information on the document about Denton Area City Schools. The statements can give the consequences of missing deadlines (*If Grace doesn't get her booster before May 7, she won't be able to register*) as well as explanations of the policies (*If a student turns five in October, he or she will have to wait until next year to enter kindergarten*).

D. Discussion...

▶ Ask representatives from each group to come to the board and write down their "to-do" list in chronological order.

▶ Have different representatives write down the list of documents.

▶ Have the class look at the lists on the board. Ask questions such as *What differences do you see? Did everyone do the same thing first? Is there anything missing from the lists?*

Workbook Link: Exercises 16, 17

▶ Do it yourself!
(A plan-ahead project) (Student page 67)

Procedure:

▶ Have students work in the four topic groups that were created at the beginning of the unit (see Lesson Plan page 1). Ask students to get out the information that they researched.

▶ Have the four topic groups compare information.

▶ Create new groups of four, consisting of one student from each of the four topic areas. Ask them to discuss the following questions: *Which process is the simplest? Which is the most complicated? Which one has the most requirements? Which one takes the longest? Which one is the most important to your family?*

LESSON PLAN, UNIT 5: REVIEW (for Student pages 68-70)

Summary of Lesson Plan

➤ **Review (Student pages 68-70)**
   Suggested teaching time: 60 minutes
   Your actual teaching time: _____

➤ **UNIT REVIEW**
   Includes expansion activities
      role play
      dialogues
      writing
      Workbook activities
      outside reading
      realia applications
      math skills applications
      civic lesson applications
      Booster Pak activities

➤ **Review (Student pages 68-70)**

Suggested teaching time: 60 minutes
Your actual teaching time: _____

Procedure:

A. Pair work or group work.

Ask and answer questions.

➤ Have students take turns asking each other questions about the picture. Model the activity with a more advanced student. Hold up the textbook and point to the woman on the phone. Ask *Who is she talking to?* (someone at the dentist's office) The student answers and then asks you a question such as *Why did the office call?* (The woman missed her appointment.) Model one more question and answer and then have students ask and answer questions with a partner.

➤ Point out the two questions asked in the directions and suggest that students ask who the different people in the picture are and what the problems are. Begin by pointing to the man reading in the background. Ask *Who do you think he is?* (the father) *What is he doing?* (reading, listening to music on his headphones) *Why isn't he helping?*

Create conversations.

➤ In pairs, students create conversations between the mother with the baby and the receptionist, and between the woman at the door and the boy doing homework.

➤ Have pairs number each person in the picture and, on a separate sheet of paper, write one line of conversation for each one.

➤ Remind students to refer to the model conversations on pages 58 and 59 for help and ideas. Circulate to offer help as necessary.

➤ Ask volunteers to role-play their conversations for the class.

Tell a story.

Option: Put yourself in another's shoes. Have students tell what they would do if they were the mother, the receptionist, the woman at the door, the boy doing homework. Give students an example such as *If I were the mother, I would ask my husband to come and get the baby. Then I would ask him to do the laundry and ...*

Option: Prioritize. Tell students to read the "to-do" list on the refrigerator. In pairs, have them prioritize the list, using A for things that must be done no matter what, B for things that the mother will do if she has enough time, and C for things someone else can do. Then imagine what advice the mother's best friend might give her.

Challenge: Tell students that sometimes stories have morals or lessons. Ask them to look at the people in the picture and imagine one lesson each might have learned from their experience. They should then express this lesson in a sentence beginning with *If*. Model the activity for students by pointing to the woman at the door and saying *If it's my turn to carpool, I'm going to call first.*

(continued on p. 13)

Book 4 Lesson Plans

Lesson Plan, Unit 5: Review (for Student pages 68–70)–*continued*

🎧 B-C.

➤ Have a volunteer read the document out loud. Ask the class to predict the topic of the listening exercise.

➤ After students listen to the conversation the first time, have students read the statements so they will know what to listen for. Allow students to listen to the conversation as many additional times as necessary to complete the exercise.

Option: Have partners rewrite the false statements in Exercise C to make them true.

D-E.

➤ Students work individually to complete the review exercises.

➤ Circulate to offer help as needed.

➤ Have students check answers with a partner. Review answers as a class.

➤ Identify any areas of difficulty that may require additional instruction and practice.

Tapescript

Male: Good morning. DMV. This is Manolo. How can I direct your call?

Female: I'd like some information about a driver's license.

Male: Is this a new license or a renewal?

Female: A new license.

Male: What's the age of the applicant?

Female: She's 15. Her birthday is June 24th.

Male: Is she planning to take driver's education in school?

Female: I'm not sure. Sometimes the classes fill up.

Male: Well, if she doesn't take driver's education, then she can't have a senior license until she's 18.

Female: That's too bad.

Male: The law is that if she wants a senior license with no restrictions before her eighteenth birthday, then she has to have completed a full three-months driver's ed course and received her certificate before she takes her driver's test.

Female: Can't she just take lessons at a driving school?

Male: No. She has to have state-certified driver's ed through a public school. I'm sorry. That's the law.

Female: OK. Well, I guess there's still time. It's only February. I'll check whether there are openings in the course.

Male: You know, if the classes are filled up at her high school, there are public adult education driver's ed courses that are given at night for adults who work during the day. You can pick that list up at the DMV or log onto our Web site for the list. That's www.dmv.st.gov.

Female: Thanks. I'll go to the Web site.

Male: OK, then. Is there anything else I can help you with?

Female: No, thanks.

Male: OK. Bye.

(continued on p. 14)

Lesson Plan, Unit 5: Review (for Student pages 68–70)–*continued*

F–G.

- Students work individually to complete the review exercises.
- Circulate to offer help as needed.
- Have students check answers with a partner. Review answers as a class.
- Identify any areas of difficulty that may require additional instruction and practice.

H. Read the overdue policy...

- Have students read the information on overdue charges from the Milwaukee Public Library.
- Make sure students understand the meaning of a *grace period* (time during which no fines are charged).
- Ask *What's the title of the overdue book?* (*Overload! It's Not the End of the World*) *When was the due date?* (March 15) *What is today's date?* (June 1) *How many days overdue is this book?* (78) Then have students figure out the amount of the fine ($5.00).

I. Composition...

- Provide students with concrete approaches to writing about the picture on page 68. Use one of the options that follow, give students a choice of options, or assign options based on students' levels of proficiency. Model what is expected of students for each option.
- Advise students to look back through the unit for help and ideas as they write.
- Circulate to offer help as needed.

Option: Have students imagine they are the woman with the baby. They should write to Joan, telling her they are on total overload, and ask for advice.

Option: Have students write a sentence beginning with *If* about each item on the "to-do" list on the refrigerator. The sentences should include a consequence of not meeting the obligation. For example, *If I don't do the laundry, the baby won't have any clean clothes.*

Option: Have students write an extended conversation for one of the pairs in the picture on page 68. Have students refer to the model conversations on pages 58 and 59 for an example of the form to use.

Challenge: Have students write a story like the group story they told on page T61. Model a beginning such as *If you miss your dental appointment, the office is going to call. If the office calls at dinner time...* Tell students to write at least six connected sentences based on the picture on page 68.

Now I can

- Read the first item in the box out loud: *Now I can understand the consequences of missing deadlines.* Elicit from the class an example such as *If I forget to return a library book, I will have to pay a fine.*
- Put students in pairs. Tell the students to take turns reading each item in the box and giving an example of what they have learned. When students can provide an example, they should check that box. If there are items students aren't able to check, have them look back through the unit for ideas.
- When students are finished reviewing with their partners, read each item out loud and elicit an example from the class.
- Refer to the piece of paper on which you wrote the students' questions about one of the objectives (from page T57). Ask what questions students answered as they worked on this unit.

Oral test (optional)

You may want to use the *Now I can* box as an informal evaluation. While students are working on the *Composition* activity, you can call them up individually and check their ability with two or three objectives.

LESSON PLAN, UNIT 6: PREVIEW/PRACTICAL CONVERSATIONS (for Student pages 71-73)

Summary of Lesson Plan

▶ **Preview and Practical conversations** (Student pages 71-73)
Suggested teaching time: 60 minutes
Your actual teaching time: _____

▶ Preview and Practical conversations (Student pages 71-73)

Suggested teaching time: 60 minutes
Your actual teaching time: _____

Warm up. What is the purpose of an estimate? Which painter would you hire? Why?

Procedure:
▶ Draw on students' prior experience by asking questions about their own home and car repairs, such as *Have you ever had your house painted? Have you ever needed car repair service? How did you decide which painter or repair person to hire? Did you get an estimate?*

▶ Point to the word *estimate* in the first illustration. Ask *What does it say next to the word "estimate"?* ($4,500, including labor and supplies) *What do you think an estimate deals with?* (the cost of something) Ask *What is an estimate?* Elicit or tell students that *an estimate* is someone's best guess about something, often referring to cost. Tell students that the word *estimate* can be either a noun or a verb. Point out the two different pronunciations (an "est<u>i</u>mit," to est<u>i</u>mate). Ask *What does the verb "estimate" mean?* (guess, approximate)

▶ To encourage critical thinking, ask *Why is an estimate important for the consumer?* (It tells the cost of a service in advance.) *Why is an estimate important for the service provider?* (It spells out exactly what the provider will do for a certain price.)

▶ Have students read the two estimates in the *Warm up* section. Check comprehension by asking questions such as *What service is the estimate for?* (painting a house) *Whose house is it?* (Mr. and Mrs. Paul Mitchell's) *Where do they live?* (45 Plainview Court, Milton, Colorado) Point out that both estimates are on company stationery, or letterhead, with the company name, address, and (for Velela Household Painting) phone number.

▶ Point to the two logos. Make sure students understand the word *logo* (a design that is a company's official sign). Ask students *What do the logos tell you about the companies?* (The paintbrush suggests painting, and the KBS logo suggests a house or building.)

▶ Put students in small groups to discuss what factors they would consider in hiring a painter. Have them list and rank these factors from 1 to 5 by importance, with 1 the least important. Write the groups' ideas on the board. The list might include these factors: *cost, time, reputation, personal knowledge of the company, friendliness, size.*

▶ Still in groups, students make a list of the differences between the two estimates. Elicit ideas and write them on the board. You may have a table like the following:

Velela	Konstantanides
• Located in Denver	• Located in Milton
• Hand-written estimate	• Typed estimate
• States the brand of paint	• No brand specified
• Includes labor and supplies	• Labor will be additional
• Cost is estimated as $4,500	• Cost is estimated as $3,600

▶ Ask students which company they would choose to paint their house. Have them explain the reasons for their choices. Ask *Which estimate do you think is most accurate?* Elicit that Velela's is more accurate because it includes the cost of labor, which is often hard for consumers to estimate. In fact, the labor cost can exceed the cost of supplies.

Unit 6 objectives

Procedure:
▶ Have students read the objectives. Ask *What do you think this unit will help you do?* (be a better consumer, know how to decide on a service provider, know about different kinds of insurance) Tell students to write down any questions they may have about the three types of insurance.

▶ Collect the questions and save them to discuss at the end of the unit.

(continued on p. 2)

Book 4 Lesson Plans

Lesson Plan, Unit 6: Preview and practical conversations (for Student pages 71-73)–continued

Model 1

Content: asking for an estimate, getting an estimate in writing, services you should get an estimate for

Procedure:

🎧 A–B.

- Have students first cover the conversation. Ask them to read the bar and then look at the photos. Ask *What do you think the people are talking about?* (an estimate) *Who do you think the customer is?* (the woman) *Who's the service provider?* (the man)

- Tell students that they are going to listen for the answers to the questions *How much?* and *How long?* With books closed or with the text still covered, students listen to the conversation.

- Then ask *How much will it cost?* ($500) *How long will it take?* (three or four days)

- Have students read the conversation silently. Check comprehension by asking questions such as *What does the caller want?* (an estimate) *Will the man write down the cost and the time it will take?* (yes) *What kind of job or service is the estimate for?* (We don't know.)

- Play the cassette or read the conversation again. Have students repeat the lines in the pauses.

🎧 Vocabulary

- Play the cassette or read the items and have students repeat.

- Read the services one at a time in random order and have students point to the pictures.

- Ask questions about the services, such as *Which services might you have done at your house or apartment?* (a paint job, construction, plumbing, electrical work) *Which ones are done at the service provider's place of business?* (an auto repair, dental work) *Which service do you think the people in the conversation were talking about? Why is it important to get an estimate for these services?* (The cost of the service varies from job to job.)

- Brainstorm other services for which consumers should get an estimate. Write the ideas on the board. Students' ideas might include *a decorating job, mowing the lawn, cutting down a tree*.

C. Pair work...

- Model the conversation with a more advanced student. Play the role of Student B, the service provider, to demonstrate how to give cost and time estimates.

- Have the students practice the conversation in pairs, switching roles to play both parts. Tell students to choose a service from the *Vocabulary* or the list on the board in order to give more realistic estimates.

Option: Write on the board *Can you give me an estimate on the _____ we talked about yesterday?* Ask a volunteer to read the line using one of the services from the *Vocabulary* or the list on the board; for example, *Can you give me the estimate on the paint job we talked about yesterday?* Note that students will have to change *a* or *an* to *the*. Students practice this modified conversation in pairs. Ask volunteers to present their conversation to the class.

Workbook Link: Exercises 1, 2, 3

(continued on p. 3)

Your notes

Lesson Plan, Unit 6: Preview and practical conversations (for Student pages 71-73)–*continued*

Model 2

Content: asking for a recommendation, benefiting from word of mouth, descriptions of good workers, service people

Procedure:

A–B.

- To set the scene for the conversation, point to the photo and ask questions such as *Who do you see in the picture?* (a man and a woman) *Where are they?* (outside, talking over a fence) *What do you think their relationship is?* (friends, neighbors) Point to the illustration and ask *What do you think they're talking about?* (a painter, a paint job)

- Have a volunteer read the bar above the conversation. Ask *What is word of mouth?* (information that one person tells another, information we get from talking about something rather than reading about it or seeing it on TV)

- After students listen to the conversation and read along silently, check comprehension by asking *What does the woman want?* (a good painter) *What is the description of the painter?* (He's reasonable and does a really good job.) *How is the neighbor going to help?* (He's going to give the woman the name of a painter.)

- Point out that *reasonable* can mean sensible or showing good judgment, but in this case it means not expensive.

- Play the cassette or read the conversation again. Have students repeat the lines in the pauses.

Vocabulary

- After students listen to and repeat the descriptions of good workers, ask questions about the items, such as *What does "reliable" mean? What is a word that means doesn't waste time?* Make sure students understand *commitments* and *delivers on promises*.

- Ask students to read the list of service providers in the box in Exercise C and think about the qualities these people should have. Brainstorm other good qualities for a service provider and write them on the board. The list might include *thorough, neat, friendly, careful,* and *responsible*.

Option: Note that using a dictionary is an important academic skill. Have students compare the definitions in the *Vocabulary* box with those in their dictionaries. Ask volunteers to read aloud the dictionary definitions.

C. Pair work...

- Model the conversation with a more advanced student. Play the role of Student A to demonstrate choosing a service provider from the box and a description from the *Vocabulary*.

- Point out that both Student A and Student B must be careful to use appropriate subject pronouns and possessive adjectives (for example, *his name, Is she reliable?*) when talking about the service provider.

Option: Have students work in pairs to match at least one desirable quality with every service person. Have them use this question as a guide: *What is the most important quality that [a painter] should have?* Students might reply *A painter should be honest and efficient*.

Option: In pairs, students decide how important each of the five descriptions of good workers is for each of the eight service people. For example, students might rank honesty as the number-one quality in a mover but reliability as the number-one quality in a dentist.

Workbook Link: Exercises 4, 5

▶ Do it yourself!

Procedure:

- On the board, write the service people from the box in Exercise C. Ask *Which service people have you used? Which one can you recommend? Did you have a problem with any of the service people? Which one?*

- Read the directions above the chart. Then point to the examples and ask questions such as *What kind of service is in the first example?* (painting) *What's the name of the company?* (Powell Company) *Was using this service provider a good experience or a bad one?* (good—Pete is reliable and does good work.) *What kind of service did Pincus Pipes provide?* (bad—The workers left a mess and were late.)

- Tell students to complete the chart with two experiences they have had with service providers.

- Have students share their experiences with a partner.

Challenge: Ask students to jot down notes about a good or bad experience they had with a service provider. Have partners take turns timing each other and trying to talk for one minute about their experience. Students can refer to their notes but should not read. Partners who are timing can also help by asking questions that will elicit more details.

LESSON PLAN, UNIT 6: PRACTICAL GRAMMAR (for Student pages 74-75)

Summary of Lesson Plan

▶ **PRESENTATION**
Practical grammar (Student pages 74-75)
Suggested teaching time: 60 minutes
Your actual teaching time: _____

▶ **Practical grammar**
(Student pages 74-75)

Suggested teaching time: 60 minutes
Your actual teaching time: _____

Note: Have students bring envelopes to class for the *Do it yourself!* activity on page 75. You will also need telephone books for this activity.

The sentence: Definition

Procedure:
▶ Ask *How can we recognize a sentence?* Discuss students' ideas. Write on the board any relevant key words that students supply, such as *verb, subject, complete thought, capital letter.*

▶ Read aloud the definition of a sentence in the box. Write the example sentence on the board and ask *What is the subject?* (The Johnsons) *What is the verb?* (know) As students answer each question, circle the subject and underline the verb.

▶ Write additional sentences on the board and have students identify the subject and verb in each one. Make sure students understand what a complete idea is. Use these sentences or write your own.
  1. I have homeowner's insurance.
  2. Paul Mitchell recommended a good painter.
  3. The plumber will give us an estimate for the job tomorrow.
  4. This estimate is too high.
  5. The painters weren't reliable.

A–B.
▶ Remind students that a sentence must have a subject and a verb. Have students circle the subjects and underline the verbs in each numbered item in Exercise A.

▶ Working individually, students put a check mark in the box next to each item that is a sentence.

▶ Read aloud the speech balloons in Exercise B. Ask *Is "Four old houses" a sentence?* (no) *Why not?* (It has no verb, It's not a complete idea.) *Is "The insurance policy is" a sentence?* (no) *Why not?* (It's not a complete idea.)

▶ Students compare answers for items 3 through 11 with a partner, explaining why each item is or is not a sentence.

Option: Discuss different kinds of verbs, including *be*, action verbs, and non-action verbs. Make sure students understand that *be* is contracted in Exercise A, items 9 and 10.

Option: Have students create complete sentences for items in Exercise A that do not express a complete idea (1, 2, 5, and 11). Give an example such as *Four old houses fell down in the storm.*

Challenge: On a separate sheet of paper, students write five items, either sentences or groups of words that do not express a complete idea. They exchange papers with a partner, and either write S next to the sentences or rewrite the groups of words to express a complete idea. Review as a class.

Workbook Link: Exercise 6

The sentence: Punctuation and capitalization

Procedure:
▶ On the board, write sentences from Exercise A (items 3, 4, 6, 7, 8, 9, 10), or ask volunteers to write sentences from the Challenge activity above. Review the key words students supplied in the earlier discussion of how to recognize a sentence. Elicit or point out that a sentence begins with a capital letter and ends with a period or a question mark. Read aloud the sentences on the board and circle the initial capital letters and end punctuation.

▶ Ask *How can we recognize a question?* Elicit the response that a question may begin with a question word such as *who* or *why*. A question may also have a verb before the subject, as in *Did she find a reliable painter? Is he also efficient?*

(continued on p. 5)

Lesson Plan, Unit 6: Practical grammar (for Student pages 74-75)–*continued*

➤ Summarize by reading aloud the rules in the box. Have volunteers read the two examples. Point out that the capital letters and end punctuation marks have been written in red for emphasis.

Option: Note that some sentences end in another type of punctuation—the exclamation point. The exclamation mark is used to express strong emotion. Write on the board item 10 from Exercise A: *She's great.* Write it a second time with an exclamation mark: *She's great!* Elicit or point out that the second sentence is stronger and more emphatic.

C. Rewrite the sentences...

➤ Working individually, students rewrite the sentences. After you review the sentences as a class, have volunteers write them correctly on the board.

Option: Write items 4 and 5 on the board using an exclamation mark as the final punctuation. Ask students what difference the exclamation mark makes (the sentences are more emphatic and stronger).

Workbook Link: Exercise 7

D. Pair work...

➤ Have pairs of students review the decisions they made in capitalizing and punctuating the items in Exercise C.

Other capitalization rules

Procedure:

➤ Tell students your full name and then spell it aloud. Begin with the word *capital* before the first letter of your first and last name; for example, *capital K-A-T-E capital M-U-R-P-H-Y*. As you spell your full name, write it on the board using a capital for the first letter in each name. Circle the capitals.

➤ Ask students why you began your first and last name with a capital letter. Elicit the response that we capitalize the first letter of a person's names.

➤ Have students work in pairs to practice asking each other's names and how to spell them.

➤ Write on the board and tell students your title together with your last name; for example, *capital M-S period capital M-U-R-P-H-Y*. Ask students why you began the title *Ms.* with a capital letter. (We capitalize the first letter of titles.)

➤ Brainstorm other titles, including *Dr., Mr.,* and *Mrs.* and write them on the board. Point out that these titles are abbreviations and therefore end with a period. Write the title *Miss* and elicit from students that it has no period because it is not an abbreviation. Point out that we do not use titles with first names; for example, we say *Dr. Svesko* or *Dr. Caroline Svesko* but not *Dr. Caroline*.

➤ Summarize the discussion of capitalization rules by having volunteers read aloud the rules and examples in the box.

➤ Point to the envelope and ask questions such as *Who is this envelope addressed to?* (Dr. Caroline Svesko) *What information goes on the line under the name?* (the street number and street name) Introduce the term *return address*. Make sure students understand that the return address is the name and address of the sender. Ask *Who is the sender?* (Solange Phillips) *What is Ms. Phillips's zip code?* (10514)

➤ Still pointing to the envelope, ask questions about capitalization and punctuation, such as *Why is the D capitalized?* (It's the first letter of the title *Dr.*) *Why is there a period after Dr.?* (It's an abbreviation.) Tell students that *NY* is a U.S. postal abbreviation and is written without periods. Elicit and write on the board other state postal abbreviations.

Option: Tell students that other common abbreviations are found in street addresses; for example, *St., Ave., Rd.* Point out the abbreviation *Pl.* in the return address on the envelope.

E. Write your name and address...

➤ Have volunteers come to the board and write their names and addresses, including street number and name, city, state, and zip code. If necessary, help students with the abbreviation for *apartment* (Apt.) and *floor* (Fl.). Review with the class, asking questions such as *What is capitalized in the name? What is capitalized in the address? Why?*

➤ Have students complete the exercise individually and then work in pairs to ask and answer questions such as *What is your address? What is your zip code? Do you have an apartment number?*

F. Rewrite the sentences...

➤ While students are working individually to rewrite the sentences and questions, have five volunteers rewrite the items on the board.

➤ Review as a class, referring to the sentences and questions on the board and correcting them as necessary.

Workbook Link: Exercises 8, 9

(continued on p. 6)

Lesson Plan, Unit 6: Practical grammar (for Student pages 74-75)–*continued*

➤ Do it yourself!
(A do-ahead project) (Student page 75)

Procedure:
- ➤ Have students get out their envelopes, or distribute those you brought in.
- ➤ Students write their return address in the upper left-hand corner on the front of the envelope, as shown on page 75. Point out that the return address can also be written on the back flap.
- ➤ Have students look up the name of a service provider in the telephone book and address the envelope to that person. If students have their own service provider, they can use that person's name and address.
- ➤ If necessary, remind students of the format for addressing an envelope. Review rules for capitalization and punctuation of names and addresses as well.
- ➤ In small groups, have students read aloud the service provider's name and address and their own return addresses. Have students exchange envelopes for correcting.

Your notes

LESSON PLAN, UNIT 6: AUTHENTIC PRACTICE 1 & 2 (for Student pages 76-79)

Summary of Lesson Plan

▶ **PRESENTATION**
Authentic practice 1 & 2:
Listening (Student pages 76-79)
Suggested teaching time: 60 minutes
  includes Cultural Discussion
Your actual teaching time: _____

Authentic practice 1
(Student pages 76-77)

Suggested teaching time: 30 minutes
Your actual teaching time: _____

Make an insurance claim

Procedure:

🎧
▶ To prepare students for the picture story, have them look at the different scenes. Ask questions such as *What is the woman holding?* (a homeowner's insurance policy) *Who do you think she is?* (She could be the homeowner or the insurance agent.) Note the man's gesture in the first scene. Ask *What do you think the people are talking about?* (the fallen tree, the damaged roof)

▶ Ask a volunteer to read aloud the bar above the picture story. Ask *What is an insurance claim?* Elicit that it is a request from the person who has the insurance policy to get money to pay for an expense covered by the policy.

▶ Play the cassette or read the text and have students read along silently.

▶ Ask students to identify the idioms used in the picture story. Write them on the board: *thank your lucky stars, you can say that again, run into a lot of money, word of mouth*.

▶ In pairs or small groups, students discuss what they think these expressions mean. Remind students that they saw the phrase *word of mouth* in Model 2 on page 73.

▶ Lead a class discussion about the meaning of the idioms using students' ideas as a springboard.

▶ Point out that *some* in *some tree* and *some storm* does not refer to an unknown amount as in *I need some milk*. Instead, it is used to emphasize the amount of damage caused by the falling tree and to express the severity of the storm. Have students express *some tree* and *some storm* in their own words. Elicit

or suggest such phrases as *What a big tree! That tree certainly did a lot of damage! That was quite a storm! That was a really serious storm.*

A. Discussion...
▶ Working individually, students answer the questions. They can compare answers with a partner or in a small group.

▶ Let students read or listen to the story again if necessary.

Option: Ask comprehension questions such as *What is the problem?* (A big storm caused a tree to fall on the roof of the house and damage it.) *Who is the man?* (the homeowner) *What does he want to know?* (if the insurance policy covers damage to the house and tree removal) Have students create additional questions about the story to ask their partners.

Challenge: Making inferences is an important academic skill. Have students give examples of information that was stated in the story and examples of information that can be inferred. Students should include the statement from the story that supports each inference. See the example:

Information that was stated	Information that can be inferred
No one was killed.	Many homes were damaged. ("I've had dozens of claims already.")

🎧 B. Check the subjects...
▶ Working individually, students check the topics discussed. Play the cassette or read the story again if necessary. Make sure students know what an *insurance adjuster* is (an agent from an insurance company who investigates claims and decides how much the company will pay).

▶ Have students underline the subjects in the picture story. Point out that being able to cite sources is an important academic skill.

▶ Review students' answers with questions such as *Do they discuss painting?* (no) *Do they discuss tree removal?* (yes) *Where can you find evidence in the story?* (In picture 2, the insurance adjuster says, "I have to check the terms of your policy about the tree removal.")

Option: Have students read the story out loud in pairs. Student A reads the role of the insurance adjuster and Student B reads the role of the homeowner. Have students switch roles for more practice.

Workbook Link: Exercises 10, 11

(continued on p. 8)

Book 4 Lesson Plans

Lesson Plan, Unit 6: Authentic practice 1 & 2 (for Student pages 76-79)–*continued*

C–D.
- Working individually, students complete the exercises.
- In Exercise D, make sure students understand the terms in item 2. Have student define *run out of money* (spend all your money so you don't have any left) and *run into a lot of money* (cost or add up to a great deal of money).
- Review the exercises as a class.

Option: Have students write sentences using the words in Exercise C that were not chosen. For Exercise D, have pairs of students create a statement or question that would elicit the response that was not underlined.

Option: Ask pairs to create an extended conversation that includes each item and response in Exercise D. Have volunteers read their conversations aloud.

E. Pair work...
- In pairs, students practice reading the items and responses in Exercise D aloud.

Option: Student B closes the book. Student A reads each item and Student B responds appropriately. Then partners switch roles.

➤ Do it yourself!

Procedure:

A. Write your own response...
- Point to the first photo. Ask a volunteer to read the speech balloon out loud. Ask *What do you think she is talking about?* Point to the other photos, have volunteers read the speech balloons, and ask questions such as *Who do you think this person is talking to? Who do you think this person is?*
- Working individually, students complete the activity. Circulate to offer help as needed.
- Students read their conversations out loud with a partner and then change roles to practice both parts.

B. Culture talk...
- Put students in small groups. Try to include students from different countries or cultures in each group.
- Using the questions as prompts, students complete a table like the one following. Write this model on the board and explain any unfamiliar kinds of insurance.

Country	Types of insurance individuals carry
United States	car, homeowner's, life, health, malpractice

(continued on p.9)

Your notes

Book 4 Lesson Plans

Lesson Plan, Unit 6: Authentic practice 1 & 2 (for Student pages 76-79)–*continued*

Authentic practice 2
(Student pages 78-79)

Suggested teaching time: 30 minutes
Your actual teaching time: _____

Note: For an activity on page 79, ask students to bring in newspaper or magazine articles that discuss damage to homes, especially damage caused by bad weather such as tornados, hurricanes, and ice storms.

Competitive bids for service

Procedure:

A–C.

➤ To set the scene for the listening activity, point to the picture and ask *What happened?* (A tree fell on the house.) Then point to the business cards and ask *What kind of service do these companies provide?* (tree removal, tree service) *What are the names of the companies?* (Speedy Tree Removal, The Chapman Chipmunk) Have students look at the logo on The Chapman Chipmunk card. Make sure students understand what a chipmunk is (a small, striped ground squirrel).

➤ Have students read the bar. Ask *What do you think the conversations will be about?* (The companies will talk about their services and prices.) Play the cassette or read the tapescript.

➤ Have students look at the chart. Ask *What three pieces of information do you need to listen for?* (when each company can start, the price, when the company will finish)

➤ Have students listen again and complete the chart individually. In pairs, students answer the discussion questions.

➤ If students have difficulty, let them listen again.

➤ Review the information on students' charts and go over the questions as a class.

Challenge: In pairs or small groups, have students discuss the advantages and disadvantages of a one-person company such as The Chapman Chipmunk vs. a larger company such as Speedy Tree Removal. Put the following chart on the board and ask students to complete it with their ideas. Compare advantages and disadvantages as a class.

How many employees?	Advantages	Disadvantages
One	Lower overhead	The jobs take longer.
Several	They may finish jobs faster.	Higher overhead

D. Role play...

➤ Read the directions for Exercise D.

➤ Have volunteers read the questions in the speech balloons on the bottom of page 78. Brainstorm other questions a homeowner might want to ask the contractors and write them on the board.

Challenge: Have students work in pairs to write a description of the damage to the house. Tell students to look at the picture at the bottom of page 78.

Tapescript

Conversation 1

A: You Mr. Adams?

B: Yes. Are you Hernan?

A: Yes, sir. From Speedy Tree. Here's my card. That's some tree fell on you. Anyone hurt?

B: Luckily, no.

A: Thank goodness.

B: You can say that again! Let's go take a closer look. [pause] Well, what do you think?

A: Whew! This job's going to take three guys a day and a half. The truck's over on the north side right now. We can start first thing tomorrow morning. It'll run you $950, plus tips for the guys, about ten bucks each.

B: So you say $950, plus $30 for tips? So that makes $980. Day and a half?

A: Give or take a few hours. We're never absolutely sure something won't go wrong.

B: And you can start tomorrow?

A: That's right. First thing.

B: And you'll finish by Wednesday, right?

A: Yes. That's right.

B: I'm going to need a written estimate for the insurance. Could you put that and your completion date in writing, on your letterhead?

A: Sure. [pause] Is this OK?

B: Yes, thanks. That's fine. I'll let you know before noon. Is that OK?

A: Sure. Just call the number on this sheet.

(Tapescript is continued on page 10.)

Lesson Plan, Unit 6: Authentic practice 1 & 2 (for Student pages 76-79)–*continued*

Tapescript *(continued from page 9)*

Conversation 2

B: Oh, hi. Are you the Chapman Chipmunk?

C: Yes, sir. Here's my card.

B: My brother Terry recommended you. Have you had a chance to see the damage?

C: Yes. You can't miss it! Everyone OK?

B: Yes, thankfully.

C: This is a big job. I work alone. It'll take me two or three days, depending. I'll charge you $700.

B: When could you start?

C: Now. My equipment's right outside.

B: And you say it'll take you two or three days?

C: Yes. Give or take.

B: So, you think you'll be finished by Thursday?

C: Yes. Thursday at the latest.

B: Can you put that all in writing? I need it for the insurance—the cost, start time, estimated completion time, number of workers. You know.

C: Sure. No problem. I have my invoices out in the truck. I'll be back in a minute.

Conversation 3

A: Hello. Speedy Tree. Hernan speaking.

B: Hernan? Mr. Adams. I'm sorry, but I've decided to go with someone else for the tree job... But thanks so much for coming out so fast.

A: No problem, Mr. Adams. Good luck with the tree.

B: Thanks. Bye.

▶ Divide the class into groups of four students each. Let students decide who will play each role: Mr. Adams, a contractor at Tip Top Roofing, a contractor at Odessa Painting, and a contractor at Universal Fencing. "Mr. Adams" should talk to each contractor in turn, asking questions such as those in the speech balloons on page 78 and others that the class brainstormed.

▶ After students have completed their role-plays, have all students fill out the contractors' estimates on page 79.

Option: To provide more practice, have the groups change parts so that each student has a chance to play all four roles.

Workbook Link: Exercise 12

▶ Do it yourself!

Procedure:

A–B.

▶ On the board, draw a chart like the one on page 79. Ask *Did you ever have damage to your home? What was the damage? When did it happen? What was the cause?* Fill in the first line of the chart with an example from the class.

▶ Have students open their books and read the questions. Point to the chart and ask *What happened?* (broken windows) *When did it happen?* (May 19, 2001) *What caused the damage?* (an earthquake)

▶ Working individually, students complete the chart according to their own experiences.

▶ In pairs or small groups, students share their stories.

Option: Collect magazine or newspaper articles that students have brought in and distribute them. After reading the accounts of natural disasters such as floods, tornadoes, or hurricanes, pairs of students take turns asking questions about the stories, such as *What kind of damage was there? When did it happen? What caused the damage?*

LESSON PLAN, UNIT : AUTHENTIC PRACTICE 3 (for Student pages 80-81)

Summary of Lesson Plan

► **PRESENTATION**
Authentic practice 3:
Reading and critical thinking (Student pages 80-81)
Suggested teaching time: 60 minutes
Your actual teaching time: _____

► Authentic practice 3
(Student pages 80-81)

Suggested teaching time: 60 minutes
Your actual teaching time: _____

Insurance basics

Procedure:

A. Read about insurance...

► Review how to scan a reading. Ask *What features should you look at before you begin to read?* Elicit or remind students of headings, subheads, boldface words, bulleted items, items in the margin.

► Check comprehension of these features by asking *What kinds of insurance are discussed in this article?* (homeowner's, auto, life, health) *What are some key terms?* (insurance, premium, liability, beneficiary, claim)

► After students have read the article, ask comprehension questions such as *What does homeowner's insurance provide? Who needs it? What does auto insurance usually cover? Who needs life insurance?*

► Have students complete the insurance self-test.

► Point out that householder's insurance covers the contents of a renter's house or apartment.

Challenge: Team questions. Divide the class into two teams. Each team creates questions on the article to pose to the other team. Each correct answer earns a point.

Challenge: Game. Divide the class into two or more teams to play this game. Write the names of the types of insurance on the board for reference. Your chart will look something like the one below. Teams take turns choosing a category and point value. Read the questions and give the teams a point for each correct answer. The team with the highest score wins.

B. Pair work...

► Have students discuss their choices on the insurance self-test with a partner. Model the activity by giving a reason of your own, such as *I need auto insurance because it is a law in this state.*

FYI...

► Remind students that *log on* means to type in a Web site address and visit that Web site on the Internet.

Option: If your students don't have access to computers, print out some of the information available at these sites.

Workbook Link: Exercises 13, 14, 5, 16

(continued on p.12)

Value	Homeowner's	Auto	Life	Health	Key terms
100	When do you need this insurance?	What requirement do most states have about auto insurance?	When does this insurance get paid?	What is one form of health insurance?	Define *insurance*.
200	What does it protect against?	What does it protect against?	Who benefits?	What does HMO stand for?	Define *premium*.
300	What is covered by this insurance?	What is covered by this insurance?	What are three short-term expenses covered?	What are three things often covered by health insurance?	Define *liability*.
400	In what three ways is your home defined?	Define *claim*.	What are two long-term expenses covered?	Who needs health insurance?	Define *beneficiary*.

Book 4 Lesson Plans

Lesson Plan, Unit 6: Authentic practice 3 (for Student pages 80-81)–*continued*

C. Read how to prepare...

- Have students read what it is necessary to include in an insurance claim. Ask for clarification of each bulleted item, such as *What is an example of road conditions?*

- Note that the past continuous is used in items (*you and the other driver were going*). Remind students that we often use the past continuous to talk about what actions we were engaged in when something else—such as an accident—happened.

Option: A group story. Begin a story about a car accident with one line such as *I had a terrible accident last night*. Each student adds to the story with a line that includes a piece of information required on an insurance claim. For example, the next line might be *It was around 8 p.m.* All students take notes on the "monitor screen" as the story unfolds.

Challenge: Put students in pairs. Student A is an insurance adjuster who asks questions based on the bulleted items; for example, *What time was it?* Student B is the driver who had the accident recounted in the group story above. Student B answers the questions using the information in the group story.

D. Betsy Harris had an accident...

- Have students cover the notes on the right side of the page. Ask questions about the picture, such as *What were the weather conditions?* (It was raining hard.) *Where was the accident?* (at the corner of Stanley Road and South Orange Avenue) *What are the people doing?* (exchanging license plate numbers and insurance information)

- Have students read the notes. Check comprehension by asking questions about new information, such as *How was the visibility?* (poor) *What time was the accident?* (7:30 p.m.) *What state was the accident in?* (New Jersey)

➤ Do it yourself!

Procedure:

- Tell students that they are going to write a description of Betsy Harris's accident for her insurance claim. As they write, they should imagine that they are Betsy Harris. They will use her notes in Exercise D as a basis for the description, but they will have to expand the notes into a narrative using complete sentences.

- Ask the class how to start the description. Refer students to the first bulleted item in Exercise C: time and date of the accident. Write on the board *I had an accident on November 27 at 7:30 p.m.* Point out that students will use *I* in their descriptions since they are writing as Betsy Harris. Remind them to use complete sentences and correct capitalization and punctuation in their description.

- Have students complete the activity individually. Review as a class.

Challenge: Telephone. In this variation on the telephone game, send several students out of the room. Have two or more volunteers come to the front of the room. Tell a story about an auto accident that you had (real or imagined). Include the date, time, location, weather and road conditions, and a brief description of what happened. During your story, students seated at their desks should take notes, but the volunteers at the front of the room should only listen. Call in one of the students who is waiting outside the class. One volunteer listener retells the story of the accident. The rest of the class adds any missing details. Repeat this process with each remaining student outside the class.

Your notes

LESSON PLAN, UNIT 6: REVIEW (for Student pages 82-84)

Summary of Lesson Plan

➤ **Review (Student pages 82-84)**
Suggested teaching time: 60 minutes
Your actual teaching time: _____

➤ **UNIT REVIEW**
Includes expansion activities
role play
dialogues
writing
Workbook activities
outside reading
realia applications
math skills applications
civic lesson applications
Booster Pak activities

➤ **Review (Student pages 82-84)**

Suggested teaching time: 60 minutes
Your actual teaching time: _____

Procedure:

A. Pair work or group work.

Ask and answer questions.

➤ Ask the class general questions about the pictures, such as *What happened on June 12?* (A tornado caused some damage.) *What happened to the house?* (The roof was torn off.) Ask at least one question about each day. Include questions about who the people are and what they're doing.

➤ In pairs, students take turns asking their partners about what happened on each day.

➤ Make sure students understand what a tornado is and what kinds of problems it can cause.

Challenge: Working individually, students list all the services the homeowner will need to take care of the problems caused by the tornado. Then have students compare lists by asking questions such as *Who does the homeowner need to talk to first? What kinds of repairs are needed? Who did she call?*

Create conversations.

➤ In pairs, students create a conversation for either the homeowner and the neighbor (June 13), the homeowner and a contractor (June 14), or the homeowner and the insurance adjuster (June 16). Have the students label the pair they chose *A* and *B*. Students write their conversations in the same format as the model conversations.

➤ Pairs copy each line of their conversations onto a slip of paper, mix up the order of the slips, and give them to another pair. The other pair must then put the conversation back in the correct order.

➤ Each pair reads the conversation they put in order to the pair who wrote the conversation. Together, the pairs add additional lines of dialogue.

Tell a story.

Option: Play a part. Have students play the role of one of the characters in the picture who is narrating the events in chronological order. Students can portray the insurance adjuster who must explain the claim to a supervisor, the homeowner talking to a friend in another town, the neighbor talking to a co-worker, or a contractor reporting to a supervisor. Encourage students to say as much as they can.

Option: One-minute stories. Have a student time you while you talk about the picture for one minute. Then, in pairs or small groups, each student talks about the picture for one minute. Encourage students to describe each of the four scenes and to say as much as they can. Tell students to continue talking until you say *Stop*, indicating that the minute is up.

Option: Insurance claim. Have students tell the story of the tornado damage from the point of view of the homeowner. Students will need to include the time and date of the accident, the location (street, city, and state), the weather conditions, and a brief description of the damages.

(continued on p.14)

Lesson Plan, Unit 6: Review (for Student pages 82-84)–*continued*

🎧 B–C.

- Tell students they are going to listen to three telephone conversations about some damage to a home.

- After students listen the first time, have them answer the questions in Exercise B.

- Have students read the statements in Exercise C before they listen again so that they will know what to listen for.

- Make sure students know that ? means that the information was not included in the conversations.

- Allow students to listen to the conversations as many times as necessary to complete the exercise. Review the answers as a class.

Option: In pairs, students rewrite the false statements to make them true.

D–E.

- Students work individually to complete the review exercises.

- Circulate to offer help as needed.

- Have students check answers with a partner. Review answers as a class.

- Identify any areas of difficulty that may require additional instruction and practice.

Tapescript

Conversation 1

Ralph: Hello. Rubin Roofing. No job too big. No job too small. This is Ralph. How can I help you today?

Woman 1: I need to discuss an emergency roof repair. My roof flew off in the storm last night.

Ralph: That was some humdinger, wasn't it?

Woman 1: Well, yes. This is kind of an emergency. Can you come out and have a look and give me an estimate today?

Ralph: Not before about three, three-thirty.

Woman 1: That'll be fine. I'm at 78 Hunter Street, on the south side of town.

Ralph: 78 Hunter Street. Let's say 4 o'clock.

Conversation 2

Woman 2: Hello. Arbor City Roof.

Woman 1: Hello. My roof got blown off in the storm last night.

Woman 2: Oh, my goodness. Was anyone hurt?

Woman 1: Luckily, no. Thanks for asking. Can you come by and give me a price quote on replacement?

Woman 2: Certainly. Where are you?

Woman 1: Hunter Street. South side. Number 78.

Woman 2: I can have someone there right away, about 20 minutes. He'll give you an estimate this morning.

Woman 1: Thanks. I'll be waiting outside. You can't miss it!

Conversation 3

Todd: Hello?

Woman 1: Todd? I'm sorry to call so early. But this is kind of an emergency.

Todd: Sure. What's up?

Woman 1: My roof. It blew off in the storm.

Todd: Oh, no. Are you OK?

Woman 1: Yes. We're all fine. But I need a good roofer in a hurry. You just had your roof repaired. Can you recommend the roofer?

Todd: Actually, yes, I can. I used Arbor City Roof. They're great. Fair, reasonable, efficient.

Woman 1: Thanks. As a matter of fact, they're on their way over to give me an estimate.

Todd: Tell them I recommended them. That way, you'll get a good deal.

(continued on p.15)

Lesson Plan, Unit 6: Review (for Student pages 82-84)–*continued*

F–G.

- Students work individually to complete the review exercises.
- Circulate to offer help as needed.
- Have students check answers with a partner. Review answers as a class.
- Identify any areas of difficulty that may require additional instruction and practice.

Option: In Exercise F, have students create original sentences using the words that were not selected.

H. Guided composition...

- Have students write a summary of the picture on page 82. Remind them to check capitalization and punctuation.
- Allow students to continue their story on a separate sheet of paper, if necessary.

Now I can

- Read the first item in the box out loud: *Now I can ask for a recommendation of a person who provides a service.* Elicit from the class an example of how to do this, such as *Do you know a good babysitter?*

- Put students in pairs, tell the students to take turns reading each item in the box and giving an example of what they have learned. When students can provide an example, they should check that objective. If there are items students aren't able to check, have them look back through the unit for ideas.

- When students are finished reviewing with their partners, read each item out loud and elicit an example from the class.

- Have students refer to the questions about insurance they had at the beginning of the unit. Ask them what answers they learned during their work on the unit.

Oral test (optional)

You may want to use the *Now I can* box as an informal evaluation. While students are working on the *Guided composition* activity, you can call them up individually and check their ability with two or three objectives.

Your notes

# LESSON PLAN∙UNIT 7: PREVIEW/PRACTICAL CONVERSATIONS (for Student pages 85-87)

Summary of Lesson Plan

➤ **Preview and Practical conversations** (Student pages 85-87)
Suggested teaching time: 60 minutes
Your actual teaching time: _____

➤ **Preview and Practical conversations** (Student pages 85-87)

Suggested teaching time: 60 minutes
Your actual teaching time: _____

Warm up. What do you know about the Constitution of the United States?

Procedure:

➤ Activate prior knowledge by asking *What do you know about the beginnings of the United States?* Write students' ideas on the board. If necessary, prompt with questions such as *Who originally lived in the area now called the United States?* (Native Americans) *When did Europeans first start settling in the United States?* (16th century) *What country did the settlers of the thirteen colonies come from?* (England) *When did the United States become independent?* (1776, late 18th century) *What document established the government of the new United States?* (the Constitution)

➤ Read the *Warm up* question. Brainstorm ideas the class has about the Constitution.

➤ Tell students that they are going to read three excerpts from the Constitution. Note that they will find some of the language old fashioned and perhaps difficult to understand. Reassure students that they do not have to understand every word of the document at this time.

➤ Point out the use of *shall* in the article and amendments. *Shall* is still commonly used in British English but rarely in American English. In this case, *shall* is a stronger form of *will*.

➤ Check comprehension with questions such as *According to Article I, what are the two parts of the Congress?* (the Senate and the House of Representatives) *What freedoms or rights are mentioned in Amendment I?* (religion, speech, press; the right to assemble peaceably) *What right does the accused have under Amendment VI?* (a speedy and public trial by an impartial jury)

Unit 7 objectives

Procedure:

➤ Read the objectives and discuss the meaning of any unfamiliar words. Elicit examples from students. For example, for *Agree and disagree respectfully*, students might say *I don't agree* or *Absolutely*. When the class can't think of an example, provide one; for example, for pros and cons of controversial issues, say *Capital punishment is a controversial issue. What are some reasons to support it? What are some reasons to be against it?*

➤ Have students underline the two objectives that are the most useful or interesting to them. Have students tell a partner why they chose those two objectives.

Challenge: Put students in small groups to brainstorm everything they already know about the Constitution, the Bill of Rights, and the U.S. justice system. Have students organize their thoughts in a K-W-L chart like the one following. Have students write their ideas in the K (what I <u>k</u>now) column and their questions in the W (what I <u>w</u>ant to know) column. Save the chart until the end of the unit so students can complete the L (what I <u>l</u>earned) column.

K What I know	W What I want to know	L What I learned
The first amendment gives me freedom of speech.	What rights do I have if I am accused of a crime?	

(continued on p. 2)

Book 4 Lesson Plans

Lesson Plan, Unit 7: Preview and practical conversations (for Student pages 85-87)–*continued*

Model 1

Content: discussing pros and cons of controversial issues; expressing opinions; arguing for and against capital punishment, government censorship of books and movies, and organized prayer in public schools

Procedure:

🎧 A–B.

▶ To set the scene for the conversation, ask questions about the photo such as *Where are the women?* (sitting on a bench in or near a playground) *Is this a formal or informal setting?* (informal) *What does the women's body language tell you?* (They are facing each other, talking, receptive, engaged.)

▶ After students listen to the conversation, check comprehension by asking questions such as *What is the topic of the conversation?* (capital punishment) *Are the two speakers in agreement?* (no)

▶ Ask students what they think "an eye for an eye" means. Elicit or explain that it means people should receive a punishment that is like the wrong they committed. This means that the punishment for killing is being killed or that the punishment for theft is taking the same things from the thief.

▶ Make sure students know that the expression "agree to disagree" is a polite way to acknowledge a difference of opinion that probably cannot be resolved.

▶ Students read and listen and then repeat after each line of the conversation.

Option: Have students listen with books closed. Read each line at a native rate of speed. Encourage students to imitate the rhythm, stress, and intonation of the conversation as closely as possible.

🎧 Opinions

▶ Play the cassette or read the opinions. Have students repeat.

▶ Ask individual students what they think about different issues such as public transportation, discrimination, or bilingual education. Tell other students to respond with an opinion.

🎧 Vocabulary

▶ Have students read the text silently before you play the cassette or read the sample pros and cons.

▶ If necessary, explain the concepts of capital punishment, government censorship, and organized prayer in public schools. Make sure that students understand prayer is allowed; the issue is whether it can be an organized student activity.

▶ After students listen, check comprehension by asking questions such as *What is one argument people might make against capital punishment?* (The punishment is as bad as what the criminal did.) *What is one argument in favor of government censorship?* (Some books and movies are too violent for people to read or see.)

▶ Brainstorm other controversial issues and write them on the board. Elicit arguments for and against each idea and write them down.

Option: Note that many of the arguments are phrased as conditional sentences. Have students underline each conditional sentence and then say which are real conditions (*If you kill someone . . . , If we execute criminals . . . , Some children are uncomfortable . . .*) and which are unreal conditions (*I think students would behave better . . .*).

Challenge: Put students in pairs. Give each pair an issue and a stance to prepare; for example, for capital punishment, against organized prayer in public schools. Make sure that each side of each controversial idea in the *Vocabulary* box is covered by at least one pair of students. Have students prepare additional arguments in support of their position. Students can also use the list of issues and arguments on the board. When students have prepared their arguments, ask students from both sides of an issue to present their arguments to the class.

C. Pair work...

▶ Model the conversation with a more advanced student. First play the role of Student A to demonstrate choosing a controversial issue. Then switch roles and play Student B.

▶ Note that in the second line, Student B must first give a positive or negative response and then give an argument to support that position. Student A's responding argument depends on whether Student B chooses a position for or against the issue. Remind students that they can begin arguments with *I believe, I think,* or *I feel*.

Workbook Link: Exercises 1, 2

(continued on p. 3)

Lesson Plan, Unit 7: Preview and practical conversations (for Student pages 85-87)–continued

Model 2

Content: agreeing and disagreeing respectfully, rules, discussing a rule you don't like

Procedure:

🎧 A–B.

- To set the scene for the conversation, point to the photo and ask questions such as *Where are the people?* (in the back of a car) *How do you think the woman on the left feels?* (upset, mad) *What is she doing?* (putting on a seat belt)

- After students listen to the conversation, check comprehension by asking *What is the woman upset about?* (wearing a seat belt) *Does the man think that wearing a seat belt is ridiculous?* (No, he says it saves lives.) *What do they agree about?* (There are too many rules.)

- Before students repeat, note that the first line is a question although it is written in statement form. The question is conveyed by the use of a question mark and a rising intonation at the end of the line. The complete form of the reduced question is *Do you want to know what I think?*

- Also point out that the phrase *You want to know* is almost always reduced in native speech to *You wanna know.*

- Listen again to the conversation and have students repeat during the pauses. Then have them practice the conversation in pairs.

🎧 Vocabulary

- After reading and listening, students repeat the rules.

- Tell students that a rule can be a law, or it can be a regulation in a school or workplace. For example, a school might have a rule that no one is allowed in a classroom until 15 minutes before the class is scheduled to begin.

- Point out that some of these rules apply to everyone in the United States (license requirements for gun ownership, voting age) and some vary according to state law (legal drinking age, seat belt and helmet requirements). Restrictions on smoking depend on local laws.

- Brainstorm other rules that people in your city must follow. Write students' ideas on the board. Ideas may include parking restrictions, pet cleanup rulings, and home window-guard restrictions.

- Have students fill in their own rule in the *Vocabulary* box.

Challenge: Have pairs of students work together to research local rules on smoking indoors in public places. Have them also find out your state's legal drinking age and whether seat belts and helmets are required. With the class, brainstorm how to find this information. Elicit or suggest the public library, a search engine on the Internet, the local newspaper.

C. Pair work...

- Write *Pro* and *Con* on the board. For each rule in the *Vocabulary*, brainstorm reasons in favor of the rule and reasons against it. Write the reasons on the board under the appropriate heading.

- Model with a more advanced student. Play the role of Student B. If necessary, prompt Student A to choose a rule from the *Vocabulary*. In response to the rule that Student A doesn't like, state one of the reasons listed on the board under *Pro*. Student A's rejoinder should be one of the reasons listed under *Con*.

- Have students choose a rule that they don't like, and practice the conversation in pairs.

Workbook Link: Exercises 3, 4

▶ Do it yourself!

Procedure:

A–B.

- Read aloud the directions for Exercise A. Tell students they can choose a rule from the *Vocabulary* box, including their own rule, or one on the board. Have students reread the controversial issues in the *Vocabulary* box on page 86.

- Tell the students to write the rule or the issue they have chosen. They should then write an argument supporting that rule or issue and an argument against it.

- On a separate sheet of paper, students write their opinions about the rule or issue, beginning with *I think, I believe,* or *I feel.* If necessary, have students review the yellow note on page 86 on how to express opinions.

- Have students share their opinions with a partner or a group.

- Students may not feel comfortable discussing what they have written about a controversial topic or one they feel is too sensitive. If they are uncomfortable sharing, invite them to choose another topic to discuss.

Copyright © 2004 by Pearson Education, Inc.
All rights reserved.

LESSON PLAN, UNIT 7: PRACTICAL GRAMMAR *(for Student pages 88-89)*

Summary of Lesson Plan

▶ **PRESENTATION**
Practical grammar (Student pages 88-89)
Suggested teaching time: 60 minutes
Your actual teaching time: _____

▶ **Practical grammar**
(Student pages 88-89)

Suggested teaching time: 60 minutes
Your actual teaching time: _____

Reporting a person's words: Direct speech

Content: quotation marks and end punctuation in quoted speech

Procedure:
- Ask students to repeat an opinion about a rule or an issue that the class has already discussed. You may choose to begin with a statement such as *I think it's a good idea for a cyclist to wear a helmet.*
- Write students' ideas on the board in two ways: first give the student's exact words, and then add the student's name and the verb *says*. For example, you might write *I'm against capital punishment* and *Maria says, "I'm against capital punishment."* Include quotation marks, commas, and end punctuation.
- Point to the quotation marks in several examples and ask *Why do we use quotation marks?* Elicit the response that quotation marks are used to write a person's exact words. Note that the period or question mark goes inside the quotation marks.
- Tell students that when we use someone's exact words, we are quoting them. The quotation marks show that the exact words are a quote. Quoting someone's exact words is also called direct speech.
- Ask a volunteer to read the first example in the box. Then point to another student and say *You are Martin. What did you say?* Make sure the student says *Censorship is wrong.* If necessary, give the response yourself. Now ask a volunteer to read the second example. Then point to another student and say *You are Nicole. What did you ask?* Make sure the student says *Why are there so many rules?* If necessary, give the response yourself.
- Write Martin's and Nicole's sentences on the board with quotation marks. Ask *Why do we need quotation marks here?* Elicit the response that the sentences give Martin's and Nicole's exact words.

- To summarize, have students silently read the bar at the top of the page and the rule and examples in the box.

A–B.
- Write the first item in Exercise A on the board. Ask a volunteer to come to the board and add quotation marks. If necessary, have the class offer corrections. Point out that the quotation marks at the end of the question follow the question mark.
- Working individually, students complete Exercises A and B.
- Students compare answers with a partner. Review as a class.

Workbook Link: Exercise 5

Use of a comma in quotations

Content: capitalization and use of a comma in quoted speech

Procedure:
- Write on the board the two example sentences from the box at the top of the page. To focus students' attention on the punctuation and capitalization, ask questions such as *Why is the M in Martin capitalized?* (It's the first letter of his name.) *Is this a statement or a question?* (a statement) *How can you tell?* (It includes the word *said* and not *asked*. It ends with a period and not a question mark.) *What kind of punctuation follows the word "said"?* (a comma) *Why do you think there's a comma there?* Elicit or tell students that we use a comma after the verb that introduces the quoted speech.
- Have students look again at Exercise A at the top of the page. Point to item 1 and ask *What kind of punctuation follows the word "asked"?* (a comma) *Why do you think there's a comma there?* (to separate the verb from the quoted speech) Continue asking questions about the items.
- Read the information in the second box. Focus students' attention on the rules by asking questions about the example, such as *What punctuation mark comes after the word "says"?* (a comma) *What letters are capitalized and why?* (T—first word in the sentence; S—first word in the quoted speech)

C. Insert a comma . . .
- Have students read the direction line and then work on the exercise individually.
- Tell students that the exercise continues on page 89. They should complete all five items.
- Have students compare answers with a partner. Review as a class.

Workbook Link: Exercise 6

(continued on p. 5)

Book 4 Lesson Plans

Lesson Plan, Unit 7: Practical grammar (for Student pages 88-89)–*continued*

Reporting a person's words: Indirect speech

Procedure:
Note: This section avoids the back shift in reported speech as this is too challenging for most students of this level.

➤ Write the first two examples from the box on the board. Do not include the parenthetical labels. Circle the pronouns *I* and *he* as well as the comma and quotation marks in the first sentence.

➤ Have volunteers read each sentence aloud. Then ask *Which sentence has quotation marks?* (the first one) *Which sentence has a comma?* (the first one) Ask what other differences students notice. Elicit that *I disagree* in the first sentence changes to *he disagrees* in the second.

➤ Tell students that the first sentence reports Paul's speech using his exact words. Elicit from the class that this is called quoted or direct speech. Then tell students that the second sentence reports Paul's speech without using his exact words. This is called indirect speech.

➤ Review the differences between direct or quoted speech and indirect speech. Write on the board a chart with the headings *Direct speech* and *Indirect speech*. Have students suggest how to fill in each column. Your completed chart should include the following:

Direct speech	Indirect speech
Quotation marks and a comma	No quotation marks or comma
A person's exact words	Not the exact words

➤ To summarize, have students read the information in the box silently. Then ask *Does using "that" to introduce the indirect speech change its meaning?* (no) Have a volunteer say the sentence without *that*: *Paul says he disagrees with that law.*

D. Report what each person says.
➤ Write the first item on the board. Ask *How can we rewrite Adam's words in direct speech?* Elicit from students and write on the board *Adam says, "I don't agree."* Ask *How can we rewrite Adam's words in indirect speech?* Elicit from students and write on the board *Adam says (that) he doesn't agree.* Remind students that indirect speech does not use quotation marks or a comma.

➤ Working individually, students rewrite items 2 through 5 as reported speech.

➤ In pairs, students compare answers. Review as a class and then have volunteers write their sentences on the board.

Note: Make sure students use *says* in this exercise and not *said*, which will require back shift in some items.

Option: Working in pairs, students rewrite the items in Exercise D as direct speech. Review as a class

Workbook Link: Exercises 7, 8

➤ Do it yourself!

Procedure:
A–B.
➤ Ask students to turn to page 87 and review the opinion they wrote. Have them write their opinion on the board and sign their name. Remind students to begin their opinion with *I think, I believe,* or *I feel;* for example, *I think censorship is a bad thing.*

➤ Students copy the opinions from the board as direct speech; for example, *Kristin said, "I think censorship is a bad thing."* They should then rewrite each quoted speech as indirect speech; for example, *Kristin said (that) she thinks censorship is a bad thing.* Then have volunteers read Ellen's opinions expressed in both direct and indirect speech.

➤ Circulate to offer help as needed. Then review the written opinions as a class.

Challenge: Opinion chain. Have students continue changing direct speech to indirect speech. Begin by expressing an opinion such as *I think non-smoking areas are very rude.* Student A reports your opinion in indirect speech: *Ms. Murphy said (that) she thinks non-smoking areas are very rude.* Student A then expresses a personal opinion, and Student B reports it in indirect speech. Continue until every student has reported someone else's opinion and has expressed his or her own opinion.

LESSON PLAN, UNIT 7: AUTHENTIC PRACTICE 1 & 2 (for Student pages 90-93)

Summary of Lesson Plan

▶ **PRESENTATION**
Authentic practice 1 & 2:
Listening (Student pages 90-93)
Suggested teaching time: 60 minutes
  includes Cultural Discussion
Your actual teaching time: _____

▶ Authentic practice 1
(Student pages 90-91)

Suggested teaching time: 30 minutes
Your actual teaching time: _____

A mistake about shoplifting

Procedure:

🎧

▶ Before students open their books, read the bar out loud. Ask students what *shoplifting* means. Elicit that it means taking something from a store without paying for it. Tell students that shoplifting is a crime.

▶ Access students' knowledge and experience by asking *How do stores try to discourage shoplifting?* (by using scanning machines at the exits, having guards patrol the store, watching shoppers) *How can you show you are not shoplifting?* (keep merchandise out in the open before purchase and in the store's bag after purchase, have the receipt available, observe rules about trying things on)

▶ Have students open their books and look at the pictures. Help them anticipate the story by asking questions such as *Who are the shoppers in this story?* (two teenage boys, Paul and Dan) *What kind of merchandise are they looking at?* (expensive watches)

▶ Have the students read along silently while they listen to the story.

▶ Some terms may be unfamiliar to students, but meanings can be inferred from the context. Check understanding of *awesome, out of my price range, I'll pass, pricey, piggy bank,* and *later*. Make sure students understand that *later* here is a reduction of *I'll see you later*. Ask *Why does Dan say, "Just my luck"?* Elicit the response or tell students that this is an ironic comment: Dan doesn't really feel lucky.

A. Read the picture story again ...

▶ After students read the story again, they work individually to write answers to the questions.

▶ While students are comparing answers with a partner, circulate and offer help as needed.

▶ Making inferences is an important academic skill. Tell students that sometimes information is stated directly, and sometimes it is implied. We have to make inferences from implied or unstated information. Ask students *What can we infer when Dan asks where the gift-wrapping department is?* (He wants to have the watch gift-wrapped.) *What can we infer from the security guard's question to Dan?* (The guard thinks Dan might be shoplifting.)

(continued on p. 7)

Your notes

Lesson Plan, Unit 7: Authentic practice 1 & 2 (for Student pages 90-93)–*continued*

B–C.

➤ Working individually, students underline the appropriate response.

➤ Students compare answers with a partner.

➤ Partners then take turns reading and responding to each item.

Option: Ask students to close their books. Read each item and elicit appropriate responses. For example, the question *Do you like this robe?* might elicit these responses: *Yes, it's beautiful; No, it doesn't look good; Sure, it's great;* or *I don't think so. It's a funny color.*

Option: Choral reading. Divide the class into two groups. The two groups take turns reading and responding to each item chorally.

D. Guided composition...

➤ Tell students to look at the picture story on page 90 again. Ask *What are Dan and Paul doing?* Note students' responses on the board. Tell students that they are going to write a composition using their answers to a series of questions. As a class, decide on one answer to use as the start of the composition. Write the answer on the board, indenting the sentence and using appropriate capitalization and punctuation.

➤ Have students read the list of questions silently. Make sure students understand the questions and can answer them. You may want to ask each question and elicit answers before students begin writing.

➤ Remind students to answer the seven questions in complete sentences, using capital letters and periods where necessary. Student can start their composition with the sentence the class chose above, or they can use the example in the text. Point out that their answers should use the same verb forms as the questions, either the present continuous or the simple present tense.

➤ When students have completed their compositions, have them exchange papers with a partner. Have students check compositions for correct information, indentation, capital letters, and periods.

➤ Review compositions as a class, having students in turn read one line of their work.

E. Discussion...

➤ In small groups, students discuss the consequences of not getting a receipt for a purchase from a store. Each small group should list the consequences.

➤ Remind students of *if* clauses in real conditional sentences: *If you don't get a receipt, ...* Review with students the verb forms that can follow *if* clauses in real conditions. (the simple present tense, the future)

➤ Call on each group, asking students to list one consequence such as *you may get stopped by a clerk, an alarm will go off*. Write the consequences on the board.

Workbook Link: Exercises 9, 10

➤ Do it yourself!

Procedure:

A–B.

➤ Have students read the speech balloons. Ask *Where do you think these people are?* (in a store) *Who do you think they're talking to?* (a friend, someone they're shopping with)

➤ Read the first speech balloon. Elicit a response such as *You're right* or *Let's look at something else.* Ask another student to respond in disagreement; for example, *I don't think so* or *It's worth it.*

➤ Working individually, students write their responses. Then they practice the conversations in pairs.

➤ Prediction is an important academic skill. In pairs or small groups, students predict what will happen next in the story. Ask students to give reasons for their predictions.

Challenge: In pairs, students discuss and then write continuations of the picture story on page 90. Have them use these questions as prompts: *Does Dan have the receipt? If so, what happens? If not, what happens?* Tell students to write at least three sentences that continue the story.

Lesson Plan, Unit 7: Authentic practice 1 & 2 (for Student pages 90-93)–*continued*

Authentic practice 2
(Student pages 92-93)

Suggested teaching time: 30 minutes
Your actual teaching time: _____

An arrest for shoplifting

Procedure:
▶ Help students anticipate the topic of the conversation by reading the bar aloud.

▶ To set the scene for the conversation, have students look at the picture. Ask questions such as *Where are the people in the picture?* (in an office) *Whose office is it?* (the man's, Hernan Guzman's) *What does the sign on the wall say?* (Hernan Guzman, Attorney at Law) *Who do you think the woman might be?* (Dan's mother)

🎧 A–B.

▶ To focus their attention, have students read the three questions in Exercise A before listening to the conversation.

▶ After listening, students work individually to write answers to the questions.

▶ Note that Dan's mother and the lawyer both call him Danny. It is not unusual for someone to have a childhood name that the family and close friends still use. More recent friends such as Paul call him Dan, an older-sounding nickname for Daniel. You may want to ask students to give personal examples of childhood names and older-sounding versions of the same name.

▶ Before listening again, students read the statements in Exercise B.

▶ After listening, students check the appropriate boxes. Review both exercises as a class.

▶ Discuss what students think will happen after the conversation between Mr. Guzman and Mrs. Ochoa. Make a list on the board of students' suggestions. Ideas should include the events mentioned in the listening (Dan's appointment with the lawyer at 3:00 p.m. on Saturday, the trial on Tuesday) and any other predictions students have.

Challenge: Have students support their answers in Exercise B by taking notes while they listen to the conversation. For example, to support their *False* answer for item 1, students should write *What brings you here on a Saturday?*

C. Vocabulary . . .
▶ Working individually, students complete the exercise.

▶ In pairs, students compare answers.

Option: Have students use all the choices in original sentences.

Option: Have students work in pairs to write definitions for all the choices.

If your students are ready . . .

Culture / Civics note: In most localities, it is up to the police whether to release an arrested person or to detain him or her. In this case, Dan was released and given a bench warrant, sometimes referred to as a summons to appear in court. Sometimes the arrested person must stay in jail until the hearing unless he or she gives a certain amount of money called bail. Bail insures that the person will appear in court for the trial. If the person shows up in court, the bail money is returned; if not, the money is forfeited. If an arrested person doesn't have enough money for the bail, he or she can get a loan from a bail bondsman. Local regulations and customs may differ in your area.

Tapescript

Mr. Guzman: Good morning, Mrs. Ochoa. What brings you here on a Saturday?

Mrs. Ochoa: Thank you for seeing me on such short notice, Mr. Guzman, but this is an emergency. My Danny was arrested for shoplifting yesterday, and we need help.

Mr. Guzman: Danny? Shoplifting? That's ridiculous. He's such a good kid.

Mrs. Ochoa: I know. Don't worry. He didn't do it, but he has to be in court on Tuesday, and he needs a lawyer. Mr. Guzman, Danny's innocent.

Mr. Guzman: Tell me what happened, Mrs. Ochoa. From the beginning.

Mrs. Ochoa: OK. Danny was at Larson's Department Store. He was looking for a Mother's Day present for me. He picked out a watch and bought it.

Mr. Guzman: OK. So far so good.

Mrs. Ochoa: Danny wanted to get the watch gift-wrapped for me, but I guess he was in a hurry or something. So he just put the watch in his backpack. He figured he would wrap it himself.

Mr. Guzman: M-hmm. Then what happened?

Mrs. Ochoa: Well, when he was leaving the store, an alarm went off and a guard at the door asked Danny to show him the backpack. It turns out the cashier didn't cut off that electronic sensor thing. When the guard saw the watch, he asked to see the receipt. And Danny didn't have a receipt.

(Tapescript is continued on page 9.)

Lesson Plan, Unit 7: Authentic practice 1 & 2 (for Student pages 90-93)–*continued*

> **Tapescript** (continued from page 8)
>
> **Mr. Guzman:** So, that shouldn't be a problem. The cashier could have backed Danny up.
>
> **Mrs. Ochoa:** Right. But when they went back to the cashier, she was gone. So Danny couldn't prove he paid for the watch. He paid cash. So the store manager called the police and they took Danny to the station. They gave him a summons for shoplifting and told him to appear in court on Tuesday with a lawyer. That's why I called you. Mr. Guzman, how serious is this? He's innocent, not guilty! My Danny never stole anything in his life. And he's going to college in September. This could ruin his whole life!
>
> **Mr. Guzman:** Mrs. Ochoa, tell Danny to be here this afternoon at 3. I'll see what we can do.

Workbook Link: Exercise 11

D. Read Dan Ochoa's arrest record.

▶ Direct students' attention to the arrest record. Have them read all 23 visible headings. Make sure students understand all the terms. If necessary, explain the difference between an alias and a nickname. (An *alias* is an assumed name that is intended to deceive people. A *nickname* is a familiar or shortened form of a name, such as Dan or Danny for Daniel.) Elicit or explain that a *common-law marriage* is an agreement between a couple who live together but who have not gone through a religious or civil marriage ceremony. Ask *What does "Unk" mean?* (It's an abbreviation for Unknown.)

▶ Check comprehension by asking questions such as *What is Dan Ochoa's full name?* (Daniel Michael Ochoa) *Is he a U.S. citizen?* (yes) *What is his birth date?* (September 17, 1987)

Option: Your students may want to discuss the categories under the headings Race and Ethic (group) on the arrest record. They may choose other categories to describe their own ethnicity or race. Remind students to express their opinions respectfully.

E–F.

▶ Have volunteers read each of the bulleted items aloud. After each item, elicit examples if appropriate. Following the first item, students might suggest saying "Yes, officer" and not saying anything like "You made a stupid mistake."

▶ Ask *What does "ASAP" mean?* (As Soon As Possible) Answer any questions students may have about language. Help students rephrase any difficult items in their own words.

▶ Then have students read the description of Dan's behavior. When students read a description indicating appropriate behavior, have them check the corresponding bulleted item in Exercise E.

▶ Ask students to identify the bullets that they did not check. Ask *Did Dan do the right things? What else should he do?* Write a list on the board of students' ideas about what Dan should do now.

Challenge: If your students have access to a computer, have them do an Internet search of the following topics: arrest rights, Miranda rights, what to do when you are arrested. One useful Web site for more information is www.infoline.org. Ask students to share their findings with the class.

Workbook Link: Exercise 12

▶ Do it yourself!

Procedure:

A–B.

▶ Ask students to think about a true story or a story from a book or movie about a person who was arrested.

▶ On a separate sheet of paper, students make notes about the events in the story. Have students use the key words *who, what, when,* and *where* as prompts for details. Have students note whether the person followed the advice on the Web site shown above. Ask students to think about the outcome of the story as well.

▶ Model the activity by telling a story about a person who was arrested. Use a movie or a newspaper article for facts. Put the words *who, what, when,* and *where* on the board and check each one as you provide details that answer that question.

▶ In pairs or small groups, students tell the story, using their notes to provide details.

Challenge: Students answer the bulleted questions to write a guided composition about someone who was arrested.

LESSON PLAN, UNIT 7: AUTHENTIC PRACTICE 3 (for Student pages 94-95)

Summary of Lesson Plan

▶ **PRESENTATION**
Authentic practice 3:
Reading and critical thinking (Student pages 94-95)
Suggested teaching time: 60 minutes
   includes Cultural Discussion
Your actual teaching time: _____

▶ Authentic practice 3
(Student pages 94-95)

Suggested teaching time: 60 minutes
Your actual teaching time: _____

The elements of the U.S. justice system

Procedure:

A. Read the excerpt...

▶ Have students preview the reading. Remind them that previewing includes skimming the first lines of each paragraph, looking at headings, subheadings, bulleted material, visuals, and specially formatted words or phrases.

▶ Ask questions about what they learned from previewing, such as *What topics are covered in this excerpt?* (the Constitution and the Bill of Rights) *In the Bill of Rights, what protections are given to people accused of crimes?* (no search without permission, a trial by jury, the right to witnesses and a lawyer)

▶ Point out that significant words or phrases are often indicated by boldface, italics, or, in this case, quotation marks. Elicit examples of important terms in quotation marks in this reading (constitutional, warrant, defendant, presumption of innocence, government). Write these terms on the board.

▶ Tell students that specially formatted terms are often defined in the sentence or paragraph. Ask students to find the definitions in the reading for the terms in quotation marks. Elicit the definitions and write them on the board next to the terms. Your board might look like this:

1. "constitutional": from or based on the Constitution
2. "warrant": permission to search an accused person's house
3. "defendant": a citizen accused of a crime
4. "presumption of innocence": jurors must consider a defendant to be innocent until the state convinces them beyond a reasonable doubt that he or she is guilty
5. "government": the state

▶ Have students read the excerpt thoroughly. Check comprehension after each paragraph or section by asking questions such as *When was the Constitution written?* (in 1787) *What does the Constitution talk about?* (how the U.S. government is organized, the limits of the powers of the government) *Why does the Constitution give citizens certain rights?* (to protect citizens from unfair punishment) *What are some rights that defendants have?* (a trial by jury of impartial people, a lawyer)

▶ Point out that the reading is very simplified and meant to be an introduction to the topic. The complete Bill of Rights appears on page 148 of the student's book.

Option: To succeed academically, students need to be able to anticipate questions that might be asked about a text. To practice this skill, have students create questions based on the reading. Put students in small groups to create 10 questions. When all the groups have finished, have them exchange and answer each other's questions.

FYI...

▶ Tell students that they can find information about the U.S. government and how it works online. The Web site given here includes the complete Constitution and all the amendments.

▶ Make sure students know that the amendments are changes and additions to the Constitution that have been made over time. The Bill of Rights is the first 10 amendments to the Constitution. They were added in 1791 to protect certain rights of citizens.

Option: Have students go to the Web site and print out other amendments, or do it yourself. Put students in small groups to read different amendments, and ask each group to explain its amendment to the class. Some amendments that concern criminal prosecutions are the 4th (protection against unreasonable search and seizure), the 6th (rights of the accused in criminal prosecutions), the 8th (protection against cruel and unusual punishment), and the 14th (right to equal protection and due process).

Workbook Link: Exercise 13

(continued on p. 11)

Lesson Plan, Unit 7: Authentic practice 3 (for Student pages 94-95)–*continued*

B. Vocabulary...

- Scanning is an important academic skill. Tell students that they should go back and scan the excerpt to find the answers, if necessary.
- Have students check answers by reading the completed statements out loud to a partner. If students are not sure of the answers, have partners identify the sentence in the excerpt that contains each definition.

FYI...

- Print out the glossary of legal terms from the Web site. Assign terms to pairs or groups to read and rephrase in their own words. Have students present the terms to the class.

Note: Students may find the definitions challenging and need help processing the information. The terms will be useful in preparing the role play below.

Option: Have individuals log on to the Web site and choose three to five words. They should study the definitions and make notes in order to present the information to the class or a group.

Option: Make flashcards with the term on one side and the definition on the other. Have pairs or groups study the terms and then quiz each other.

C. Culture talk...

- With the class, brainstorm questions for students to use as prompts. You may want to use the textbook excerpt on page 94 as a basis for the questions. Suggestions may include *Does your country have a document like the U.S. Constitution? When was it written? Are defendants entitled to a trial by jury?*
- Have students suggest additional questions that are not based on the textbook excerpt.
- Have students work in small groups to compare and contrast justice systems in their home countries.

▶ Do it yourself!

Procedure:

- Tell the students that there are two attorneys at a trial. One is the defense attorney (in this case, Hernan Guzman) who represents the person accused of the crime (Dan Ochoa). The other is the prosecutor or state's attorney (Marion Wilkens) who tries the case for the government.
- Brainstorm with the class the important information that must be presented at the trial. Ask students to think of movies or television shows they have seen that include courtroom scenes. Write students' ideas on the board. Elicit that we need to know the following: Dan's story, what Paul saw and heard before he left Dan, what the cashier remembers, and what the guard saw. Students may also suggest that evidence should be presented about Dan's character, the day's receipts from the register at the watch counter, the fact that Dan had money before the sale and not after, and so on.
- Put students in small groups to make two lists of questions, one for the prosecutor to ask and one for the defense attorney.
- Collect the questions. Assign every student a role. There are eight non-juror roles, so everyone else can be jurors or assistants to the two attorneys. Other possible roles are the manager of Larson's Department Store, the arresting officer, and the officer who gave Dan the summons to appear in court. Give the attorneys the questions provided by the small groups. If you think it would help organize the role play, play a role yourself, such as that of the judge.
- Give all the students a few minutes to think about what they need to do in their roles. Tell jurors that they can take notes at this trial, although this is not permitted at a real trial. Remind the class that the jury verdict must be unanimous.
- After the role play, discuss the court proceedings and the verdict.

Challenge: Trial witnesses often have to make a written statement. Tell students to imagine that they are one of the witnesses (Paul Yon, the cashier, or the guard). Have them write a brief report about what happened from that person's perspective. Collect the reports and read them aloud.

Workbook Link: Exercises 14, 15

Copyright © 2004 by Pearson Education, Inc.
All rights reserved.

LESSON PLAN, UNIT 7: REVIEW (for Student pages 96-98)

Summary of Lesson Plan

➤ **Review** (Student pages 96-98)
Suggested teaching time: 60 minutes
Your actual teaching time: _____

➤ **UNIT REVIEW**
Includes expansion activities
   role play
   dialogues
   writing
   Workbook activities
   outside reading
   realia applications
   math skills applications
   civic lesson applications
   Booster Pak activities

➤ **Review** (Student pages 96-98)

Suggested teaching time: 60 minutes
Your actual teaching time: _____

Procedure:

Note: The format of this exercise is somewhat different from those in other *Review* sections. There are no general questions about who the characters are or where they are, and the task requires students to summarize and synthesize information from the *Authentic practice* sections on pages 90 through 95.

A. Pair work or group work.

Ask and answer questions.
➤ Ask the class general questions about the pictures, such as *What is Dan doing in the first scene?* (paying for the watch) *Where is Dan in the third scene?* (at the police station) *What are the people talking about in the fourth scene?* (Dan's arrest for shoplifting, his need for a lawyer) *What is happening in the last scene?* (Dan's friend Paul Yon is answering questions on the witness stand.) In pairs, students take turns asking and answering questions about what happened on each day.

➤ Point to the jurors in the jury box. Ask *How many people are on this jury?* (12) Tell students that a jury may include one to two additional jurors called alternates. They are present during the entire trial in case one of the regular jurors gets sick.

Option: Working in pairs, students write factual questions that can be used by the trial lawyers. An example of a factual question about the first scene is *Who saw Dan give the cashier the money?* (Paul Yon) Then have one pair of students join another pair to ask and answer the questions they have written.

Create conversations.
➤ Assign pairs of students one of the scenes and have them create a conversation for the characters. Have five pairs read their conversations in order to the class.

Option: Have pairs number the speech balloons and, on a separate sheet of paper, write one line of conversation for each person.

Option: Each student assumes the role of a character in the story (Dan, Paul, the cashier, the guard, the police officer, Mr. Guzman, or Mrs. Ochoa). Students say as much as they can about what happened from their character's point of view. They should keep talking until you say *Stop*.

Challenge: Remind the class about capitalization and punctuation. In pairs, students write one of the conversations using quoted speech. Then have pairs take turns reading aloud each part.

Challenge: Have students report one of the conversations using indirect speech. For scene 1, students might report *Dan says he has the exact change, even the pennies.* If necessary, refer students to Exercise D on page 89.

(continued on p. 13)

Lesson Plan, Unit 7: Review (for Student pages 96-98)—*continued*

🎧 B–C.

- Tell students they are going to listen to Paul Yon's testimony. Make sure students understand that a *testimony* is evidence presented orally by a witness during a trial.
- After students listen the first time, have them read the six statements in Exercise B so they will know what to listen for. Allow students to listen to the conversation as many additional times as necessary to complete the exercise individually.
- Have students check answers with a partner. Then have pairs change the false statements to make them true.
- Tell students to read Mr. Guzman's questions in Exercise C. As students listen again, they should take notes, focusing on Paul Yon's answers.
- Working individually, students report Paul's answers in indirect speech.
- In pairs, students check their statements. Review as a class.

D. Read each sentence...

- Students work individually to complete the review exercise.
- Circulate to offer help as needed.
- Have students check answers with a partner. Review answers as a class.
- Identify any areas of difficulty that may require additional instruction and practice.

Tapescript

Mr. Guzman: Now, Paul, could you please tell me where you were on Friday afternoon at about 4:45?

Paul: I was at Larson's Department Store, Mr. Guzman.

Guzman: Who, if anyone, were you with?

Paul: I was with my friend, Dan Ochoa.

Guzman: And could you please tell me in your own words what happened on that occasion?

Paul: Everything?

Guzman: Just the facts.

Paul: Sure. Well, we were shopping for Mother's Day presents and Dan picked out a watch. We went to the cashier and Dan paid for the watch.

Guzman: How did he pay for the watch?

Paul: What do you mean, "How did he pay?"

Guzman: Did Dan charge the watch? Did he pay by check? Cash?

Paul: He paid cash. I remember that because he had exact change. He said, "I have exact change, even the pennies."

Guzman: Did he get a receipt?

Paul: I don't know.

Guzman: You don't remember?

Paul: No, it's not that. I left to look for a robe for my mom. I didn't see if he got a receipt or not.

Guzman: But you're sure he paid for the watch?

Paul: Absolutely sure. Dan paid for the watch.

Guzman: No further questions.

Female: You may step down, Mr. Yon. Thank you for your testimony.

(continued on p. 14)

Your notes

Lesson Plan, Unit 7: Review (for Student pages 96-98)–*continued*

E–F.

▶ Students work individually to complete the review exercises.

▶ Circulate to offer help as needed.

▶ Have students check answers with a partner. Review answers as a class.

▶ Identify any areas of difficulty that may require additional instruction and practice.

G. Composition ...

▶ Provide students with concrete approaches to writing about the picture on page 96. Use one of the options that follow, give students a choice of options, or assign options based on students' levels of proficiency. Model what is expected of students for each option.

▶ Advise students to look back through the unit for help and ideas as they write.

▶ Circulate to offer help as needed.

Option: Students tell the story of Dan Ochoa's arrest and trial in chronological order. They can refer to the guided composition they wrote in Exercise D on page 91 to begin the story and add details to complete the story.

Option: Have students choose any scene on page 96 and write an extended conversation between the characters. Students should refer to the model conversations on pages 86 and 87 for an example of the format to use.

Option: Have students write an extended conversation for any two characters on page 96. Tell students to use direct speech. Remind them to use correct capitalization and punctuation.

Challenge: Have students write an *Ask Joan* letter from Mrs. Ochoa, who wants advice following her son's arrest.

Now I can

▶ Read the first item in the box out loud: *Now I can discuss pros and cons of controversial issues.* Elicit from the class an example of how to discuss an issue, such as *I'm against capital punishment.*

▶ Put students in pairs, tell the students to take turns reading each item in the box and giving an example of what they have learned. When students can provide an example, they should check that objective. If there are items students aren't able to check, have them look back through the unit for ideas.

▶ When students are finished reviewing with their partners, read each item out loud and elicit an example from the class.

▶ Have students take out the K-W-L charts they created at the beginning of the unit. Ask them to complete the L section with what they have learned.

Oral test (optional)

You may want to use the *Now I can* box as an informal evaluation. While students are working on the *Composition* activity, you can call them up individually and check their ability with two or three objectives.

LESSON PLAN, UNIT 8: PREVIEW/PRACTICAL CONVERSATIONS (for Student pages 99-101)

Summary of Lesson Plan

➤ **Preview and Practical conversations** (Student pages 99-101)
Suggested teaching time: 60 minutes
Your actual teaching time: _____

➤ **Preview and Practical conversations** (Student pages 99-101)

Suggested teaching time: 60 minutes
Your actual teaching time: _____

Note: For a discussion on page 105, have students bring in ads from newspapers or magazines for miracle products.

Note: If you are interested in educator materials related to food and nutrition, go to the home page for the food and nutrition information center at www.nal.usda.gov.fnic. You can click on the Food Guide Pyramid for information on this specific topic, or go to teacher resources for other materials.

Warm up. Do you know what this chart is? What can you use it for?

Procedure:

➤ Introduce the topic of the Food Guide Pyramid by asking questions about the illustration, such as *What shape is this chart?* (a pyramid) *What is pictured in each section of the pyramid?* (different kinds of food) *What kind of food is in the biggest section?* (grains) *What kind of food is in the smallest section?* (fats, oils, and sugars)

➤ Read the first question and elicit or tell students that it is the Food Guide Pyramid. Ask *What can you use it for?* (identifying foods in each group, making food choices)

➤ Put students in pairs or small groups to identify all the categories of food and the examples shown in the chart. Elicit students' ideas and create a table on the board like the one following. At the left, write foods from the section at the top of the pyramid. Continue with foods from the remaining sections, ending with foods from the bottom of the pyramid.

Unit 8 objectives
Procedure:

➤ Have students read the objectives. Explain any unfamiliar terms, such as *quackery* (practices or treatments that pretend to cure an illness).

➤ Working individually, students rank the objectives from 1 to 5, with 1 being the objective that is most important to them.

➤ Have students form groups based on which objective they ranked as 1. So, for example, all students who ranked "Suggest a remedy" as the most important objective form one group. Students then brainstorm questions they have about the objective.

(continued on p. 2)

Fats, oils, sweets	Milk products	Meats, poultry	Vegetables	Fruits	Grains
oil	milk	egg	carrots	apple	bread
sugar	yogurt	fish	celery	bananas	cereal
cookies	cheese	meat	eggplant	orange	rice
		poultry	onion	pear	pasta
		nuts	pepper	grapes	crackers
		beans	Brussels sprout	watermelon	
			potato		

Book 4 Lesson Plans

Lesson Plan, Unit 8: Preview and practical conversations (for Student pages 99-101)–*continued*

Model 1

Content: expressing regret; *shouldn't have*; expressing sympathy; ways to take care of health problems; fattening, salty, and fatty foods

🎧 A–B.

▶ To set the scene for the conversation, point to the photo and ask questions such as *Where are the people?* (in a restaurant) *What have they been eating and drinking?* (pretzels, soft drinks) *What expression does the man have on his face?* (regretful, a little upset)

▶ To access students' experience, ask *Have you ever eaten something and then wished you hadn't?* Elicit examples or give one of your own: *I was eating cookies and watching TV. All of a sudden, I realized I'd eaten the whole bag! I was sorry I had eaten so much fat and sugar!*

▶ After students listen to and read the conversation, check comprehension by asking questions such as *What did the man regret eating?* (pretzels) *Why?* (He has to limit his salt.) *What is his health problem?* (high blood pressure)

Option: Before students listen to and read the conversation, have them cover the conversation and look at the photo. Read the first line of the conversation. Then ask students *Why not? Why shouldn't he have eaten the pretzels?* Elicit reasons he might not want to eat pretzels.

Option: Play the role of Student A and have the class respond chorally with Student B's lines. Then switch roles.

🎧 Vocabulary

▶ Have students read and listen to *Ways to take care of health problems*.

▶ Check students' understanding of the relationship of ideas by asking questions such as *Why does the man have to watch his weight?* (because he is overweight) *The woman has high blood pressure. What does she have to do?* (limit her salt)

▶ Make sure students understand that *watch one's weight* means to keep one's weight low, not to gain weight. Also, *fatty foods* are foods that contain a lot of fat.

▶ Have students write down another health problem, such as having diabetes, and what the person has to do (not eat foods with sugar).

Option: Begin a chart on the board with the headings *Health problem, Contributing food,* and *Solution / advice*. Begin with the information in the *Vocabulary* section and elicit ideas from the class to fill in the chart.

Health problem	Contributing food	Solution / advice
Overweight	Fattening foods (desserts, fast food, junk food)	Watch your weight, avoid fattening foods
High blood pressure	Salty foods (chips, fries)	Limit salt intake
High cholesterol	Fatty foods (fast food, junk food, meats)	Avoid fatty foods

Brainstorm other health problems that certain kinds of foods can exacerbate, and continue completing the chart. You may have examples like the following:

Health problem	Contributing food	Solution / advice
Diabetes	Foods with sugar (sweets)	Lose weight, avoid sweets
Ulcers	Spicy foods (chili peppers)	Avoid spicy food
Lactose intolerance	Dairy products (milk, ice cream)	Reduce dairy intake
Migraines	Caffeine (coffee, tea, colas)	Cut down on coffee, tea

C. Pair work...

▶ Point out that *fatty foods* contain a lot of fat such as butter, lard, or oil. *Fattening foods* contain a lot of calories. Elicit some examples of fattening foods that may not be fatty foods, such as soda and candy. There will be some overlap between these two categories.

▶ Give students time to brainstorm foods that fit into the three categories in the box. Opinions will vary and conversation will be lively. Allow discussion.

▶ When students have completed their lists, model the conversation with a more advanced student. Play the role of Student A to demonstrate how to express regret for eating a certain food and how to give a reason for the regret. Make sure the class understands that Student A states both a way to take care of the health problem and the health problem.

▶ In pairs, students practice making the appropriate substitutions. Have volunteers read their conversations aloud.

Workbook Link: Exercises 1, 2

(continued on p. 3)

Lesson Plan, Unit 8: Preview and practical conversations (for Student pages 99-101)–*continued*

Model 2

Content: asking about ailments, negative *yes-no* questions, suggesting a remedy

Procedure:

A–B.

- To set the scene for the conversation, point to the photo and ask *Where are the women?* (sitting at a table) *What are the women doing?* (drinking tea or coffee, talking, looking at a magazine)

- After students listen to the conversation, check comprehension by asking questions such as *What problem does the woman in red have?* (migraines) *What is the remedy that the woman on the left suggests?* (Rackinusha)

- Play the cassette or read aloud the conversation. Have students repeat the lines in the pauses and then practice reading the conversation in pairs.

- Circulate, correcting students' pronunciation if necessary.

C. Pair work...

- Have students read the ad for Rackinusha. Ask questions such as *Have you ever heard of this remedy?* (no) *Do you need a prescription to buy it?* (No, it's an over-the-counter medication.) *Does it sound too good to be true?* (yes) *Why?* (It says it cures many ailments, probably too many.)

- Write the conversation with substitution slots on the board. Walk the students through each line, eliciting a word or phrase that could go in each slot. You may get a conversation like this:

   A: Don't you have *(name of an ailment, possibly from the Rackinusha ad)*?

   B: Yes, I do. *(follow-up question such as "Why?" or "What's up?")*

   A: They say *(a remedy, possibly Rackinusha)* cures *(a pronoun, or repeat name of the ailment)*.

   B: *(questions about the information)*?

   A: *(source of information)*. It couldn't hurt to give *(the pronoun or the remedy)* a try.

- Brainstorm other ailments. Write examples on the board. Next to each ailment, write the names of remedies (real or fictitious) that students suggest.

- Have pairs practice the conversation, using an ailment and a remedy from the board or the ad.

Workbook Link: Exercises 3, 4

➤ Do it yourself!

Procedure:

A–B.

- Remind students that a remedy can be a medicine, a supplement, a food, or another treatment that they have used.

- Have students complete the charts individually.

- When students have finished their charts, have pairs or small groups discuss the remedies. Have them use these questions as a guide for discussion: *Did you list ailments in common? Which ones? What remedies do you use? Which remedies are the most effective?*

Option: Have pairs of students create an ad for one of their remedies. Remind them to include what the product is for, good things about it, and a picture or other visual.

LESSON PLAN, UNIT 8: PRACTICAL GRAMMAR *(for Student pages 102-103)*

Summary of Lesson Plan

▶ **PRESENTATION**
Practical grammar (Student pages 102-103)
Suggested teaching time: 60 minutes
Your actual teaching time: _____

▶ **Practical grammar**
(Student pages 102-103)

Suggested teaching time: 60 minutes
Your actual teaching time: _____

Should have / shouldn't have

Procedure:

Note: If students have difficulty with past participles, refer them to the list of irregular verbs on page 145.

▶ Refer students to the model conversation on page 100. Read aloud the first line: *I shouldn't have eaten those pretzels.* Ask *How does the man feel?* (regretful, sorry) *Why?* (He shouldn't have eaten all the pretzels.) *Have you ever done something you wish you hadn't?* Elicit students' experience or tell your own, such as *I shouldn't have gone to that movie. It got a terrible review; I shouldn't have left the house so late. I missed my bus.*

▶ Tell students that we use *shouldn't have* plus a past participle to talk about regrets—when we've done something but wish we hadn't. Tell them that we can also express regret with *should have: I should have gone to the new movie across the street, I should have left the house at 7:30.* We use *should have* when we haven't done something but wish we had. Elicit students' regrets with *should have* plus a past participle.

▶ Point out that in speech both *should have* and *shouldn't have* are usually contracted, or reduced. It sounds like the speaker is saying *should of* and *shouldn't of*.

▶ Write on the board *You shouldn't have* and *You should have*. To check that students understand how these expressions are used, tell them that you will make some statements about behavior you regret. They will comment either *You shouldn't have* for things you did or *You should have* for things you didn't do. Create your own or use these statements: *I didn't call my mother on her birthday! I just ate the whole pie. I quit my job. I didn't ask my boss for a raise. I didn't study for the test.*

A. Complete each sentence ...

▶ Write the first item on the board. Include the blank and the words *not buy* below the line. Read the directions aloud and ask the class to suggest the completion of the first item.

▶ Working individually, students complete sentences 2 through 6.

▶ In pairs, students compare answers. Review as a class and answer any questions.

Workbook Link: Exercises 5, 6

Negative *yes-no* questions

Procedure:

▶ Refer students to the model conversation on page 101. Read aloud the first line: *Don't you have migraines?* Point out that the speaker believes that the other woman does have migraines and is seeking confirmation. In fact, her belief is confirmed: *Yes, I do.* Note that the response is a short answer and stands for *Yes, I do have migraines.*

▶ Ask a series of negative *yes-no* questions to confirm information you think is correct and elicit short answers from the class. Use these questions or create your own: *Didn't you drive here today? Wasn't it beautiful yesterday? Didn't I see you on the street the other day?*

▶ Tell students that negative *yes-no* questions are used both to get confirmation or agreement and to express surprise or disbelief. When expressing disbelief, a negative question can sound accusatory: *Can't they turn down their TV?*

▶ Read each of the examples in the box and have volunteers answer the questions.

(continued on p. 5)

Lesson Plan, Unit 8: Practical grammar (for Student pages 102-103)–*continued*

B. Complete each negative *yes-no* question.

➤ Write the first item on the board. Include the blank and the words *you / see* below the line. Read the directions aloud and ask the class to suggest the completion of the first item.

➤ Tell students that they should complete the exercise using the simple present tense or the simple past tense. As a class, go over the items and decide whether the verb should be written in the simple present tense or the simple past tense. Have students point out the words that helped them decide. (1: simple past tense, "last night"; 2: simple present tense, "yet"; 3: simple present tense, "yet"; 4: simple past tense, "were"; 5: simple present tense, "usually")

➤ Working individually, students complete sentences 2 through 5.

➤ In pairs, students compare answers. Review as a class and answer any questions.

➤ In item 5, students may ask about the word *anything*. Tell them that either *anything* or *something* is appropriate in the question: *Doesn't she usually take something for her back pain?*

C. Complete each conversation ...

➤ Write the first item on the board. Include A's blank line and the words *cake / be delicious* under the blank.

➤ Tell students that they will use the words *cake / be delicious* to create a negative *yes-no* question that leads to B's answer, *Yes, it is*.

➤ Remind students that a short answer follows a *yes-no* question. The verb used in the answer can help students identify the auxiliary verb they will need to form the question. B's answer in item 3, for example, *Yes, I do*, tells students to use a form of *do* in the question. Remind them that they need a negative form: *Don't you have insomnia?*

➤ Working individually, students write questions.

➤ Have students check answers with a partner and then review as a class.

Option: After correcting the exercise, students work in pairs to practice asking and answering the questions in the exercise.

Challenge: Have students work in pairs to create conversations that include one of the items in the exercise. They must use both question and answer in the conversation, which should be at least six lines long.

Challenge: Although a negative *yes-no* question usually seeks confirmation or agreement, sometimes the listener disagrees. Have students write negative responses to the questions. For item 1, for example, the response might be *Actually, I don't really like cake.*

Workbook Link: Exercises 7, 8

➤ Do it yourself!

Procedure:

A–B.

➤ On the board, write the two headings *I should have* and *I shouldn't have*. Under the first heading, write *I should have bought milk yesterday. Now we're out.* Under the second heading, write *I shouldn't have drunk all that coffee after dinner!* Read the sentences and tell students they are both regrets about your recent behavior. Ask students for examples of regrets they have about their recent behavior. Write two or three students' ideas under the appropriate heading.

➤ Tell students to look at the chart in their books. Working individually, students write down two regrets about something they didn't do (*I should have*) and two regrets about something they did (*I shouldn't have*).

➤ Working in pairs, students take turns telling each other about their regrets.

Challenge: After Student A expresses a regret, Student B asks a negative question about the behavior. For example, if Student A says *I should have bought milk yesterday*, Student B might ask *Didn't you write it on your list?* Or if Student B says *I shouldn't have drunk all that coffee after dinner*, Student A might ask *Didn't you have trouble sleeping later?*

LESSON PLAN, UNIT 8: AUTHENTIC PRACTICE 1 & 2 (for Student pages 104–107)

Summary of Lesson Plan

▶ **PRESENTATION**
Authentic practice 1 & 2:
Listening (Student pages 104-107)
Suggested teaching time: 60 minutes
Your actual teaching time: _____

▶ **Authentic practice 1**
(Student pages 104-105)

Suggested teaching time: 30 minutes
Your actual teaching time: _____

Avoid quackery.

Procedure:

▶ To set the scene for the picture story, point to the pictures and ask general questions such as *Where are the two women?* (sitting outside on a bench) *What are they doing?* (talking, looking at magazines)

▶ Have students read along silently as they listen to the picture story.

▶ Some terms may be unfamiliar to students, but the meaning can be inferred from the context. Elicit the meanings of *breakthrough, a thing of the past, gullible, pass up, couch potato, don't fall for that, take my word for it, there's no free lunch, no pain, no gain*.

▶ Explain that *my word* is used to represent *my statement* or *my promise*, so *take my word* means believe me, believe what I say.

▶ Check understanding by asking questions such as *What is Sophie reading about?* (Fat-B-Gone) *What is Fat-B-Gone?* (a new weight-loss product, perhaps a pill) *Why might Sophie have a weight problem?* (She can't pass up food and she doesn't exercise.) *Does Sophie believe the claims for Fat-B-Gone?* (yes) *Does Helen believe the claims?* (no)

Option: Write *Fat-B-Gone* on the board. Tell students that this is the name of a new weight-loss product and that you're going to dictate portions of an ad that tells all about its benefits: *It makes dieting a thing of the past. Eat what you want, when you want. Fat-B-Gone goes to work when you go to sleep . . . Does the dieting for you. No annoying exercise. Guaranteed. Lose up to 30 pounds the first week, or your money back! Completely natural. Made from the bark of the ancient chinchona tree, found only in the La Mancha region of Spain.* While students are writing individually at their desks, have volunteers write the sentences on the board. Read each sentence aloud again as students look at the board. After each claim, ask *Does this sound too good to be true?* If students say *yes*, put a check mark next to the statement.

Option: Have pairs of students read the conversation between Sophie and Helen.

A. Discussion . . .

▶ Working individually, students write answers to the questions.

▶ Being able to give support for answers is an important academic skill. Have students underline the information in the story that supports their answers. For example, if students answer the question *What's Sophie's problem?* by saying that she wants to lose weight, they might underline *I'm going to send away for this miracle weight-loss breakthrough* or *I just can't pass up food. And I'm a real couch potato.*

▶ In pairs, students compare answers.

▶ Review answers as a class. Note that Sophie might have two problems: wanting to lose weight (or being overweight) and being gullible.

Option: Read the part of Sophie and have students respond chorally with Helen's lines.

Challenge: Have students write an *Ask Joan* letter from Helen about Sophie's problem and her plan to buy Fat-B-Gone. Remind students to use indirect speech or quoted speech where appropriate in describing the product claims and Sophie's statements. Students can exchange letters and write responses from Joan giving advice.

(continued on p. 7)

Book 4 Lesson Plans

Lesson Plan, Unit 8: Authentic practice 1 & 2 (for Student pages 104-107)–*continued*

B. Vocabulary...

➤ Have students read the statements in Exercise B.

➤ Then have them reread the picture story, scanning for the underlined words or phrases. Remind students to use the context to check meaning.

➤ Working individually, students check *True* or *False* for each statement.

➤ Review answers as a class. Ask students to explain their answers, giving support from the text.

Challenge: Have students create original *True-False* statements using other words or phrases from the picture story. Make sure statements demonstrate the meaning of the words. An example might be *"No free lunch" means Sophie will have to buy her lunch today.* (False) Have volunteers write their sentences on the board. Have students copy the sentences and write *True* or *False* next to each one.

C. Read each sentence or question...

➤ Point out that *Come on!* can have different meanings: to encourage someone to go with you or to express disbelief.

➤ Working individually, students select a response. In pairs, they compare answers.

Option: Read each item and have students respond chorally with the correct response.

Option: Have pairs of students take turns reading the items and responses.

D. Reread the picture story...

➤ Tell students to reread the story on page 104.

➤ Tell them to write down on a separate sheet of paper at least five claims made for the product.

➤ Elicit the claims and write them on the board.

E. Discussion...

➤ Have students read the questions. Put students in small groups to discuss the answers.

➤ Elicit examples of products that make exaggerated claims, such as weight-loss, memory improvement, better muscle tone, or baldness remedies. Ask *Where might you find out about a product like Fat-B-Gone?* (ads on TV or radio or in magazines or newspapers, word of mouth, direct mail ads)

➤ Point out that the answer to the second question is not given in the picture story. Students will have to come up with their own ideas to discuss as a group.

Challenge: Out-of-class assignment. Ask students to watch television or listen to the radio for ads. They should take notes on product claims that may be too good to be true. After a few days, ask students to report on products they discovered, claims they heard, and any other information they would like to share.

Workbook Link: Exercises 9, 10

➤ Do it yourself!

Procedure:

A. Write your own response...

➤ Have a volunteer read the first speech balloon out loud. Model an appropriate response such as *Don't be so gullible* or *The only way to build muscle is to exercise.*

➤ Have volunteers read the other speech balloons aloud. Point out that, like Sophie, the three speakers sound as though they believe the product claims they're talking about. Have students decide whether they want to respond sympathetically or take the opposite attitude toward the claims.

➤ Point out that *cream* in the second speech balloon may also be written as *crème* when referring to cosmetics.

➤ Working individually, students write responses to the speech balloons.

➤ In pairs, students compare answers and practice their conversations.

Challenge: Have students write a response to each speech balloon using a negative *yes-no* question; for example, *Don't you think this ad sounds ridiculous?*

B. Discussion...

➤ Ask students to take out the ads they collected, and supply some of your own.

➤ If possible, put students in small groups according to the type of product represented in their ads, such as weight-loss programs, muscle development, or health promotion. In small groups, students list the different claims made for the products.

➤ In each group, have students classify the claims as believable or unbelievable. Ask students to be prepared to give reasons for their classifications.

➤ Have groups share examples of products and claims with the class.

(continued on p. 8)

Lesson Plan, Unit 8: Authentic practice 1 & 2 (for Student pages 104-107)–*continued*

Authentic practice 2
(Student pages 106-107)

Suggested teaching time: 30 minutes
Your actual teaching time: _____

Nutrition, diet, and health

Procedure:

A. Take the self-test...

➤ Make sure students understand that a *myth* is a story or an idea that is widely believed but not actually true.

➤ Working individually, students check whether each statement is a fact (true) or a myth (false).

➤ Tell students that they will check their answers after listening to the report on nutrition and health.

🎧 B–D.

➤ Students listen to the report twice. After the second listening, they check their answers on the self-test according to the information they heard in the report. The answers are at the bottom of the page.

➤ Working in small groups, students discuss their answers.

➤ Elicit examples of information that students found surprising and write them on the board.

Option: Determining meaning from context is an important academic skill. Sometimes a definition for an unfamiliar term appears as an appositive—it's next to the word it explains. In written material, an appositive may be set off by commas, parentheses, or dashes (as it is in the previous sentence). In the listening comprehension, there are two appositives; they define the words *obese* and *myths*. Have students listen to the report again and note the definitions.

FYI...

Option: If your students have access to computers, assign each student or pair one or more of the following questions. Ask them to find the answers on the Web site listed on page 106.

1. How has the prevalence of overweight and obesity in adults changed over the years?
2. What is the prevalence of overweight and obesity in minorities?
3. What is the prevalence of overweight and obesity in children and adolescents?
4. What is the prevalence of overweight and obesity in people with diabetes?
5. What is the prevalence of overweight and obesity in people with hypertension (high blood pressure)?
6. What is the prevalence of overweight and obesity in people with high cholesterol?
7. What is the prevalence of overweight and obesity in people with cancer?
8. What is the mortality rate associated with obesity?
9. What is the cost of overweight and obesity?
10. What is the cost of hypertension (high blood pressure) related to overweight and obesity?
11. How much do we spend on weight-loss products and services?
12. How physically active is the U.S. population?

Tapescript

Sinclair: Good evening, viewers. I'm Martin Sinclair with tonight's nutrition update.
More than half the U. S. population is overweight, and about 25 percent are obese—very overweight. This evening's guest is Dr. Prunella Kazan, nutritionist and expert on healthy weight control and weight loss. [pause] Good evening, Dr. Kazan. What's tonight's subject?

Kazan: Good evening, Martin. Tonight we turn our attention to common myths about diet and weight loss.

Sinclair: Myths?

Kazan: Yes. There are a lot of myths, or misconceptions, about how to lose weight. Since so many people are always trying to lose weight, I thought I would talk about four common myths many people think are facts.
First: Many people think that an effective way to lose weight is to skip meals.

Sinclair: Isn't it? That's what I do.

Kazan: No. Not a good idea. If you skip meals during the day, you are likely to eat more at the next meal. Studies show that people who skip breakfast tend to be heavier than those who eat a nutritious breakfast.

Sinclair: No kidding! I'm never hungry at breakfast, so I thought skipping it was a painless way to cut down on calories. What else do you have on your list?

(Tapescript is continued on page 9.)

Lesson Plan, Unit 8: Authentic practice 1 & 2 (for Student pages 104–107)—*continued*

Tapescript *(continued from page 8)*

Kazan: The second myth is that eating at night makes you gain weight.

Sinclair: You mean that's not true either?

Kazan: Nope. It doesn't matter what time of day you eat—it's how much you eat during the whole day and how much exercise you get that make you gain or lose weight. The best way to lose weight is to eat many small meals throughout the day and to exercise. The secret is just using more calories than you eat, and exercise burns calories.

Sinclair: Hmm. That's interesting.

Kazan: Three. Many people believe that some foods burn fat and make you thin. Certain foods, such as grapefruit, celery, and cabbage, have the reputation as fat burners, but there is absolutely no truth in this. It's possible that these myths were created by people marketing products that include grapefruit or other foods. Don't believe it.

Sinclair: Are you sure?

Kazan: Yes. Grapefruit, celery, and cabbage are great low-calorie foods that fill you up so you don't want to eat high-calorie things. But they don't have any magical powers to "burn" fat.

Sinclair: And what's myth number 4?

Kazan: This one's my favorite. People think that when they see a label that says "Low fat" or even "No fat" that the food has no calories. People need to understand that they are fooling themselves if they fill up on low-fat cookies, cakes, or candies. Those foods often have lots of sugar, and they are often as fattening as foods with fats. It's important to educate yourself about both the concepts and the vocabulary of diet and weight loss.

Sinclair: Well, that's really interesting. Unfortunately, our time is up. See you next week at the same time. This is Martin Sinclair, thanking Dr. Prunella Kazan for tonight's nutrition update.

Workbook Link: Exercise 12

➤ Do it yourself!

Procedure:

A. Study the food classes.

Vocabulary

➤ Play the cassette or read the classes of foods. Have students repeat.

➤ Call out classes of foods and have students point to the pictures. Ask students to identify the items they see in each category.

Challenge: Classification Game. Divide the class into two or more teams. Members on each team brainstorm as many examples as they can of each class of foods. Then have a member of Team A call out a food. A member of Team B must state the food class it belongs to. Each correct classification earns 1 point for the team.

Challenge: Alphabet Game. Divide the class into two or more teams. Members on each team brainstorm foods that begin with each letter of the alphabet. Then teams take turns stating foods for all the letters in the alphabet. When stating a food, the team member must say the letter, the food, and the class it belongs to: *A, artichoke, vegetable*. If Team A names a food beginning with a letter and Team B cannot, Team A gets 1 point. When teams come to the end of the alphabet, the team with the highest number of points wins.

B. Classification ...

➤ Working individually, students complete the chart with the names of single-ingredient foods that they like.

➤ Circulate and offer help as needed.

➤ Have students put a check mark next to the foods they listed that they think are healthful.

C. Discussion ...

➤ With the class, brainstorm criteria for healthful foods. Criteria might include the following considerations: low in fat, high in vitamins, high in fiber, protein-rich, and so on. Write students' ideas on the board.

➤ In small groups, students discuss which of the foods they listed that they consider healthful. Have students explain why they consider a particular food healthful.

Challenge: Have students work in pairs to list the ingredients of a recent meal they ate at a restaurant. Remind them to list all the ingredients in each dish. Circulate to offer help as necessary. Then have students refer to the criteria for healthful foods on the board and rate their restaurant meals on a scale of 1 to 5, with 1 being most healthful and 5 being least healthy. Have students compare their findings.

Workbook Link: Exercise 13

LESSON PLAN, UNIT 8: AUTHENTIC PRACTICE 3 (for Student pages 108-109)

Summary of Lesson Plan

▶ **PRESENTATION**
Authentic practice 3:
Reading and critical thinking (Student pages 108-109)
Suggested teaching time: 60 minutes
   includes Cultural Discussion
Your actual teaching time: _____

▶ Authentic practice 3
(Student pages 108-109)

Suggested teaching time: 60 minutes
Your actual teaching time: _____

The Food Guide Pyramid

Procedure:

A–B.

▶ Have students look at the Food Guide Pyramid and read the name of each group. Have them also read the number of recommended servings for each group.

▶ Put students in groups of three. Assign one the role of facilitator, one the role of recorder, and one the role of reporter. The facilitator asks the questions and makes sure everyone responds. The recorder takes notes on the answers, and the reporter tells the class about the discussion.

▶ When groups have finished their discussion, elicit the answers to the questions from the group reporters.

Challenge: Have students look at the Food Guide Pyramid in their books for one minute. Draw an empty pyramid on the board with the six compartments but no other information. Have volunteers come to the board one at a time, and give them each the name of a food pictured in the Pyramid. They write the food in the correct compartment. Ask the rest of the class to make sure the categorizations are correct.

Challenge: Tell students that the United States Department of Agriculture had trouble designing a graphic that conveyed the information about nutrition in the most effective way. Ask pairs of students to design another graphic to inform people about different kinds of foods and persuade them to eat nutritious food.

C. Write all the foods you ate yesterday.

▶ Write on the board *Breakfast / Quantity* and tell students that they are going to list what they ate for breakfast yesterday. Write *toast—2 slices* and any other food that you ate. Ask volunteers for the foods they ate. Make sure students include the amounts.

▶ Have students look at the chart on page 108. Tell them to complete the chart with everything they ate yesterday and the amount.

Option: On a separate sheet of paper, students copy the chart. They interview a partner and complete the chart with the partner's information. Partners look at the two charts and discuss similarities and differences.

D. Discussion...

▶ Ask students to look at their charts and write a letter next to each entry to indicate what group it belongs to: G—grains, V—vegetables, and so on.

▶ Write the names of the groups of foods on the board. As you read each group, ask students to raise their hands if that is the group that most of their foods came from yesterday. Put tally marks next to the groups.

(continued on p. 11)

Lesson Plan, Unit 8: Authentic practice 3 (for Student pages 108-109)–*continued*

E. Read about the Food Guide Pyramid.

➤ After students read the information from the United States Department of Agriculture (USDA) Web site, check comprehension by asking questions such as *What is the Pyramid designed to help you do?* (eat better every day) *What group should you eat the least from?* (fats, oils, and sweets) *How many servings from the meat group should you have each day?* (two to three) *What is one serving of bread?* (one slice) *What is one serving of peanut butter?* (two tablespoons) *What is one serving of milk?* (one cup)

Option: Have students create five comprehension questions based on the reading. Then have students exchange papers with a partner and answer their partner's questions.

Option: Have students create a food pyramid based on the diet of their home country or culture. For example, instead of bread, students from northern Africa might list couscous in the grains group at the bottom of the pyramid.

Option: Have students log on to the following Web site and look up a pyramid for their culture or a culture similar to theirs:
www.semda.org.info/pyramid.
If students have created their own cultural food pyramid, they can compare them to the ones on the Web site.

Option: Students can get more information about each food group by visiting the following Web site and clicking on the group:
www.nal.usda.gov:8001/py/pmap/htm.

➤ Do it yourself!

Procedure:

A–B.

➤ Remind students to use the Food Guide Pyramid in planning their food choices. Have them refer to the USDA information on serving sizes.

➤ Tell students that their plans should be realistic and include foods and portions they will probably really eat tomorrow. For example, they shouldn't write down 3 ounces of fish if they know they won't have time to buy any.

➤ In pairs or small groups, students talk about their completed meal plans. Put these questions on the board to guide discussion: *Have I included enough food from each group? Have I included too few servings from any group or groups? Where do I need to improve my choices? Have I included too many fattening, fatty, or salty foods?*

C. Culture talk...

➤ If students created food pyramids based on the diet of their home country or culture, ask them to get them out.

➤ Put students in small groups by country or culture, if possible. Have students list typical foods eaten in their countries and the usual amounts of those foods. Ask students to indicate which of those foods are healthful.

➤ Restructure the groups so that the new groups consist of members from different countries or cultures. Have them compare diets.

➤ Lead a class discussion, asking questions such as *What do your diets have in common? What are some significant differences? How do the diets in your home countries compare to the diet of this country?*

Option: Put students in small groups to discuss how their eating habits have changed since their arrival in this country.

Workbook Link: Exercises 14, 15

LESSON PLAN, UNIT 8: REVIEW (for Student pages 110-112)

Summary of Lesson Plan

▶ **Review (Student pages 110-112)**
Suggested teaching time: 60 minutes
Your actual teaching time: _____

▶ **UNIT REVIEW**
Includes expansion activities
- role play
- dialogues
- writing
- Workbook activities
- outside reading
- realia applications
- math skills applications
- civic lesson applications
- Booster Pak activities

▶ **Review (Student pages 110-112)**

Suggested teaching time: 60 minutes
Your actual teaching time: _____

Procedure:

A. Pair work or group work.

Ask and answer questions.

▶ Ask questions about the picture, such as *Where are the man and woman in the first scene?* (a restaurant) *What is the man looking at in the second scene?* (an ad for Fat-B-Gone) *What is he doing in the last scene?* (cooking a healthy meal)

▶ Partners take turns pointing to different things in the picture and asking and answering questions.

Option: Let pairs of students study the picture for one minute. Then have Student A close his or her book while Student B asks questions about the three scenes.

Option: Let partners study the picture for one minute. Then have both students close their books and list as many objects in the scenes as they can remember. Have partners compare lists.

Create conversations.

▶ Focus students' attention on the first scene. Tell them to imagine that the man is sorry that he's eaten so much dessert. Have pairs complete this sentence for the man: *I shouldn't have . . .* Tell them to continue the conversation between the couple.

Challenge: Talkathon. Ask pairs of students to come to the front of the room and role-play a conversation between the couple. Time each pair. The pair that can sustain a logical conversation for the longest period of time wins.

Tell a story.

▶ Tell students that although the same man is shown in all three scenes, many details are needed to connect the scenes so the picture as a whole tells a coherent story. Ask students to describe the events in each picture and to add as much information as they can to make the scenes connect more smoothly. Before students begin, you may want to brainstorm possible questions to answer, such as *How much time has gone by between each scene? What was the man's experience with Fat-B-Gone? Why did he decide to use the Food Guide Pyramid for help in meal planning? Does he have any regrets now?*

Option: Ask *Who do you think the woman is?* Have students tell her story. They should include information about how long she has known the man, how she feels about her weight, whether she has any health problems, any regrets she has about her recent behavior.

Option: Divide the class in half. Have half the students imagine they are the man in the picture and that he has lost a lot of weight. Now he makes inspirational speeches to groups and describes his experience successfully losing weight. Tell students to create a talk for the man to give to the class. Have the other half of the class think up questions to ask the speaker, such as *What do you think of Fat-B-Gone? Do you have any healthful recipes to share? Do you ever eat dessert now?*

(continued on p. 13)

Lesson Plan, Unit 8: Review (for Student pages 110-112)–*continued*

🎧 B–C.

➤ Tell students that they are going to listen to a radio call-in show on nutrition.

➤ Brainstorm questions that callers might have for a nutritionist. Write examples on the board.

➤ After students have listened the first time, ask *What did the caller want to know?* (how to use the Food Guide Pyramid)

➤ Have students read the advice in column A of Exercise C. Then have students listen to the call-in show again and match the advice in column A with its purpose in column B.

➤ Note that reasons in column B are written as infinitives of purpose. Remind students that they saw this structure in Unit 3.

➤ When students have completed the matching activity, check answers by asking *why* questions such as *Why should you eat a variety of foods?* Students should answer with an infinitive of purpose: *to get necessary nutrients*.

Option: In pairs, have students ask and answer *why* questions about the advice in the listening.

D–E.

➤ Students work individually to complete the review exercises. Tell students that Exercise E continues on page 112 and that they should complete the entire exercise.

➤ Circulate to offer help as needed.

➤ Have students check answers with a partner. Review answers as a class.

➤ Identify any areas of difficulty that may require additional instruction and practice.

Tapescript

Edwin: This is Edwin Crane. Welcome to "Ask the Nutritionist." Today's questions relate to the Food Guide Pyramid. Our first caller is Meredith. Meredith, you're on the air.

Meredith: Hello, Edwin. Thank you for taking my call. I don't understand how to use this Pyramid thing that everybody's talking about. Can you help me?

Edwin: Sure, Meredith. What specifically do you want to know about the Pyramid?

Meredith: Well, first, do I have to eat all these things at every meal? If I do that, I'll be fat as a house!

Edwin: No, of course not. The Pyramid tells you how much you need in a day, not in a meal.

Meredith: Oh, that makes sense. Another question: You know the milk, yogurt, and cheese group?

Edwin: Yes.

Meredith: Well, I absolutely hate yogurt!

Edwin: You don't have to eat yogurt just because it's in the Pyramid. That group also contains milk and cheese. You can have two to three servings of any of those.

Meredith: You mean I can have three servings of cheese? I love cheese.

Edwin: Of course. The Pyramid doesn't tell you *what* to eat, it just gives you guidelines to follow.

Meredith: The Pyramid is still too complicated for me. Can't you just give me some general advice?

Edwin: Sure. Here's some advice. It's not complete, but I hope it helps:

Eat a variety of foods to get all the nutrients you need.

Balance the foods you eat with exercise, to maintain or improve your weight.

Choose a diet with lots of grains, fruits, and vegetables to help you avoid eating too much fat.

Choose a diet low in fat and cholesterol to reduce your risk of heart disease.

Choose a diet moderate in sugars to help avoid tooth decay.

Choose a diet moderate in salt and sodium to help reduce your risk of high blood pressure.

If you drink alcoholic beverages, do so in moderation to avoid accidents, addiction, and health problems.

Meredith: That's easy as pie! Thanks, Edwin!

(continued on p. 14)

Lesson Plan, Unit 8: Review (for Student pages 110-112)–*continued*

F–G.

➤ Students work individually to complete the review exercises.

➤ Circulate to offer help as needed.

➤ Have students check answers with a partner. Review answers as a class.

➤ Identify any areas of difficulty that may require additional instruction and practice.

Option: Students practice reading Exercise G in pairs.

H. Composition...

➤ Provide students with concrete approaches to writing about the picture on page 110. Use one of the options that follow, give students a choice of options, or assign options based on students' levels of proficiency. Model what is expected of students for each option.

➤ Advise students to look back through the unit for help and ideas as they write.

➤ Circulate to offer help as needed.

Option: Tell students to imagine what the man is thinking in scenes 2 and 3. Have them write his thoughts; for example, *Wow! That's a terrific offer! I could lose 50 pounds in a week!* Ask volunteers to read their thought balloons aloud.

Option: Have students write a conversation between the man and woman in the first scene. They can look at the model conversation on page 100 for an example of the format to follow.

Option: Have students write a letter of complaint to the maker of Fat-B-Gone or Muscle Man Cream in which they complain that the claims were not true. The letter should include when the product was purchased, how long it was used, and what the results were.

Challenge: Have students write a public service announcement to encourage people to follow the Food Guide Pyramid in making their daily food choices.

Now I can

➤ Read the first item in the box out loud: *Now I can express regret.* Elicit from the class an example of how to do express regret, such as *I shouldn't have eaten that pizza.*

➤ Put students in pairs, tell students to take turns reading each item in the box and giving an example of what they have learned. When students can provide an example, they should check that objective. If there are items students aren't able to check, have them look back through the unit for ideas.

➤ When students are finished reviewing with their partners, read each item out loud and elicit an example from the class.

Oral test (optional)

You may want to use the *Now I can* box as an informal evaluation. While students are working on the *Composition* activity, you can call them up individually and check their ability with two or three objectives.

Copyright © 2004 by Pearson Education, Inc.
All rights reserved.

LESSON PLAN, UNIT 9: PREVIEW/PRACTICAL CONVERSATIONS (for Student pages 113-115)

Summary of Lesson Plan

➤ **Preview and Practical conversations** (Student pages 113-115)
Suggested teaching time: 60 minutes
Your actual teaching time: _____

➤ **Preview and Practical conversations** (Student pages 113-115)

Suggested teaching time: 60 minutes
Your actual teaching time: _____

Warm up. Is this a good opportunity? Would you call 1-800-BIG-SIGN? Why or why not?

Procedure:

➤ Put students in small groups to look at the picture and answer these questions: *Would you want to go into business with this man? Why or why not?* Elicit reasons why working with this man might not be a good idea and write them on the board; for example, *There are many indications that he is running an unprofitable business, such as peeling paint, hand-lettered signs, a bare light bulb. He is unprofessionally dressed in a T-shirt.*

➤ Tell students that the slogan *Get rich quick* is often a clue that a business may be using unethical schemes. Point out the unorthodox spelling: *Earn x-tra $$$* instead of *Earn extra money.*

➤ Now read the *Warm up* questions and elicit responses: *Is this a good opportunity?* (probably not) *Would you call 1-800-BIG-SIGN? Why or why not?* (maybe, you don't know until you call, it doesn't look like a good business opportunity to get involved with)

Option: Have students write a one-paragraph description of the office. Remind them to indent the first line and use appropriate punctuation and capitalization. They can comment on the list on the board of reasons why working with this man might not be a good idea.

Option: Students from some cultures may be shocked by the man's disrespectful posture, especially the placement of his feet. Explain that the man is supposed to look sleazy and unreliable and that he is probably a scam operator, running a business that may not be quite legal. You may want to use this picture as a point of departure for a brief discussion on behavior that different cultures find rude or offensive. Remind students to express their opinions respectfully.

Unit 9 objectives

Procedure:

➤ Tell students that sometimes objectives relate to knowledge gained and sometimes to skills acquired. Ask students to read the objectives and write an S next to the skills and a K next to the knowledge-based objectives.

➤ Have each student identify the objective that he or she thinks will be hardest to meet. Write 1 through 8 on the board to indicate the objectives. Read the objectives aloud and have students raise their hands for the one that seems most difficult. Tally the results next to each objective.

➤ Some of these objectives may be treated differently in other cultures. Allow students to discuss how their home cultures view the borrowing and lending of money.

➤ Refer students to objective 6. Tell them that the picture shows a work-at-home scheme. Note that the word *scheme* often has a negative connotation, implying something manipulative or dishonest.

(continued on p. 2)

Lesson Plan, Unit 9: Preview and practical conversations (for Student pages 113-115)–*continued*

Model 1

Content: borrowing money from a friend, giving a reason, committing to repay, ways to agree or decline

Procedure:

🎧 A–B.

▶ Before students listen and read, ask *What would you do if you got to work and discovered you had left your money at home?* Elicit attitudes about borrowing and lending money at work. Discuss possible solutions to the problem.

▶ To set the scene for the conversation, ask questions about the photo, such as *Where are these people?* (in an office, at work) *What do you think their relationship is?* (co-workers) *What is happening?* (The man is giving the woman money.) *Why do you think he is giving her money?* (maybe he is returning a loan, maybe she is borrowing money)

▶ After students listen to the conversation, check comprehension by asking questions such as *What does the woman want?* (to borrow $10) *Why?* (She left her wallet at home.) *Does the man lend her the money?* (yes)

▶ Before students repeat the lines, tell them that although native speakers often say groups of words quickly, pauses at the end of sentences are also important. Ask them to focus on the number of sentences in each line of the conversation (2, 2, 2, 1). Then have students repeat, making sure to pause appropriately at the periods.

Option: Put students in pairs or small groups to discuss attitudes toward borrowing money. Ask them to list different people they would feel comfortable borrowing money from, such as a relative or a good friend. Then have students discuss how much money they would be willing to borrow from these people. Lead a class discussion to compare students' attitudes.

🎧 Ways to agree and decline

▶ Have students listen to and repeat the statements.

▶ Brainstorm other polite ways to agree and decline and write them on the board. Suggestions may include *Sure, You're in luck* and *Sorry, I don't have that much.*

▶ Tell students *A co-worker just asked me for $10, but I only have $8.* Point out that sometimes a middle option is appropriate: *I'm sorry, I don't have $10, but would $5 help?*

🎧 Vocabulary

▶ Have students listen to and repeat the reasons to borrow money from a friend.

▶ Brainstorm other reasons to borrow money. Prompt with *Why might you need money and not have it?* Elicit examples such as *I have to buy a book, I forgot my lunch, I lost my wallet.* Write students' ideas on the board.

C. Pair work...

▶ Note that Student B can either agree or decline to lend the money. If Student B declines, Student A does not say *Thanks so much. I'll pay you back tomorrow.* Brainstorm other responses Student A might make, such as *That's okay, Thanks anyway.* Discuss possibilities for Student B's last line, such as *I'm really sorry* or *Maybe Student C has cash today.*

▶ Model the conversation with a more advanced student. Play the role of Student A, demonstrating how to give a reason to borrow money, request a dollar amount, and respond appropriately to Student B's agreement or refusal.

▶ Have pairs practice the conversation, using reasons from the *Vocabulary* and the ways to agree or decline.

Option: Ask students what expressions they have heard for not having money. On the board write ideas such as *I'm broke, I'm tapped out, I'm strapped for cash, I'm low on funds.* In pairs, students can use these expressions in the conversation. They can also use them to practice declining invitations, as in this conversation:

A: Can you go to the movies tonight?

B: Sorry, I'm broke.

Workbook Link: Exercises 1, 2

(continued on p. 3)

Lesson Plan, Unit 9: Preview and practical conversations (for Student pages 113-115)–*continued*

Model 2

Content: sharing your wishes and dreams, offering advice on financial aid, wishes and dreams, ways to fund dreams that are hard to afford, *but* to connect ideas

Procedure:

🎧 A–B.

➤ After students listen to the conversation, check comprehension by asking questions such as *What does the woman on the left want to do?* (go to college) *What is the problem?* (It's so expensive.) *What does the woman on the right suggest?* (Her friend should apply for a scholarship.)

➤ Preview the grammar topic by saying *The woman on the left would love to go to college.* Then ask *What information contradicts her wish to go to college?* (It's so expensive.) *What key word tells you that the second part of the sentence contradicts the first?* (but)

➤ Remind students that *Why don't you* begins a negative question, but it is used to make a suggestion. Elicit examples of other ways to make a suggestion, such as *You could ...* or *You might....* An imperative can also be used to make a suggestion: *Just do it!*

➤ Tell students that the letter *o* can be pronounced in several different ways. In this conversation, the following words contain different vowel sounds: *love, college, don't,* and *do*. Have students repeat these words after you.

➤ Tell students to concentrate on saying the correct vowel sounds as they repeat the conversation.

🎧 Wishes and dreams

➤ Ask *What are wishes and dreams?* Elicit that both words express something that is wanted or hoped for.

➤ After students repeat the phrases in the book, elicit examples of their own wishes and dreams and write them on the board.

🎧 Vocabulary

➤ Make sure students understand the meaning of *scholarship, college loan, tuition assistance, credit union, finance,* and any other difficult terms.

Option: Have students work in small groups and tell a true story about using one of the ways to fund dreams.

C. Pair work ...

➤ Model the conversation with a more advanced student. Play the role of Student B to demonstrate choosing a way to fund dreams from the *Vocabulary*.

➤ In pairs, students practice the conversation.

➤ Circulate to offer help as needed.

Workbook Link: Exercises 3, 4, 5

➤ Do it yourself!

Procedure:

A. Complete the chart ...

➤ On the board, copy the chart from the book. Ask students if getting married is really free. Elicit or point out that although weddings can cost a lot of money, a simple civil ceremony can be had for the price of a marriage license, so it is practically free.

➤ Ask students to think about their wishes and dreams that require money and those that don't. Since it may be easier to think of wishes and dreams that cost money, brainstorm examples that are free, such as *I'd like to get in shape, spend more time with my family, get in touch with my old friends*.

➤ Working individually, students complete the chart in their books. Students can refer to the examples of wishes and dreams on the board or think of their own.

B. Discussion ...

➤ On one side of the board, write *The best things in life are free*. Ask students to explain this saying (really important things don't cost money) and offer examples, such as health, a positive outlook, good family relationships.

➤ On the other side of the board, write *You get what you pay for*. Ask students to explain this saying (things that have value also cost something) and offer examples, such as buying an appliance on sale that you can't get parts for. Elicit or point out that the two sayings are almost opposite in meaning.

➤ Put students in small groups to brainstorm other sayings on the same topic from their home cultures or from this one. Elicit examples and write them under one of sayings on the board; for example, *There's no such thing as a free lunch* and *Money is the root of all evil*.

➤ In small groups, students discuss which idea they agree with most and why.

LESSON PLAN, UNIT 9: PRACTICAL GRAMMAR *(for Student pages 116-117)*

Summary of Lesson Plan

▶ **PRESENTATION**
Practical grammar (Student pages 116-117)
Suggested teaching time: 60 minutes
Your actual teaching time: _____

▶ Practical grammar
(Student pages 116-117)

Suggested teaching time: 60 minutes
Your actual teaching time: _____

Common misspellings

Procedure:

▶ Write on the board the three example sentences using *two*, *too*, and *to*. Read the sentences aloud and circle the words *two*, *too*, and *to*. Ask *What's the meaning of each of these words?* Elicit that *two* is a number, *too* refers to added information, and *to* plus a base form is an infinitive.

▶ Tell students that *two*, *too*, and *to* are examples of homonyms, or words with the same sound but different meanings and usually different spellings. Because even native speakers can make mistakes with these words, students are going to study the spelling of some of the more common homonyms.

▶ Write on the board the three example sentences with *they're*, *it's*, and *you're*, but do not use the contracted forms: *They are writing a resume right now*, *It is 5:15*, *I hope you are happy here*. Tell students that if they can rewrite a sentence with a pronoun and a form of *be* then the term is a contraction and is spelled with an apostrophe. Model this pattern with by reading the sentences on the board with contractions (*They're*, *It's*, and *You're*).

▶ Write on the board *The book's cover is red* and *The books have red covers*. Elicit or point out the difference between *'s* (to show possession) and *s* (to make a noun plural). Remind students not to use an apostrophe to make a noun plural.

▶ Have volunteers read aloud each of the example sentences in the box. Make sure students understand the differences in meaning among the homonyms.

Option: Bring to class and hand out paragraphs from newspapers or magazines. Have students work in pairs to find examples of the homonyms they've studied here. Read the material beforehand to insure that the paragraphs contain enough examples.

A. Choose the correct word...

▶ Write the first example on the board, including the word choices below the line. Elicit the correct choice and write it in the blank. If necessary, focus students' attention on *they're* and ask them to try reading the sentence with the uncontracted form, *they are*.

▶ Working individually, students complete the sentences. Tell them to refer to the examples in the box if necessary.

▶ Review answers as a class.

Option: Spell check game. Divide the class into teams with three or four members each. Have each team create 12 different flashcards on which students write one of the homonyms. Read a sentence from the box or Exercise A that contains one of the homonyms: *They're writing a resume right now*. Student 1 from Team 1 holds up the correct flashcard when he or she hears the homonym: *they're*. Holding up the correct card earns 1 point. Student 1 from Team 2 responds to the next sentence, and so on, until everyone has had a turn. In a variation of this game, teams compete at the same time.

Challenge: Dictation. Each student dictates a sentence for the rest of the class to write. Have students use sentences from the box or Exercise A.

Challenge: Have students brainstorm other homonyms that cause confusion. Write them on the board and elicit or explain meanings. Students can add these words to the list in their books and include them in the *Option* and *Challenge* activities above.

Workbook Link: Exercise 6

(continued on p. 5)

Lesson Plan, Unit 9: Practical grammar (for Student pages 116-117)–*continued*

Connecting ideas with *but* and *so*

Procedure:

- Write on the board the following pairs of sentences: *I asked for money. They lent it to me* and *I asked for money. They didn't lend it to me*. Also write the three connecting words *and*, *but*, and *so*. Read the first pair aloud. Then ask students what word they would use to connect the sentences. Elicit *and* to join two sentences when the second sentence gives additional information. Rewrite the sentences as two connected clauses and include a comma: *I asked for money, and they lent it to me*.

- Repeat the procedure with the second pair of sentences. Elicit the connecting word *but* to connect two sentences when the second sentence gives contradictory information. Rewrite with a comma.

- Write this sentence from Model 2, page 115: *I'd love to go to college, but it's so expensive*. Point out the comma and the connecting word *but*. Ask *Why do we connect these two sentences with "but"?* Elicit the fact that the second sentence gives contradictory information. Remind students of the earlier discussion.

- Write on the board a third pair of example sentences: *They didn't give me the loan. I borrowed the money from my family*. Repeat the procedure. Elicit the connecting word *so* to connect two sentences when the second sentence gives a result. Rewrite with a comma.

- Ask *What is a sentence?* Elicit that a sentence has a subject and a verb and expresses a complete thought. Ask *What is a clause?* Remind students that a clause is like a sentence in that it has a subject and a verb, but that it is part of a larger sentence. You may want to review the discussion of clauses and sentences in Unit 5. Have the students read the information in the box.

- Point out the comma before *and*, *but*, and *so*. Note that even educated writers sometimes omit the comma. The use of the comma also varies depending on the style of writing; for example, it is often dropped in newspaper articles. Tell students that they will practice connecting sentences with *and*, *but*, and *so* and a comma.

B. Complete each sentence ...

- Write the first sentence on the board with the blank rule. Read it aloud and ask *Does the second clause introduce a result, or does it provide contradictory information?* Elicit that it is a result. Ask *Should we complete the sentence with "but" or "so"?* Elicit the answer *so* and write it on the line.

- Tell students to read each remaining sentence and decide if the second clause introduces a result or provides contradictory information. Then they can decide whether to use *but* or *so*.

- Working individually, students write the appropriate conjunction on the line.

- In pairs, students compare answers.

C. Complete each clause ...

- Write the first item on the board and read it aloud. Elicit possible completions such as *I'm going to take out a loan*, *I decided to buy a bicycle*.

- If necessary, remind students what a clause is (it is like a sentence in that it has a subject and a verb, but that it is part of a larger sentence). Make sure students know when to use *but* and *so* (to introduce a contradiction; to introduce a result).

- Students complete the sentences by writing original clauses that tell a result or provide contradictory information.

- In pairs, students read their sentences.

Workbook Link: Exercises 7, 8

▶ Do it yourself!

Procedure:

A-B.

- Write on the board the two following sentences: *I'd like central air conditioning*, *I'd like to get married*, and the conjunctions *but* and *so*. Ask volunteers to add a clause beginning with *but* or *so* to one of the sentences. Students may offer *I'd like central air conditioning, but I can't afford it* or *I'd like to get married, so I'm dating a lot of new people*.

- Tell students to look at the chart on page 115 that they completed with their own wishes and dreams. Have them write each wish or dream on a separate line. Then have them add to each one a clause beginning with *so* that expresses a result or a clause beginning with *but* that expresses contradictory information.

- In pairs, students read their sentences.

Challenge: An extended conversation. After Student A reads a sentence, Student B responds appropriately, as if in a conversation. For example, if Student A says *I want to renovate my house, but it's very expensive*, Student B might respond *Why don't you take out a loan?* Have students continue the conversation with as many exchanges as possible.

Workbook Link: Exercises 9, 10

LESSON PLAN, UNIT 9: AUTHENTIC PRACTICE 1 & 2 (for Student pages 118-121)

Summary of Lesson Plan

▶ **PRESENTATION**
Authentic practice 1 & 2:
Listening (Student pages 118-121)
Suggested teaching time: 60 minutes
 includes Language Notes (10 minutes)
Your actual teaching time: _____

▶ Authentic practice 1
(Student pages 118-119)

Suggested teaching time: 30 minutes
Your actual teaching time: _____

Work-at-home schemes

Procedure:

🎧

➤ Before students open their books, ask if they have ever heard of jobs where employees can work at home. Elicit examples of jobs such as telemarketing and stuffing envelopes. Point out that sometimes a reputable company allows employees to work from home on the computer. This arrangement differs from a typical work-at-home scheme because it is a flexible benefit rather than a condition of employment.

➤ Have students open their books and read the bar. Point out that *schemes* here has a negative meaning.

➤ Have students read along silently as they listen to the conversation. Then check comprehension by asking questions such as *What's the name of the man's company?* (Get Rich Quick Inc.) *Does the company seem profitable and well run?* (no) *Why not?* (It's in a room and not an office, the wall is peeling, there are paint cans on the floor, the man is dressed sloppily) *Does the woman take the job immediately?* (no) *Why not?* (She wants to think about paying $2500 to get started.)

➤ Discuss the meanings of any unfamiliar terms such as *make your own hours, beats, right up my alley, got it, zap, start-up fee, put you down, on second thought, never mind, suit yourself.*

A. **Read the picture story again...**
➤ Have students write complete sentences in response to the questions. Ask volunteers to read their answers aloud.

Option: Have two or more students write their answers on the board. Check content as a class. Review capitalization and punctuation as well.

B. **Vocabulary...**
➤ Model the exercise. Read the first item aloud. Ask *What phrase do I have to define?* (in your free time). Have students read the two responses. Ask *Which response means in your free time?* (when you're not working) Remind students to indicate their answers by filling in the ovals.

➤ Working individually, students complete the remaining seven items, including those on page 119.

➤ Have students compare answers with a partner.

Option: Have students work in pairs to create original conversations that begin with the first line in each item. Students add an appropriate rejoinder, as in the following example:

A: Earn extra cash in your free time!

B: Well, what do I have to do?

As a variation, students can create extended conversations that include the first line.

If your students are ready...

Language note: The phrase *work-at-home* is hyphenated because it is a phrasal modifier, meaning that the whole phrase together conveys one idea that modifies the noun *scheme*. It requires hyphens between each word in the phrase. A phrasal modifier is different from a string of adjectives, each of which modifies a noun: *an interesting, productive computer job.* In this example, the job is interesting and productive and in the field of computers. The three modifiers give three different pieces of information. On the other hand, the modifier *work-at-home* conveys only one idea about the job—the employee works at home. You can ask students to find these other phrasal modifiers in the story: *sign-making (job, machine), start-up (fee).*

(continued on p. 7)

Book 4 Lesson Plans

Lesson Plan, Unit 9: Authentic practice 1 & 2 (for Student pages 118-121)–*continued*

C. Critical thinking...

➤ Have students read the questions and then look at the picture story again.

➤ Working individually, students answer the questions.

➤ In small groups, students discuss the pros and cons of the job offer. Have them create a table to list advantages and disadvantages. See the example below for possible entries.

Advantages	Disadvantages
Work at home Set your own hours Could make $12.50 to $15/hour	Start-up cost of $2500 May not make a good wage because you don't work fast enough Equipment might be messy and need a lot of space No benefits Pushy manager

➤ When students have finished their charts, write their ideas in a similar chart on the board. Ask *Do you think the woman should take the job?*

Challenge: In this two-part activity, students first write a letter to *Ask Joan* asking for advice on this job opportunity. Remind students to include the information from the picture story. When finished, students exchange letters with a partner. In response, partners write a letter of advice from Joan. Partners should refer to some of the disadvantages listed in their charts.

Workbook Link: Exercises 11, 12

➤ Do it yourself!

Procedure:

A. Write your own response...

➤ Have students look at the pictures of the man on the phone. Point out that since the same person appears in all three pictures, this is meant to be one consecutive conversation.

➤ Read the first speech balloon. Ask *Who do you think this person is?* (a scam operator, a sleazy business person) *What do you think of the start-up fee?* (It's not "low," The amount makes me suspicious.)

➤ Working individually, students write responses to each of the speech balloons. Have them compare responses with a partner.

➤ In pairs, students read their conversations out loud.

B. Discussion...

➤ Read the first question in the directions. Remind students that *scheme* has a negative connotation and suggests a business that is not altogether legal.

➤ Elicit examples of work-at-home schemes such as telemarketing and stuffing envelopes. Point out that usually such jobs are based on piecework, that is, workers get paid for how many pieces of work are finished, not how long they work. Ask students if they think this is a good way to pay people.

➤ Ask students if they have ever had such a job or if they know someone who has. Put students in small groups to discuss the terms of any work-at-home schemes they know about and whether or not they decided to get involved. Have students give reasons for their decision.

Option: Have students look for work-at-home notices in local magazines and newspapers as well as in flyers and brochures. Ask them to bring in the notices or copy the information. They can also report on phone solicitations they have received for work-at-home possibilities. Have students note the type of work, what costs must be paid up front, and other terms of the offers.

(continued on p. 8)

Lesson Plan, Unit 9: Authentic practice 1 & 2 (for Student pages 118-121)–*continued*

Authentic practice 2
(Student pages 120-121)

Suggested teaching time: 30 minutes
Your actual teaching time: _____

Loans

Procedure:

🎧 A–B.

➤ Point to the handwritten note and ask *What is this?* Elicit that it is an IOU, which stands for I owe you. It is a note that says the writer promises to repay money. *Who would you write an IOU to?* (a friend, a co-worker, a relative) Make sure students understand that writing an IOU is a way we commit to repaying a personal loan. It is more formal than a verbal promise.

➤ Ask questions about the other two documents, such as *What information is given on the Metro Credit Union document?* (consumer loan rates, car loan rates) *What does the other document promise?* (cash until payday)

➤ Make sure students know that a credit union is an organization that people can join, often at a workplace. One of the benefits a credit union offers to its members is loans at low interest rates. Tell students they will learn more about credit unions on the next page.

➤ Tell students that they are going to listen to three short conversations about money.

➤ After students have listened the first time, have them read the statements in Exercise B. As they listen the second time, have them check the appropriate boxes for each conversation. If necessary, have students read the statements for only one conversation at a time, and then have them listen to just that conversation.

Option: Have pairs of students rewrite the false statements to make them true.

Challenge: Have students take notes during the listening. As a way of supporting their answers, they should write down as much of the conversation as they can that relates to each statement. For example, next to item 1 under Conversation 1, students might write *I really appreciate your lending me this cash on such short notice, George.* After students have listened to the three conversations, elicit examples of the notes, and ask how the information pertains to the statement. Students might say, for example, that George lent the money, not a bank, and that using the first name implies a personal relationship.

FYI...

Option: If students have access to the Internet, assign each pair of students two to three terms from the glossary. Have them make notes on the glossary definitions, put them into their own words, and share the information with the class.

Tapescript

Conversation 1

Man 1: I really appreciate your lending me this cash on such short notice, George. It came right in the nick of time. I can pay you back by the end of February. Is that all right?

Man 2: Sure, no problem. But I'd feel more comfortable if you'd sign an IOU. Amelia would never forgive me if I didn't ask you for one.

Man 1: Absolutely. I understand. *My* wife would feel the same way. How should we do this?

Man 2: I could draft a note. Look it over and see if you agree to the terms. OK?

Man 1: Good plan.

Conversation 2

Woman: What kind of loan rates can we get at the Credit Union?

Man: The Credit Union—good idea! I'll check. Credit unions are usually fairer than dealers. What's the Web address?

Woman: Metro.cu.org/rates.

Man: OK. Here it is. Not bad. Have a look.

Woman: That <u>is</u> pretty good. Much better than the rates in this car ad.

Conversation 3

Man: You need some fast cash?

Woman: You bet. And my credit's not great. What should I do?

Man: You can always get a payday loan. There's this place that advertises, on the corner of First and Elm. Easy, fast. Why don't you pass by and see about a loan?

Woman: Are you sure? There must be some catch. Something that looks too good to be true usually is.

(continued on p. 9)

Lesson Plan, Unit 9: Authentic practice 1 & 2 (for Student pages 118-121)–*continued*

C. Read the information...

➤ Scanning for specific information is an important academic skill. Before students read about credit unions and payday loans, write several questions on the board. You can use the ones listed below or create your own. Remind students that when they scan, they are looking for key words that will help them locate specific pieces of information. Often phrases in the question itself are repeated in the sentence where the information can be found.

1. What is a <u>credit union</u>?
2. <u>How many people</u> are <u>served</u> by credit unions?
3. How can you <u>join</u> a credit union?
4. What is <u>a payday loan</u>?
5. Is <u>this kind of credit</u> cheap?
6. What are some other <u>names</u> for <u>payday loans</u>?

➤ Organizing information from readings in charts and tables is another important academic skill. After students read about the two topics, have them summarize the information with bulleted items. To review as a class, put a similar table on the board and elicit students' ideas. See the following table for an example.

CREDIT UNIONS	PAYDAY LOANS
Nonprofit financial institutions	Small, short-term, high-rate loans
Owned and run by members	Very expensive rates
Safe, reasonable	Also called cash advance loans, check post-dated check loans, deferred deposit check loans
Serve a specific community	

➤ To encourage critical thinking, ask *If you needed a loan, where would you rather go, to a credit union or a place that offered payday loans? Why?*

Option: In pairs, students underline all the adjectives used to describe the two different services. Elicit examples and write them on the board. Your lists should resemble the following: <u>Credit union:</u> nonprofit, cooperative, financial, safe, reasonable. <u>Payday loans:</u> small, short-term, high-rate, expensive.

D. True story...

➤ Tell students that there are many types of loans—some informal, some formal contracts. Put students in pairs to talk about any experience they have had borrowing money. They can use these questions as prompts: *Did you borrow from a financial institution or a person? How long did you have to pay the money back? What kind of fee or interest did you have to pay on the loan? Was it a good experience? What kind of advice would you give about borrowing money?* If students are comfortable sharing this information, they can also say how much money they borrowed.

➤ Lead a class discussion about borrowing money, drawing on students' experience. Ask questions such as *Who borrowed money from friends or relatives? Who took out a bank loan? What advice would you give someone who needed to borrow money?*

Workbook Link: Exercises 13, 14, 15

➤ Do it yourself!

Procedure:

A-B.

➤ Put students in pairs or small groups to answer the two questions. Tell them to support their opinions with reasons and examples. Encourage students to jot down their ideas on a separate sheet of paper.

➤ Then put students in small groups that include people from different countries. Have them compare and contrast borrowing and lending customs in their home countries and in this one.

Option: Have each small group make a list of situations when it is not a good idea to borrow money. Then have groups share their ideas with the whole class.

Challenge: Have students present the findings from their discussion in a chart or Venn diagram. In a chart, they should list the countries across the top and the various features down the left column. If they decide to use a Venn diagram, they should compare only two or three countries at a time.

LESSON PLAN, UNIT 9: AUTHENTIC PRACTICE 3 (for Student pages 122-123)

Summary of Lesson Plan

▶ **PRESENTATION**
Authentic practice 3:
Reading and critical thinking (Student pages 122-123)
Suggested teaching time: 60 minutes
Your actual teaching time: _____

▶ Authentic practice 3
(Student pages 122-123)

Suggested teaching time: 60 minutes
Your actual teaching time: _____

Note: For the plan-ahead project on page 123, ask students to bring in car ads and ads for credit and for work-at-home opportunities. Suggest that students look in magazines and newspapers.

"Neither a borrower nor a lender be."

Procedure:

A. Read and listen to the letters.

➤ Have students read the bar. Ask them to rephrase the quotation in their own words; for example, Don't borrow or lend money. Ask *Do you agree or disagree with the advice?* Have students give reasons to support their opinions. Ask *What do the quotation marks tell us?* Elicit that this is quoted speech, somebody's actual words. Tell students that it is a quotation from *Hamlet*, a play by Shakespeare.

➤ After students read and listen to the letters, check comprehension by asking questions such as *What is Shelly's problem?* (A co-worker keeps borrowing money and doesn't pay it back.) *What does Joan advise her to do?* (Tell the co-worker how much she owes and ask for the money.) *What is Gus's problem?* (He took out a payday loan.) *What are some loan options that the FTC suggests?* (a credit union loan, a pay advance, a loan from family or friends, a cash advance on a credit card, a business loan from a local community-based organization)

➤ Explain any unfamiliar terms such as *be short a dollar or two, take the bull by the horns, exorbitant, cash advance*. Pronounce the word *stingy* and explain if necessary. Make sure students know what a *budget* is (a plan for spending money).

Challenge: In developing academic reading skills, students need to answer interpretive or critical thinking questions as well as literal questions. A literal question asks for information that is directly stated in the reading, such as *Are the people in Shelly's office all of the same nationality?* (No. There are a lot of people of different nationalities.) Interpretive questions ask for information that is implied in the reading, such as *Do you think Shelly has trouble refusing to loan Jenna money?* (Yes. Shelly continues to lend Jenna money even though Shelly feels angry inside and doesn't enjoy the lunches anymore.) Ask students to write one literal question and one critical thinking question about the letters. Have students exchange questions with a partner and discuss the answers.

B. Role play ...

➤ Put students in pairs. Let them decide who will play the borrower and the lender. Have them create two conversations, one in which the borrower agrees to repay the loan and another in which the borrower doesn't repay. Refer students to the conversation on page 114 for suggestions.

➤ Circulate to help students with their conversations.

➤ Have volunteers perform their role play for the class.

C. Discussion ...

➤ As a class, brainstorm different ways of getting money. Refer students to the documents on page 120 and to the boxed information in the *Ask Joan* column.

➤ In small groups, students discuss the advantages and disadvantages of different ways of getting money.

Option: Put students in groups of four and assign each group one way of getting money, such as a bank loan, a credit-union loan, a credit card advance, tuition assistance, or a car loan. Tell students that group members must each have a role: facilitator, recorder, reporter on advantages, and reporter on disadvantages. When students have completed their discussions, have groups present the pros and cons of the methods they discussed.

Workbook Link: Exercises 16, 17

(continued on p. 11)

Lesson Plan, Unit 9: Authentic practice 3 (for Student pages 122-123)–*continued*

➤ Do it yourself!
(A plan-ahead project) (Student page 123)

Procedure:

A. Read the ads.

➤ After students have looked at the ads, ask questions such as *Which work-at-home opportunity pays a better rate?* ($5 for every envelope) *Is the interest rate higher on a 15-year loan or a 30-year loan?* (the 30-year loan) *How much is the Honda Accord?* ($15,495 or $17,060 with all its equipment)

➤ Elicit or tell students that a *SASE* is a self-addressed stamped envelope. Ask *Why should you send a self-addressed stamped envelope?* (to receive more information) Explain any terms or abbreviations that are difficult or unfamiliar.

B–C.

➤ Ask students to take out the car ads and ads for credit and for work-at-home opportunities they found in magazines and newspapers. Contribute some of your own as well.

➤ Assign students to groups depending on the type of ad they brought in: all the car ads in one group, the ads for credit in another, and the ads for work-at-home opportunities in a third. If necessary, subdivide groups so that there are only five members in each group.

➤ Have groups create two lists, one for elements of the ads that are similar and one for elements that are different.

➤ Create new groups of three students consisting of a member from each of the original groups (one car ad, one credit ad, one work-at-home opportunity). Have group members tell about typical features of the ads they studied.

Option: Based on their ad research, have pairs or small groups create a car ad, an ad for credit, or an ad for a work-at-home opportunity. Have them first discuss the elements that make each type of ad attractive, eye-catching, or interesting.

Your notes

Copyright © 2004 by Pearson Education, Inc.
All rights reserved.

LESSON PLAN, UNIT 9: REVIEW (for Student pages 124-126)

Summary of Lesson Plan

➤ **Review (Student pages 124-126)**
Suggested teaching time: 60 minutes
Your actual teaching time: _____

➤ **UNIT REVIEW**
Includes expansion activities
- role play
- dialogues
- writing
- Workbook activities
- outside reading
- realia applications
- math skills applications
- civic lesson applications
- Booster Pak activities

➤ **Review (Student pages 124-126)**

Suggested teaching time: 60 minutes
Your actual teaching time: _____

Procedure:

A. Pair work or group work.

Ask and answer questions.

➤ Ask the class general questions about the pictures, such as *What do you think the women in the restaurant are talking about?* (the bill, a loan) *What kind of ad is on the bus stop wall?* (an ad for a work-at-home scheme) *What do you think the woman at the bottom left is doing?* (getting a payday loan) *What is the man at the bottom right filling out?* (a credit union membership application)

➤ For each picture, have partners take turns answering these questions: *What is happening? What are the people doing?*

Challenge: Divide the class into two teams. Tell the teams that they must create questions about the pictures using the following question words: *why, where, who, what,* and *when.* They should write three questions for each question word. Elicit one or two examples and write them on the board, such as *Why is the woman on the right in the top picture holding some money? Where is the man filling out an application?* Collect all the questions. In random order, ask the questions, alternating between the two teams. Each correct answer gets 1 point.

Create conversations.

➤ Have pairs number the speech balloons and, on a separate sheet of paper, write one line of conversation for each person in the pictures. Then have students read their lines aloud for the rest of the class to guess who is speaking.

Option: In pairs, students create conversations for each of the four interactions pictured. Have volunteers read one of the conversations aloud.

Option: Have pairs choose one of the pictures and create an extended conversation for the characters.

Challenge: Assign half the class the role of the borrower in the top picture and half the role of the lender. Allow students a few minutes to look back through the unit for ideas. Then have students stand up and form two concentric circles, with the students on the inside playing the role of the lender and the students on the outside playing the role of the borrower. Students face each other, pair up, and have a conversation. After a minute, the "borrowers" walk to their right, pairing up with the new "lender," who is one student down from the previous partner. These two students then have a conversation. Repeat until all students have had an opportunity to practice the conversation with several partners. After students have practiced with two partners, you can change the scenario and have the lender ask for the money back.

Tell a story.

Option: One-minute speech. Assign each student one of the pictures. Give students several minutes to look at the picture and review ideas from the unit. Each student must then describe what is going on in the picture, talking for one minute if possible.

Option: Create a character. Have students choose one person in the pictures and tell what he or she is doing and thinking at the moment. Have students imagine a reason why the character might need extra money.

Option: Fortuneteller. Ask students to choose one of the four situations and predict what will happen in the future.

(continued on p. 13)

Lesson Plan, Unit 9: Review (for Student pages 124-126)–*continued*

🎧 B. Listening comprehension...

➤ Tell students that they are going to hear two speakers talk about financial matters.

➤ After listening, students work individually to write advice to each of the speakers.

➤ In pairs, they compare answers.

Challenge: Have students create their own statements about a money problem, and then read their statements to a partner. The partners offer advice orally or in writing.

C–D.

➤ Students work individually to complete the review exercises.

➤ Circulate to offer help as needed.

➤ Have students check answers with a partner. Review answers as a class.

➤ Identify any areas of difficulty that may require additional instruction and practice.

Tapescript

1. **Male:** Look at this ad for making flags! "Work your own hours, in the comfort of your own home!" How hard could *that* be?

2. **Female:** I saw this great deal on a used computer, and I can buy it for only four hundred dollars! The original cost was eleven hundred and ninety-nine dollars! The problem is I don't have that kind of money. I think I'll get a payday loan.

(continued on p. 14)

Your notes

Lesson Plan, Unit 9: Review (for Student pages 124-126)–*continued*

E–G.

➤ Students work individually to complete the review exercises.

➤ Circulate to offer help as needed.

➤ Have students check answers with a partner. Review answers as a class.

➤ Identify any areas of difficulty that may require additional instruction and practice.

Challenge: For Exercise E, have students write a new ending for the sentences. They should use the other conjunction and an original clause. For example, students might rewrite item 1 as *Joan advised Gus not to borrow money from a check-cashing business, but he did it anyway.*

H. Composition...

➤ Provide students with concrete approaches to writing about the picture on page 124. Use one of the options that follow, give students a choice of options, or assign options based on students' levels of proficiency. Model what is expected of students for each option.

➤ Advise students to look back through the unit for help and ideas as they write.

➤ Circulate to offer help as needed.

Option: Students write a description, in paragraph form, of what happened in one of the pictures. The paragraph should have at least five sentences. One of the sentences should use *but* and one should use *so*. Remind students to indent the first sentence and to use correct punctuation and capitalization.

Option: Students write an IOU for the woman borrowing money in the first picture. They can follow the model on page 120 and make up names for the two women.

Option: Students write an extended conversation between any two speakers in the pictures. Refer them to the conversation on page 114 for format and ideas.

Challenge: Students write down the information they think would be asked for on a loan application.

Now I can

➤ Read the first item in the box out loud: *Now I can borrow money from a friend or co-worker.* Elicit from the class an example, such as *I'm out of cash. Do you think you could lend me $5?*

➤ Put students in pairs. Tell students to take turns reading each item in the box and giving an example of what they have learned. When students can provide an example, they should check that objective. If there are items students aren't able to check, have them look back through the unit for ideas.

➤ When students are finished reviewing with their partners, read each item out loud and elicit an example from the class.

Oral test (optional)

You may want to use the *Now I can* box as an informal evaluation. While students are working on the *Composition* activity, you can call them up individually and check their ability with two or three objectives.

Your notes

LESSON PLAN, UNIT 10: PREVIEW/PRACTICAL CONVERSATIONS (for Student pages 127-129)

Summary of Lesson Plan

➤ **Preview and Practical conversations** (Student pages 127-129)
Suggested teaching time: 60 minutes
Your actual teaching time: _____

➤ **Preview and Practical conversations** (Student pages 127-129)

Suggested teaching time: 60 minutes
Your actual teaching time: _____

Warm up. Look at the resume. What's the purpose of a resume?

Procedure:

➤ Before students open their books, brainstorm initial contacts with a potential employer. If necessary, prompt with questions such as *When does a potential employer have the first contact with you? What are some ways an employer can form an impression of you?* Elicit responses, including *a phone inquiry, an application form, a resume, an interview.* List students' ideas on the board.

➤ Brainstorm ways to create a good impression through each of the contacts listed on the board. You may end up with a list like this one.

A phone inquiry: Be polite; get all the necessary information
An application form: Be neat, thorough, and truthful; spell words correctly
A resume: Be neat and clear; use good grammar and spelling; tailor the resume to the job
An interview: Be punctual, well-groomed, prepared, and polite; ask good questions; answer questions completely

➤ Have students open their books. Read the *Warm up* question and elicit responses. Make sure students know that *a resume* is a summary of a person's work and educational experience. Writing a resume is generally part of a job application process.

➤ Ask students what Carlos Sinkoff has included on his resume. They should respond with the resume headings *objective, summary of qualifications, strengths, work experience, education,* and *references.*

➤ Note that the word *resume* is spelled like the verb *resume,* but it is pronounced *rayzumay,* because it was originally a French word. Students may also see the word spelled with accent marks: *résumé.*

Challenge: Working individually, students create questions about the information covered on the resume. They should phrase the questions as if they were addressing Carlos Sinkoff; for example, *What kind of education do you have?* Or *Can you tell me about your educational background?* Review questions briefly and then put students in pairs to take turns asking and answering the questions.

Challenge: Have students research various methods of getting a job. Students with Internet access can check resume-posting Web sites such as monster.com. Other class members can investigate the free resources at the public library, such as resume and interviewing workshops, the classified section of the local paper, and computers with word-processing and resume-writing programs. Have students share their findings with the class.

Unit 10 objectives

Procedure:

➤ Have students read the objectives.

➤ Have students count off by 6 (the number of objectives). Direct all the 1s to one area of the room, 2s to another, and so on, until six groups have formed. Ask groups to list steps they would follow in meeting that objective. For example, the 1s might include *Look into other job opportunities by checking the classified ads.* Ask groups to put their lists on transparencies or big sheets of paper. Then have the groups present their ideas. Save the transparencies or sheets to refer to at the end of the unit.

Workbook Link: Exercises 1, 2

(continued on p. 2)

Lesson Plan, Unit 10: Preview and practical conversations (for Student pages 127-129)–*continued*

Model 1

Content: applying for a better job, reasons to apply for a better job, resume excerpts

Procedure:

A-B.

► To set the scene for the conversation, ask students questions about the photo, such as *Where are the two speakers?* (in an office) *Whose office is it?* (the woman's) *How do you know?* (The phone is facing her, She is writing.) *Why do you think the man is in her office?* (Maybe he's a co-worker or a job applicant.)

► After students read and listen to the conversation, check comprehension by asking questions such as *What questions does the interviewer ask?* (How long have you been in your current job? Why do you want to change jobs?) *Why does the job applicant want a new job?* (He's completed his degree, and he's ready for a bigger challenge.)

► Tell students that we often alternate strongly stressed syllables with more weakly stressed ones. The longer sentences in this conversation have a distinctive rhythm that students should try to attune their ears to.

► Ask students to listen to the conversation again and put a dot above each syllable. They should use a small dot for a weakly stressed syllable and a large dot for a strongly stressed syllable.

► Write the sentences in the conversation on the board. Read each sentence and elicit information about the stress of each syllable. Place an appropriately sized dot above each syllable. Finally, have students repeat the sentences after you.

Ideas

► After students listen and repeat, brainstorm other reasons to apply for a better job, such as *a better schedule* or *the opportunity to learn new skills*. Write the ideas on the board.

Option: Have students rewrite the ideas using clauses introduced by *but* (item 5) or *so* (items 1, 2, 3). They will have to rewrite item 4 to use a clause with *but*.

C. Pair work...

► Have students read the four resume excerpts.

► Ask students to assume the role of one of the four job applicants. Give them time to think of answers to the following questions: *How long have you been in your current job? Why do you want to change jobs? What are your career goals?*

► Model the conversation with a more advanced student. Play the role of Student B, the job applicant, to demonstrate giving a reason to apply for a better job.

► In pairs, students practice the conversation, first giving reasons for one of the job applicants and then for themselves.

Challenge: Working in pairs, students extend the conversation to include more of the job interview. As a class, first brainstorm questions the interviewer might ask. Then, alternating the roles of the interviewer and the applicant, students role-play a job interview. They can answer for themselves or assume the role of one of the four applicants.

(continued on p. 3)

Your notes

Lesson Plan, Unit 10: Preview and practical conversations (for Student pages 127-129)–*continued*

Model 2

Content: telling your employer about a job offer; getting a counteroffer; telling someone about a hard choice; perks, benefits, and other features of good jobs

Procedure:

A–B.

- To set the scene for the conversation, ask questions about the photo, such as *Where are the two speakers?* (in an office) *Whose office do you think it is?* (the man's) *Why do you think so?* (The woman is entering, He's behind the desk.)

- Discuss appropriate ways to enter a co-worker's or supervisor's office. Elicit ideas such as *Knock, say "Excuse me," and ask if you can interrupt.*

- After students read and listen to the conversation, check comprehension by asking questions such as *What does Oliva want to talk about?* (a job offer) *Does John want her to leave?* (No. He asks if there is some way they can get her to stay.) *What is better about the other position?* (The salary is much higher.)

- Before listening to the conversation again and repeating, tell students to listen for the stressed words and syllables. Then have them mark the text with a large dot for a strongly stressed syllable and a smaller dot for a weakly stressed syllable, as they did for Model 1.

Telling someone about a hard choice

- Students listen to and repeat ways to tell someone about a hard choice.

- Read the conversation with the class playing the role of Student B. Play the role of Student A and substitute one of the ways to tell someone about a hard choice.

Vocabulary

- Tell students that *a perk* is a benefit or advantage. It is a short form of the word *perquisite*.

- Have students listen and repeat.

- Brainstorm other features of good jobs and write them on the board, such as *more flexibility* or *a better schedule*.

Option: Have students rank the perks, benefits, and other features of good jobs from 1 to 6. Let 1 be the most important feature to them. Put students in small groups to discuss the reasons for their rankings.

C. Pair work...

- Model the conversation with a more advanced student. Play the role of Student A. Demonstrate telling someone about a hard choice and describing a perk or benefit. Choose a feature from the *Vocabulary* box or from the list on the board.

- Have pairs practice the conversation, alternating the roles of Students A and B. Make sure they first choose names for the characters.

Workbook Link: Exercises 3, 4

▶ Do it yourself!

Procedure:

- Have students refer to page 128 to see how the job seekers in Exercise C set up their resumes.

- Explain that a *draft* is a first attempt at writing something. A draft for a resume needs to be rewritten in order to include all relevant details under the appropriate headings; to polish the wording; and to check spelling, capitalization, and punctuation.

- Copy the form from the book on the board and fill it out for yourself. Read the information aloud and answer any questions about format.

- Tell students to begin their own resumes by writing their names on the top line. In the first slot on the second line, they should write the month and year or just the year that they began their current job.

- Note that *to present* on a resume indicates that the job applicant is still employed in that same capacity at that same company. If students are no longer working, they should adapt the form as follows: 2000 (the year they began) *to* 2003 (the year they stopped working).

- In the remaining space, students write their position, the company, and the company address.

Option: In pairs, students ask and answer questions about their resumes, such as *How long have you worked there? What is your present position?*

LESSON PLAN, UNIT 10: PRACTICAL GRAMMAR (for Student pages 130–131)

Summary of Lesson Plan

▶ **PRESENTATION**
Practical grammar (Student pages 130-131)
Suggested teaching time: 60 minutes
includes Language Note (10 minutes)
Your actual teaching time: _____

▶ Practical grammar
(Student pages 130-131)

Suggested teaching time: 60 minutes
Your actual teaching time: _____

The past unreal conditional

Procedure:

▶ Review with students the information on unreal conditional sentences from Unit 5. Put on the board a series of unreal conditions; for example, *If I wanted to save money, If I paid my bills on time*. Brainstorm result clauses and write students' ideas on the board, making sure to use *would*; for example, *I would buy a used car, I wouldn't have to pay a late fee*. Ask *Are these real situations?* (no) Tell students that unreal conditional sentences express hypothetical or imaginary situations.

▶ Tell students that we can explain the consequences of unreal conditions in the past using the past unreal conditional. Write on the board *If I had wanted to save money, I would have bought a used car; If I had paid my bills on time, I wouldn't have had to pay a late fee*. Underline *had* and the past participle in the *if* clause and *would have* and the past participle in the result clause.

▶ Focus students' attention by asking questions such as *What verb form do we use in the "if" clause?* (had + past participle) *What verb form do we use in the result clause?* (would have + past participle).

▶ Reread the sentences on the board, giving the result clause first. Remind students that the order of the clauses does not change the meaning. However, when the *if* clause comes first, it is separated from the result clause by a comma.

▶ Have students read the information in the box. Create other examples of past unreal conditions and write them on the board. Use these clauses or your own: *If I had applied for the job, If the company had gotten your resume, If she had completed her degree*.

Have students suggest clauses to complete the sentences, making sure to use *would have* or *could have* plus a past participle in the result clause.

A. Distinguish ...

▶ Have students read item 1. Ask *Did Al leave?* (no) *Did they offer him an opportunity to advance?* (yes) Tell students to fill in the first oval because that statement is closer in meaning to the underlined *if* clause.

▶ Tell students that in this exercise the underlined *if* clauses express something that didn't happen. Tell them to select the statement that tells what did happen.

▶ Working individually, students complete the exercise. Have pairs compare answers, and then review as a class.

Option: A story about the past. To help students practice formation of the past unreal conditional, explain that you are going to tell a story about the past. After each sentence you say, students are to ask a question beginning with *What if*. Begin by saying *I went to college*. Elicit the question *What if you hadn't gone to college?* Give an answer such as *If I hadn't gone to college, I couldn't have become a teacher*. Continue this activity until students can ask *What if* questions quickly and accurately.

Challenge: Have students work in pairs to rewrite the sentences in Exercise A. In each item, the *if* clause should match the meaning they didn't choose. In item 1, for example, the sentence would read *Al wouldn't have left if they had offered him an opportunity to advance*.

B. Choose the correct forms ...

▶ Review with students the verb forms in past unconditional sentences: *had* + past participle in the *if* clause, *would / could have* + past participle in the result clause. For practice, have students identify the verb forms in Exercise A.

▶ Have students work individually to complete the exercise. Remind them that the exercise continues on page 131.

▶ After students have compared answers with a partner, review as a class. Ask students to support their verb form choices; for example, *In item 1, the situation described is unreal. It takes place in the past. I can't use "would have" in the "if" clause. Therefore the correct form is "had offered."*

(continued on p. 5)

Lesson Plan, Unit 10: Practical grammar (for Student pages 130-131)— *continued*

C. Complete each of the following...

- Complete item 1 with the class. Have students underline the *if* clause. Ask *What verb form is used?* (had + past participle). Ask *What verb form is used in the result clause?* (would / could have + past participle)
- Have students look through the remaining sentences and underline the *if* clauses. Remind them that *if* clauses in past conditional sentences use *had* + past participle and result clauses use *would / could have* + past participle.
- Working individually, students complete the sentences. Review as a class. Check that students completed the sentences with the past unreal forms since the sentences also make sense as present unreal conditionals.
- The last sentence is very challenging, and students may need help. Be sure students see the passive construction in the result clause. Compare the differences in items 5 and 6. Item 6 can serve as a model if students want to produce the passive in the *Do it yourself!* activity.

Option: You might wish to contrast the meaning of the following:
1. If she applied for that job, she would get it.
2. If she had applied for that job, she would have gotten it.

Elicit from students that the first implies a future consequence of a present condition. The second implies a past consequence of a past condition.

Option: Have students make the sentences negative: *If she hadn't applied for that job, she wouldn't have gotten it.*

If your students are ready...

Language note: Unreal past conditionals can also be formed using inversion rather than an *if* clause. It's not important for students to be able to manipulate this grammatical form, but they may hear it and should understand what it means. For example, item 1 in Exercise A on page 130 would appear as *Had they not offered him an opportunity to advance, Al would have left.* Item 2 could be rewritten *Had she known about the job in quality control, she would have taken it.* The meaning is the same, but the clause that states the condition is formed by inverting the auxiliary verb *had* and the subject. This is not a question formation but a different type of inverted form. The past unreal conditional expressed with inversion occurs in the last frame of the picture story on page 132.

Workbook Link: Exercises 5, 6

▶ Do it yourself!

Procedure:

A–B.

- Tell students that when we speculate we think about unreal situations—what might happen or might have happened.
- Model Exercise A with a sentence about yourself, such as *If my first language had not been English, I could have learned it in school.*
- Working individually, students complete the sentences. Students exchange sentences with a partner to check for the correct verb forms in the clauses.
- When students have finished, write the two *if* clauses as headings on the board.
- Students write their result clauses under the appropriate *if* clauses.
- Have the students read the sentences aloud.

Option: Put students in small groups to compare and contrast their result clauses. Elicit from each group the ways in which their speculations were similar or different.

Option: Brainstorm other life-changing or life-defining situations. Elicit ideas by asking *What events or conditions have determined the way your life has turned out?* Write these ideas on the board as *if* clauses; for example, *If I hadn't gotten married, If I hadn't gone to college, If I had been an only child.* Have students create endings for several of the sentences.

Workbook Link: Exercises 7, 8

LESSON PLAN, UNIT 10: AUTHENTIC PRACTICE 1 & 2 (for Student pages 132-135)

Summary of Lesson Plan

▶ **PRESENTATION**
Authentic practice 1 & 2:
Listening (Student pages 132-135)
Suggested teaching time: 60 minutes
    includes Cultural Discussion
Your actual teaching time: _____

▶ Authentic practice 1
(Student pages 132-133)

Suggested teaching time: 30 minutes
Your actual teaching time: _____

Consider a counteroffer.

Procedure:

▶ Help students focus their attention before they listen to the picture story. Write on the board questions such as *Why is Mike talking to Fred? What is Fred's reaction to Mike's news?* Tell students to listen for answers to these questions.

▶ With books still closed, have students listen to the picture story. If necessary, let them listen again.

▶ Elicit responses to the two questions on the board: *Mike wants to tell Fred he got another offer and is giving notice; Fred wants Mike to stay, so he makes a counteroffer.*

A. Check...

▶ Have students read the statements. Then have students read the picture story while they listen again.

▶ Some expressions may be unfamiliar to students. Have students find and circle *spring this on you, give you notice, it would be a shame, take my word, hang in there, no harm in trying*. Ask them to think of a different word or phrase for each of these. For example, instead of *Sorry to spring this on you*, you could say *Sorry to give you this unexpected news*.

▶ Ask students to locate the past unreal conditional in this story (frame 4: *Had we known ...*). Remind them that inverting *had* and the subject has the same meaning as an *if* clause in a past unreal conditional. If necessary, refer students to the *Language note* on page T131.

▶ Working individually, students check the appropriate boxes. Have students compare answers with a partner.

Option: Making inferences is an important academic skill. Have students identify the statements that require the reader to look beyond the literal information given in the story. For example, no one says that Mike's work is very good, but Fred says he's not surprised that Mike got another offer and that it would be a shame to lose him. From these statements, we can infer that Mike's work is good. For each statement that requires making inferences, ask students to cite the information in the story that led to their answers.

B. Listen...

▶ Play the cassette or read the tapescript.

▶ Students respond to the three items.

Option: Dictation. Have the students write each of the three items. Let them listen as many times as necessary to complete the activity.

C. Check the subjects...

▶ Make sure students complete the exercise on page 133.

▶ Students work individually to check the subjects discussed.

▶ For each topic discussed, students underline the supporting information in the story.

▶ In pairs, students check their answers.

Tapescript

1. Fred? Excuse the interruption. Have you got a minute?
2. It would be a shame to lose you.
3. Would you be willing to hang in there till the end of the day? I could get back to you by three.

(continued on p. 7)

Lesson Plan, Unit 10: Authentic practice 1 & 2 (for Student pages 132-135)–*continued*

D–E.

➤ Put students in pairs. Student A opens the book to page 133 while Student B listens with closed book.

➤ Student A reads each item. Student B responds appropriately.

➤ Student B opens to page 133, and pairs choose the appropriate responses together.

➤ In pairs, students take turns reading the items and the appropriate responses.

Option: Have students create original sentences or questions that could lead to the other responses. In item 1, for example, the question *Why do you want to leave?* could lead to the response *Forgive me for saying this, but* ...

Option: Give students time to review the responses, and then have them close their books. Read the items in random order and have students answer chorally with the appropriate response.

F. Critical thinking ...

➤ Working individually, students answer the question.

➤ Put students in small groups to compare answers. Ask students to discuss what contributes to job satisfaction. Have them create a list of these factors and reach a consensus on which two or three factors are most important.

➤ Lead a class discussion about what the groups decided were the most important factors in job satisfaction. Write their ideas on the board.

Challenge: Tally the results for each factor listed on the board that contributes to job satisfaction. Have students present these findings as a pie chart. See the sample below.

Friendly work environment	6
Good pay / benefits	11
Challenge	5
Opportunity for advancement	8

Workbook Link: Exercises 9, 10, 11, 12

➤ Do it yourself!

Procedure:

A. Write your own response ...

➤ Have students read the speech balloons. Ask *Who is talking?* (a boss, a supervisor) Point out that since the same person appears in all three pictures that this activity is meant as a single conversation.

➤ Have a more advanced student read the first speech balloon out loud. Model an appropriate response such as *Maybe, but the other position pays a much higher salary.*

➤ Have students write responses individually and then compare responses with a partner.

➤ In pairs, students practice their conversations.

B. Culture talk ...

➤ Put students in groups with others from the same or a similar culture. Have them discuss what people do when they get an offer for another job.

➤ Have the students create a role play about the situation. Ask volunteers to perform their role plays for the class.

➤ Lead a discussion about the different responses that were presented in the role plays.

(continued on p. 8)

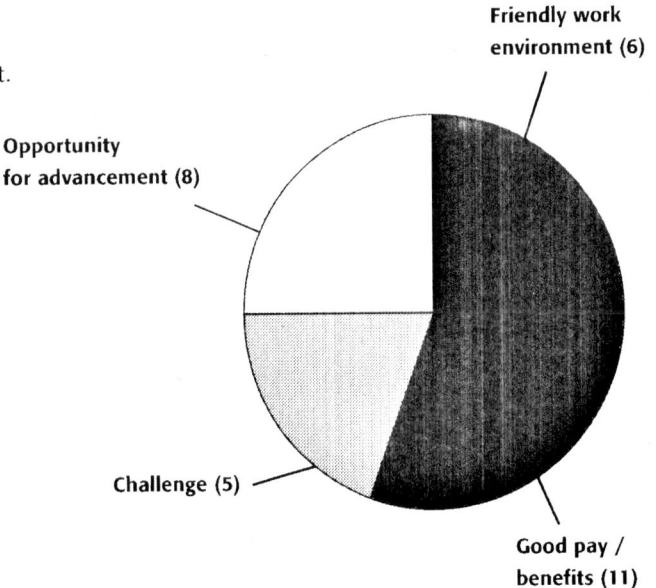

Friendly work environment (6)

Opportunity for advancement (8)

Challenge (5)

Good pay / benefits (11)

Lesson Plan, Unit 10: Authentic practice 1 & 2 (for Student pages 132-135)–*continued*

Authentic practice 2
(Student pages 134-135)

Suggested teaching time: 30 minutes
Your actual teaching time: _____

How to get a better job

Procedure:

A. Listening comprehension...

➤ To set the scene for the listening activity, have students look at the picture. Ask questions such as *Where are the speakers?* (in a cafeteria) *What kind of relationship do you think they have?* (friends or co-workers)

➤ Have students read the questions. Ask students why immigrants are often underemployed in their new country. Elicit reasons such as the following: *Immigrants don't know the language, The educational requirements for some jobs are different.*

➤ Play the cassette or read the tapescript. Have students write answers to the questions.

➤ Put students in pairs to compare answers.

B. Read the statements...

➤ Students read the statements and possible completions.

➤ Have students listen to the conversations again and then select a completion for each statement.

➤ Review as a class.

C. Role play...

➤ Have a volunteer read the man's speech balloon. Ask *What advice could you give this man?* Write students' suggestions on the board.

➤ Tell students that they are going to create a role play between two co-workers. One wants to move up, and the other gives advice.

➤ Put students in pairs to brainstorm ideas. Refer students to the list on the board.

Tapescript

Conversation 1

Mary Lou: Hey, Sara, why the long face?

Sara: Mary Lou, I just can't stand it any more. I've been in this same assembly job now for two and a half years, and there's no way to move up. What should I do?

Mary Lou: Have you told Evan?

Sara: No. I'm afraid he'd get mad. After all, who would do all this work?

Mary Lou: Believe me, if you got another job, they'd find someone to do the work. Speak up.

Sara: What do you mean?

Mary Lou: Well, you've got nothing to lose. If you'd spoken up two years ago, you'd be earning a whole lot more by now.

Sara: Do you think? What do I tell Evan?

Mary Lou: Just tell him that in Venezuela you were a plant manager. Now that your English is better, you'd like to find work at a higher level—like you used to do. Ask him if there are any possibilities for you to move up.

Sara: Hey, look. There's Evan, and he's alone.... I'll go talk to him now. Wish me luck.

Conversation 2

Sara: Evan? Excuse the interruption, but I really need to talk to you.

Evan: Sure, Sara. Something wrong?

Sara: Well, not wrong, but... I just need to know if there's any possibility you might consider promoting me to a more... managerial spot. I've been on the assembly line for a couple of years now. But compared to what I did in Venezuela, I feel a little underemployed.

Evan: What kind of work did you do in Venezuela?

Sara: I was plant manager in a manufacturing business. I had 35 people reporting to me. I have a college degree.

Evan: No kidding. If you'd told me that a while back, I would have kept an eye open for a higher-level position.

Sara: It's not your fault. When I first got here, my English was pretty weak. But I've been studying at night, and now with my American husband and my in-laws and everything, my English has really improved. I'm sort of bored in this job. I think it's time to move on. That's why I wanted to talk to you.

Evan: Well, I'm glad you spoke up. I'll be on the lookout. I think I heard there's something in the Center Street branch. Just hang in there. I'll give the chief a call today and get back to you soon.

Sara: Thanks, Evan. I appreciate it.

(continued on p. 9)

Lesson Plan, Unit 10: Authentic practice 1 & 2 (for Student pages 132-135)—*continued*

D. Culture talk...

➤ On the board, write two headings: *My job now* and *My last job in my home country*. Ask students what factors they might consider as they compare the jobs they have now with the jobs they had in their home countries. Students may suggest salary, medical insurance, paid vacations, and other ideas. If necessary, remind students of the discussion generated during the critical thinking exercise on page 133 of factors that contribute to job satisfaction.

➤ Working individually, students jot down notes about the jobs they had in their home countries and the jobs they have now. Students who don't work now or who didn't work before can jot down notes about how their lives in general are the same or different. Have them list several factors to consider, such as household chores, child care, and contact with friends.

➤ Have students display the similarities and differences in a Venn diagram.

➤ In pairs or small groups, have students explain their diagrams.

➤ Lead a group discussion on any patterns that students noticed when comparing past and present jobs or lives. If necessary, prompt with questions such as *Are most students employed now? Is their standard of living better or worse? Have their goals changed? How?*

➤ Do it yourself!

Procedure:

➤ Tell students that they are going to fill out the employment history section of a job application. Students who do not have an employment history can use that of a friend or relative, or work with partner.

➤ Have students read the directions under *Employment History*. Make sure students understand the terms and abbreviations on the application by asking questions such as *What does "mo" stand for?* (month) *What does "yr" mean?* (year) *What does "wk" mean?* (week) *What is a base salary?* (the salary before any tips or overtime is added on) *What is a starting position title?* (the name of the position you had when you began work at the company)

➤ Remind students to begin with the position they have now. If they are not working, they should discuss the last job they had.

➤ Note that salaries can be figured by the week or by the year. Students should circle *wk* or *yr*, depending on which one applies to them.

➤ Tell students to look at the *Ideas* box on page 128 and the *Vocabulary* box on page 129 for examples of reasons for leaving a job. Students should phrase this reason as a positive step; for example, they might cite *no opportunities for advancement* rather than *boring job*.

➤ Tell students that when they are listing duties and responsibilities they should follow parallel structure. For example, they might want to list everything as a gerund: *filing, answering the phone, keeping a correspondence log, operating and maintaining the fax machine.*

Option: Have students exchange forms and practice peer review on the job applications. Provide these and similar questions as guidelines: *Are all names, addresses, and phone numbers complete? Can you read the handwriting? Are dates and dollar amounts clear? Are the duties and responsibilities listed in parallel structure?*

Option: Have students list on a card or slip of paper their duties and responsibilities without any further description. Collect the cards and read the duties and responsibilities aloud. Have other students guess the job position.

Challenge: Have students work in pairs to roleplay an interviewer and a job applicant. The questions and answers should be based on the information in the employment history. Make sure the job applicant describes the duties and responsibilities in complete sentences rather than just a list; for example, *I was responsible for all the filing and answering the phone. I also kept the correspondence log and was responsible for operating and maintaining the fax machine.*

Workbook Link: Exercise 13

Copyright © 2004 by Pearson Education, Inc.
All rights reserved.

LESSON PLAN, UNIT 10: AUTHENTIC PRACTICE 3 (for Student pages 136-137)

Summary of Lesson Plan

▶ **PRESENTATION**
Authentic practice 3:
Reading and critical thinking (Student pages 136-137)
Suggested teaching time: 60 minutes
Your actual teaching time: _____

Authentic practice 3
(Student pages 136-137)

Suggested teaching time: 60 minutes
Your actual teaching time: _____

Writing a resume

Procedure:

A. Read and listen to the letters.

➤ Have students read along silently as they listen to the letters. Check comprehension by asking questions such as *What was Carlos's job in his country?* (He was a commercial artist and draftsman.) *What has he done in this country?* (He's driven a taxi and worked as a painter.) *What is his problem?* (He wants to go back to his profession, work as a commercial artist and draftsman.) *What does Joan advise Carlos to do?* (write a resume)

➤ Have students read the *Tips for a winning resume*. Check comprehension by asking questions such as *What are two types of resumes?* (chronological and functional) *How are they different?* (A chronological format organizes information by date, with the most recent date first. A functional format presents information according to skills and accomplishments.) *Who should use a functional resume?* (people changing careers or people who have been out of the job market for a number of years) *What are some things you should not put on a resume?* (salary information, reasons for leaving jobs, personal statistics, names of supervisors, names and addresses of references)

➤ Some terms may be unfamiliar to students. Make sure they know the meaning of *setting off, showcase,* and *red flags*.

Option: In small groups or pairs, have students speculate about Carlos and what his life might have been like if it had taken a different turn. Put on the board past unreal conditional *if* clauses such as *If Carlos had not left his country, If Carlos hadn't married an American, If Carlos hadn't learned English.* Elicit speculations such as *If Carlos had not left his country, he might have found another job as a commercial artist, If Carlos hadn't gotten married, he might not have come to this country.*

Option: Creating a timeline can be a helpful way to organize information. Ask students to create a timeline for Carlos, including everything they know about him. Have students underline information in his letter that they will use, such as *eight years ago, two years—taxi driver, painter*. Put an empty timeline on the board and elicit information that corresponds to specific dates; for example, *1995—lost my job as a commercial artist and draftsman*.

Challenge: When students have finished creating a timeline for Carlos, have them create an employment and education timeline for themselves. Tell them to include all education and training as well as employment experience. Have students share their completed timelines in pairs.

Challenge: Put students in pairs or small groups to compare Carlos's employment experience to that of Sara. Have them create a graphic organizer such as a Venn diagram to present the similarities and differences. Students can then use their ideas about Carlos and Sara to write a paragraph that compares their work histories.

B. Critical thinking...

➤ Direct students' attention to the *Resume red flags*.

➤ Ask *Why shouldn't you put this information on a resume?* Working individually, students jot down their ideas.

➤ In pairs or small groups, students compare ideas.

➤ Then lead a class discussion about reasons not to put this information on a resume. Elicit students' ideas and write them on the board. Ideas might include the following: *Salary information is best discussed in a private conversation, Giving salary information might limit the amount a potential employer would be willing to offer, Giving reasons for leaving a job might appear too negative, Listing names of supervisors adds unnecessary length to a resume.* Tell students that personal statistics are irrelevant to most jobs and, in fact, it is illegal for a perspective employer to ask about some of them.

(continued on p. 11)

Lesson Plan, Unit 10: Authentic practice 3 (for Student pages 136-137)–*continued*

C. Discussion ...

➤ Review with students the features of the two types of resumes.

➤ Put students in small groups to discuss which format Carlos should use for his resume. Have them give reasons for their choices.

➤ Ask students which type of resume they think they should write for themselves. Have volunteers explain their reasoning.

Workbook Link: Exercises 14, 15

➤ Do it yourself!

Procedure:

A. Look at Carlos Sinkoff's resume.

➤ Have students read Carlos's resume. Check comprehension by asking questions such as *What kind of resume did Carlos write—functional or chronological?* (functional) *What are his strengths?* (visual creativity and careful execution of projects on a timely basis) *What commercial art experience has Carlos had?* (He was an illustrator and layout person for eight years in Chile.) *Where did he go to school?* (University of the West, Vina del Mar, Chile) *What kind of job does Carlos want now?* (a position as an architectural draftsperson or commercial artist)

Option: Using the resume as a reference point, students work in pairs to develop a role play between Carlos and an interviewer. The interviewer should ask Carlos questions about his education, job experience, and goals. Have students switch roles to practice both parts.

Option: If your students have access to the Internet, have them research resume formats. If possible, they should print out a variety of resume formats and bring them to class. In small groups, students compare the various formats and select one for their own use.

B. Write your own resume ...

➤ Have students decide on the format and general categories that they want to use in their resume. Tell students to review the resume tips on page 136 and Carlos's resume on this page. They may want to change the categories Carlos used or add others.

➤ Have students draft a resume on a separate sheet of paper.

Option: Ask how students feel about sharing the information in their resumes. If appropriate, have students exchange resumes and practice peer review. They should check spelling, punctuation, use of parallel structure, and consistent formatting.

Your notes

LESSON PLAN, UNIT 10: REVIEW (for Student pages 138-140)

Summary of Lesson Plan

▶ **Review (Student pages 138-140)**
Suggested teaching time: 60 minutes
Your actual teaching time: _____

▶ **UNIT REVIEW**
Includes expansion activities
role play
dialogues
writing
Workbook activities
outside reading
realia applications
math skills applications
civic lesson applications
Booster Pak activities

▶ **Review (Student pages 138-140)**

Suggested teaching time: 60 minutes
Your actual teaching time: _____

Procedure:

A. Pair work or group work.

Ask and answer questions.

▶ Ask the class general questions about the picture, such as *Where is the woman in the first picture?* (in her home country, in a drugstore) *What do you think her job was there?* (pharmacist) *When did she come to this country?* (in 2000) *What kind of job did she have when she first came here?* (She worked in a restaurant.)

▶ Partners take turns pointing to different things in the picture and asking questions. For each picture, students should ask *What is happening? What are the people doing?* in addition to their own questions.

Option: On a separate sheet of paper, have groups write as many questions as they can about each picture. Students should put questions for each picture under the appropriate date. Have groups exchange questions. Students take turns reading the questions, and the group discusses the answers.

Create conversations.

▶ Have pairs of students create a conversation between the woman and the pharmacist at Health Note or the woman and the restaurant manager. Or students may choose to create a conversation for one of the earlier dated pictures, even though no speech balloons are used.

▶ If students need help or ideas, they can look back over the unit.

▶ Ask volunteers to role-play their conversation for the class. Have pairs present their conversations in chronological order so that the conversations create a continuous story.

Tell a story.

Option: Scenes. Assign students one of the six pictures. Give them a few minutes to look at the picture and review ideas from the unit. Each student must explain what is going on in the picture, including the date and place and who the characters are. Ask students to talk for one minute if they can.

Option: The woman's story. Have students tell the woman's story, alternating the simple past tense with past unreal conditional sentences. For example, a student might begin *Tina used to be a pharmacist in her country. If she had stayed there, she might have owned her own pharmacy.* In a variation, you could have one student begin in the simple past tense, have the second speculate in the past unreal conditional, the third advance the real story in the simple past tense, and so on.

Option: Sequencing. Dictate the following sentences. Have students write down the sentences and then put them in the correct order (3, 4, 6, 2, 5, 7, 1).

She went to talk to the restaurant manager.

She took English classes so she could speak the language better.

She used to work as a pharmacist.

She arrived in her new country.

One day she decided to try returning to her profession.

She got a job in a restaurant.

She had an interview with a pharmacist at Health Note.

(continued on p. 13)

Book 4 Lesson Plans